RAINBOW
FLEUR DE LIS

RAINBOW FLEUR DE LIS

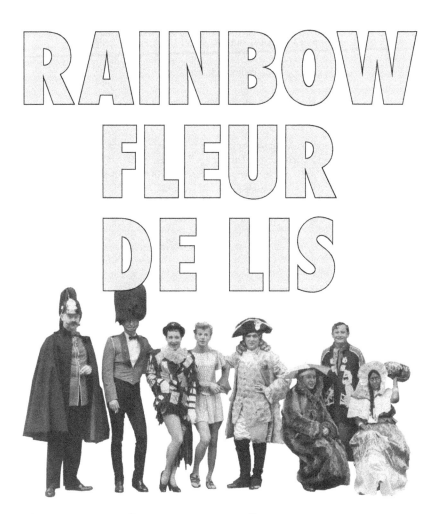

ESSAYS ON QUEER NEW ORLEANS HISTORY

FRANK PEREZ

University Press of Mississippi / Jackson

The University Press of Mississippi is the scholarly publishing agency of the Mississippi Institutions of Higher Learning: Alcorn State University, Delta State University, Jackson State University, Mississippi State University, Mississippi University for Women, Mississippi Valley State University, University of Mississippi, and University of Southern Mississippi.

www.upress.state.ms.us

The University Press of Mississippi is a member of the Association of University Presses.

Publisher: University Press of Mississippi, Jackson, USA
Authorised GPSR Safety Representative: Easy Access System Europe - Mustamäe tee 50, 10621 Tallinn, Estonia, gpsr.requests@easproject.com

Photo of Mardi Gras maskers (p. iii) from The Historic New Orleans Collection, Gift of Mr. Clay Watson, Acc. No. 1982.147.2.

Library of Congress Cataloging-in-Publication Data

Names: Perez, Frank, 1968– author.
Title: Rainbow fleur de lis : essays on queer New Orleans history / Frank Perez.
Description: Jackson : University Press of Mississippi, 2025. | Includes bibliographical references and index.
Identifiers: LCCN 2024052557 (print) | LCCN 2024052558 (ebook) | ISBN 9781496857583 (hardcover) | ISBN 9781496857590 (epub) | ISBN 9781496857606 (epub) | ISBN 9781496857613 (pdf) | ISBN 9781496857620 (pdf)
Subjects: LCSH: Sexual minorities—Louisiana—New Orleans—History. | Gay people—Louisiana—New Orleans—History. | Gay community—Louisiana—New Orleans—History. | Gay culture—Louisiana—New Orleans—History. | AIDS (Disease)—Social aspects. | New Orleans (La.)—History.
Classification: LCC HQ73.3.L8 P47 2025 (print) | LCC HQ73.3.L8 (ebook) | DDC 306.7609763/35—dc23/eng/20250120
LC record available at https://lccn.loc.gov/2024052557
LC ebook record available at https://lccn.loc.gov/2024052558

British Library Cataloging-in-Publication Data available

For Rip and Marsha

CONTENTS

ACKNOWLEDGMENTS

BECAUSE THE EIGHTY-FIVE ESSAYS IN THIS VOLUME WERE WRITTEN OVER a twelve-year period, it would be impossible to list every person I interviewed when composing the original articles. I am grateful to all who agreed to be interviewed. A handful of people were helpful in the compilation of the present volume. These include Rip and Marsha Naquin-Delain, who offered me a column in *Ambush* so many years ago; current *Ambush* owner and publisher Tomy Acosta; Ellis Anderson, founder and publisher of *French Quarter Journal*; Robert Ticknor of the Williams Research Center at The Historic New Orleans Collection; the staff of the Louisiana Research Collection at Tulane University; Robert Fieseler, author of *Tinderbox*; and my partner, Chris Trentacoste.

RAINBOW
FLEUR DE LIS

INTRODUCTION

ONE AFTERNOON IN THE FALL OF 2012, WHILE I WAS SITTING AT CAFÉ Lafitte in Exile, Rip Naquin and his partner Marsha Delain entered the bar and sat next to me. Rip congratulated me on the recent publication of my book, *In Exile: The History and Lore Surrounding New Orleans Gay Culture and Its Oldest Gay Bar*. He then asked me if I would be interested in writing a history column for *Ambush Magazine*. I immediately said yes and thus began a close friendship that lasted until his death in 2017. It is now 2024, twelve years later, and I'm still writing the column.

I had seen Rip and Marsha in the bars for years, though I didn't formally meet them until I interviewed them for *In Exile* in 2010. They had founded *Ambush* in 1982 and in the decades that followed had become something of legends in the French Quarter. In addition to publishing *Ambush*, essentially a tabloid bar rag, they also formed the Krewe of Queenateenas in 1987, hosted numerous fundraisers for many local charities, produced the Gay Easter Parade, and hosted websites for Southern Decadence and Gay Mardi Gras.

Before meeting them, my impression of them was vague. The first thing I noticed was that Rip and Marsha were inseparable. I never saw one without the other. And they were mysterious, even unapproachable. Observing from a distance, the contrasts between them were obvious— Rip was loud and gregarious; Marsha was quiet and subdued. Rip was masculine; Marsha was feminine. Rip could be aggressive; Marsha tended to be more submissive. But there were similarities too—they both loved to eat (neither was thin) and they both loved to drink (mostly vodka). I also noticed people either loved or hated them. As a unit, they were magnetic—attractive and polarizing all at once. This, more than anything, intrigued me. In short, Rip and Marsha fascinated me.

So, I was thrilled when Rip asked me to write for *Ambush*. Not only would I have the chance to get know Rip and Marsha, I would also have an opportunity to learn more about local queer history. I first became interested in queer history when I came out in the early 1990s. I've always been something of a history buff and after I made peace with my sexuality, I naturally devoured any book I could find on gay history. Edmund White's *States of Desire: Travels in Gay America*, Vito Russo's *The Celluloid Closet*, Urvashi Vaid's *Virtual Equality*, Charles Kaiser's *The Gay Metropolis*, and Christopher Isherwood's *The Berlin Stories* especially intrigued me. The more I read, the more I realized there was so much more I didn't know about gay history. And it made me more than a little angry. Events and people that are conventional reference points among gay folk—Stonewall, Harvey Milk, the veneration of Bette Davis for example—had totally escaped me in my closeted years. The more I read, the more ignorant I felt. Stamping out that ignorance became a personal crusade.

It was only a matter of time before I turned my attention to gay New Orleans history. Having grown up in south Louisiana, New Orleans always occupied a privileged position in both my heart and my mind. After visiting the Cabildo for the first time (I must have been around ten or eleven), my mother bought me a copy of Leonard Huber's *New Orleans: A Pictorial History*. It was the beginning of a love affair with books about New Orleans that persists to this day. When I lived away from the city, I visited New Orleans every chance I could. The uneven cobblestone banquettes, the magic of Carnival, the majestic live oak trees, the intricate cast iron dripping from ancient buildings, the scent of jasmine hanging in the sweltering humidity, the sight of men in seersucker suits eating oysters in restaurant windows—these all, along with a hundred other sensual images, made me feel at home. And whenever I left the city to return to whatever humdrum place my career had me at the time, I ruefully concluded that I must have lived in New Orleans in a previous life, and I vowed that I would live in New Orleans again. It was a self-fulfilling prophecy for in 2008, due to a series of circumstances that requires a book of its own, I found myself moving to New Orleans.

Since then, I've written four books about New Orleans queer history and edited an anthology on the same topic. I cofounded a nonprofit organization, the LGBT+ Archives Project of Louisiana, which works to preserve queer history. I've also found moderate success with my Rainbow Fleur de Lis Walking Tour and as a public speaker. None of that would have happened without Rip's support and friendship.

Rip passed away in August of 2017 and Marsha followed four months later. When Rip died, *Ambush* was in its thirty-fifth year of publication and many feared it would die as well. But a community angel stepped forward and saved the venerable magazine. Before Marsha died, she sold *Ambush* to local attorney Tomy Acosta. Acosta knew nothing about the publishing business, but he believed *Ambush* was important for the community.

Ambush remained in print until 2020, long after many LGBT+ periodicals had faded away or gone exclusively digital. Due to the economic effects of the COVID-19 pandemic, *Ambush* ceased print publication in July 2020 and revamped its website. It continues to publish content today.

In addition to writing for *Ambush*, I'm also a columnist for *French Quarter Journal*—an online publication that launched in 2019. I'll never forget the sunny day when Ellis Anderson showed up at my office on St. Ann Street. She introduced herself and told me about a new project she was working on, *French Quarter Journal*. Her vision for the magazine resonated with me. It would feature stories about the neighborhood—its residents, its businesses, its architecture, and its vibe—in an effort to explore the French Quarter as a community, not a commodity. She then asked me if I would write a regular column focusing on the LGBT+ heritage of the sacred enclave. How could I say no?

The essays collected in this volume were originally published in *Ambush Magazine* and *French Quarter Journal*. This anthology is not an exhaustive collection of everything I've written for both publications; I've written a number of news stories and investigative reports for *Ambush*, and in addition to my Rainbow History column, I also have a Civic Beat regular feature in *French Quarter Journal*. Those pieces are not included here.

Arranged topically, the eighty-five articles published here offer not only an expansive glimpse into the history of LGBT+ New Orleans, but also a broad overview of the contributions queer folks have made to the city's colorful history. My hope is that this book will constitute a small step in the reclaiming of a significant and dynamic history, much of which unfortunately remains in the closet.

With the exception of some minor editing to reduce redundancy and to conform to the publisher's guidelines, the essays in this volume appear as they did when they were originally published. The original publication date of each essay and where it was published—*Ambush Magazine* or *French Quarter Journal*—follow each entry. Endnotes indicate relevant updates and developments regarding the topics covered, as well as explanations of references that may not be familiar to contemporary readers.

GAY CARNIVAL

In many ways, the LGBT+ history of New Orleans is not unlike that of other cities. There was a time in New Orleans when homophobia was de rigueur, the closet was pervasive, discrimination was rampant, and police raids of bars were common; nevertheless, there are a few things that make New Orleans queer history distinctive. The phenomenon of Gay Carnival is one of those things. At a time when being gay could get someone arrested, fired, evicted, or committed to a mental asylum, Gay Carnival afforded gay men an opportunity to not only be themselves, but also an outlet for their creative and artistic talents. The essays in this section examine the early years of Gay Carnival, its birth in 1958 and its growth in the subsequent decades until the advent of the HIV/AIDS crisis. "Dixie's, Yuga, and Gay Carnival" details the origins of the first gay krewe and its ill-fated 1962 ball, as well as the role of Dixie's Bar of Music in Gay Carnival. "The Children of Yuga" outlines the impact Yuga had by providing brief sketches of the krewes the members of Yuga would go on to found. "The Lost Krewes of Gay Carnival" identifies the krewes that have faded away or folded over the years. "Mardi Gras and Mythology" dispels the misconception that Mardi Gras is nothing more than a massive street party filled with drunken people and explains why gay men are so drawn to it. "Remembering Polyphemus" offers an inside glimpse into the founding of a krewe, the internal drama that characterizes krewes, and the effect AIDS had on this unique New Orleans institution.

DIXIE'S, YUGA, AND GAY CARNIVAL

IN THE 1950S, THE EPICENTER OF GAY MARDI GRAS IN NEW ORLEANS was the intersection of Bourbon and St. Peter Streets. There, on the downriver side, were Dixie's Bar of Music and, across the street, the Bourbon House. Above the side entrance to Dixie's on St. Peter was a sign that read "For Male Bachelors Only." Several of the bachelors in that line would eventually form the first Gay Carnival krewe—the Krewe of Yuga.

Mardi Gras, that sacred day of days marked by wanton abandonment and baroque fantasy, has long been revered by gay men. Much like the Quarter itself, Carnival is a wonderfully complex cultural phenomenon, replete with layers of meaning and symbolism. It is revelry, pageantry, and fantasy; who better to embody it than gay men?

Drag, of course, has always been a part of Mardi Gras. In fact, a man in drag is the subject of the first written reference to Mardi Gras in New Orleans. In 1729, Marc-Antoine Caillot, a bureaucrat working for the Company of the Indies (whose offices were along Decatur between St. Peter and Toulouse Streets), wrote in his journal:

> The next day, which was Lundi Gras, I went to the office where I found my companions bored to death. I proposed to them that we mask and go to Bayou St. John . . . As for myself, I was dressed as a shepherdess, all in white. I had a corset of white bazin, a muslin skirt, a large pannier . . . I had some beauty marks too. I had my husband, who was the Marquis of Carnival . . . What made it hard for people to recognize me was that along with having shaved very closely that evening I had a number of beauty marks on my face and even on my breasts, which I had plumped up . . . unless you looked at me very closely, you could not tell that I was a boy.[1]

In the twentieth century, one of Mardi Gras' great appeals to gay men was that it was the one day out of the year when cross-dressing and masking were permitted. This is evident in the Bourbon Street Awards—a costume contest held annually on Mardi Gras afternoon that, for the most part, features elaborate costumes made for the tableaus at the Gay Carnival balls earlier in the season. The Bourbon Street Awards was founded in 1964 by Arthur Jacobs, owner of the Clover Grill, as a way to drum up business for his diner.

While Mardi Gras is still immensely popular among gay men, it's safe to say that Southern Decadence has surpassed Fat Tuesday as the premier gay holiday in the city. For the gay krewes, none of which parade, the Carnival balls are the pinnacle of the season.

The first gay krewe—Yuga—grew out of a house party. Doug Jones lived on Carrollton Avenue and each year would host a parade viewing party for the Krewe of Carrollton parade. Among his friends were Elmo Avet, John Bogie, Claude Davis Jr., John Dodt, Stewart Gahn, Tracy Hendrix, Jim Schexnayder, Clay Shaw, and others.

In 1958, these men, many of whom were members of the mysterious (and enduring) Steamboat Club, which had been founded in 1953, formalized their annual party by calling it a ball and proclaiming themselves the Krewe of Yuga. Yuga was a group of older, well-established men who escaped their straight, Uptown lives by congregating in the Quarter at Miss Dixie's.

Dixie, herself a lesbian, affectionately called them "the cuff-link set." From the hub of Dixie's, they would frequent other "queershops," as the police derisively called them, such as Tony Bacino's, Café Lafitte in Exile, and the Starlet Lounge.

Jones was a Carnival enthusiast and appreciated its history. His family had ties with the Krewe of Proteus, and it was the 1889 Proteus parade theme—"Hindoo Heavens"—that inspired the name Yuga. In Hindu mythology, the Kali Yuga was an epoch of time.

Yuga's first two balls were held at Jones's home. Just about everyone was in drag and the parties, which featured "debutramps" instead of debutantes, were enormously popular. Otto Stierle is quoted in *Unveiling the Muse* as remembering "everyone arriving at the house had to be in costume and climb a large staircase in front of the house to reach the second-floor entrance, a spectacle for an otherwise quiet neighborhood."[2]

By the third year, it was clear the ball would have to be held elsewhere. In 1960, Yuga left Uptown for the lakefront and held their ball at Mama Lou's jazz club on Lake Pontchartrain. The following year the ball moved to Metairie to a venue called the Rambler Room, which was a dance studio attached to a day care facility at which one of the krewe's members worked. The location was perfect, and Yuga scheduled their fifth ball there. But the fifth Yuga ball was ill-fated.

The 1962 ball was off to a good start. The costumes were fabulous, alcohol was flowing, and aging French Quarter legend Elmo Avet, who owned an antique store on Royal Street, dressed as Mary Queen of Scots awaited being crowned Yuga Regina V.

But it was not to be. Before the tableau began, Jefferson Parish police arrived at the Rambler Room, kicked open the doors, and raided the ball. Pandemonium ensued and many fled the building by jumping out of windows. Several ran into the adjacent woods but were stopped when the police dogs approached. Nearly one hundred men were arrested.

Those who escaped arrest eventually made it back to the safety of the French Quarter. Miss Dixie, upon being alerted of the raid, dispatched her attorney with a wad of cash from her bar safe to bail everyone out of jail. The morning following the raid, Elmo Avet and Bill Woolley, both of whom avoided arrest, sat at the Bourbon House across from Dixie's and debriefed the previous evening's fiasco.

So, who tipped off the police? It's easy to assume the conservative, suburbanite housewives of Metairie in 1962 naturally called the police when they saw a bunch of men dressed in drag entering their local day care facility, but a much more tantalizing theory involves a jilted drag queen. Hell hath no fury . . .

Candy Lee hailed from Cajun country and found her way to New Orleans, where she secured work as a "female impersonator" at the legendary Club My-O-My. She also worked as a bartender at Tony Bacino's, which in 1958 was raided several times by the police. Candy Lee was arrested multiple times.

Convinced the raids were the result of a tip to the police from a fellow queen who had a proverbial axe to grind with her, Candy Lee, never one to be soft-spoken, loudly and repeatedly told several people whom she thought had snitched on Tony Bacino's. Her accusation was never verified, and it may not have been true at all since the mayor's "Committee on the Problem of Sex Deviates"—created to rid the French Quarter of homosexuals—harassed several "queershops."

Candy Lee raised so much hell about the raids that by the early 1960s she had been banned from the two gay krewes at the time—Yuga and Petronius—and was generally considered a persona non grata.

In the aftermath of the 1962 Yuga raid, many speculated, among them Yuga founder Doug Jones, that Candy Lee had tipped off the police that a wild stag party involving cross-dressing homosexuals was occurring at the Rambler Room, thus exacting her revenge.

Candy Lee became something of a legend when she inspired Tennessee Williams's *And Tell Sad Stories of the Death of Queens*. Lee and Williams had become friends, and the playwright was fascinated by her life story. Lee often regaled Williams with the various tales of woe that constituted her life at bars in the Quarter and at her apartment on Decatur Street.

Lee and Williams and Jones and Dixie and Yuga are long gone now, but Gay Carnival survives and continues to add layers of complexity to a tradition begun on Shrove Tuesday 1699, when Iberville and his younger brother Bienville, who lived into his eighties and never married, docked their pirogues and made camp near present-day New Orleans. They dubbed a nearby bayou "Bayou Mardi Gras" and called the settlement "Pointe du Mardi Gras." (Take that, Mobile!)

Although Yuga was the first gay krewe, the origins of Gay Carnival in New Orleans stretch back nearly ten years before Yuga was formed. The next essay explores that genesis as well as the gay krewes that arose out of Yuga after its demise.

French Quarter Journal, January 26, 2020

NOTES

1. Marc-Antoine Caillot, *A Company Man*, ed. Erin M. Greenwald (New Orleans: The Historic New Orleans Collection, 2013).

2. Howard P. Smith, *Unveiling the Muse: The Lost History of Gay Carnival in New Orleans* (Jackson: University Press of Mississippi, 2017).

THE CHILDREN OF YUGA

THE SEVENTY-THIRD YEAR OF GAY CARNIVAL IS UPON US. FOR THOSE familiar with it, Gay Carnival usually means formal balls produced by krewes such as Petronius, Amon-Ra, Armeinius, Lords of Leather, Mwindo, and Narcissus. But Gay Carnival did not start out with krewes or balls. It began with a group of gay men who decided to do lunch.

It all began in 1949 when Bob Demmons brought five out-of-town friends to lunch at Brennan's. During the lunch, and much to his guests' surprise, Demmons produced a bouquet of flowers and a tiara and crowned one of his friends "Queen of the Lunch." After the meal, a carriage was waiting for the group, and they began making their way around the French Quarter tossing gladiolas to those they passed. Thus was born a tradition that survives today—the Fat Monday Luncheon.

It was also in 1949 that Dixie Fasnacht relocated her "Bar of Music" from the 200 block of St. Charles to the intersection of Bourbon and St. Peter Streets. In the 1950s, Dixie's became ground zero for gay men on Mardi Gras. At the time, Dixie's was the epicenter of gay nightlife in the Quarter. Across the street was the Bourbon House, a popular eatery among gay and lesbian folks who lived in the Quarter. A half a block away was Pat O'Brien's, which featured a bar "for bachelors," code for "gay man" in that era. And nearby were popular gay bars Tony Bacino's and Café Lafitte in Exile.

Among the queer denizens that frequented Dixie's was Doug Jones. It is also likely that Jones attended the Fat Monday Luncheons in the 1950s (although membership records no longer exist and this supposition cannot be verified). Jones lived across town on South Carrollton Avenue, along the Krewe of Carrollton parade route.

Each year, he hosted a parade viewing party for his friends. Among these friends were Elmo Avet, John Bogie, Claude Davis Jr., John Dodt, Stewart Gahn, Jerry Gilley, Tracy Hendrix, JoJo Landry, Carlos Rodriguez, Jim Schexnayder, Otto Stierle, and Bill Woolley. In 1958, these men (many of whom were also members of the mysterious Steamboat Club, which had been founded in 1953) decided to change their casual parade party into something more formal, a mock ball, replete with costumes and royalty. They called themselves the Krewe of Yuga.

Before the tableau at the 1962 Yuga ball began, Jefferson Parish police arrived, kicked open the doors, and raided the ball. Pandemonium ensued and many fled the building by jumping out of windows. Several ran into the adjacent woods but were stopped when police dogs approached. Nearly one hundred men were arrested.

That was the end of the Krewe of Yuga, but from its ashes arose other gay krewes. The men who founded and later joined Yuga would eventually go on to start other gay krewes:

Petronius: Elmo Avet, Bill Woolley, John Dodt, William McKenzie, Otto Stierle Jr., Carlos Rodriguez, Brad Lysholm, JoJo Landry, Don Fitzpatrick, and Joseph Barcellona
Amon-Ra: Brad Lysholm and Jim Schexnayder
Armeinius: Tracy Hendrix
Ganymede: JoJo Landry
Celestial Knights: Bill Woolley, William McKenzie, Otto Stierle Jr., Carlos Rodriguez

Since Yuga was formed, there have been close to twenty gay krewes, including Ganymede, Apollo, Olympus, Memphis, Polyphemus, Ishtar (the only lesbian krewe), Lords of Leather, Mwindo, Rue Royale Revelers, Narcissus, and Stars. In recent years, some krewes have departed from the Bal Masque format. The Radical Faeries hosts the St. Brigid Ball, which crowns an Empress but is less formal than the traditional balls. Stars presents a Show Ball and the Krewe de la Rue Royale Revelers hosts a Twelfth Night party.

In addition, there have been, since Yuga, lesser-known or very short-lived krewes, most of which did not produce balls but rather celebrated Carnival in other ways. These krewes include Kancellation, The Queen's Men, Phoenix, Satins and Sequins, Jason, Desime, Dionysus, David, Eros, Vesta, Tragoidia, Queenateenas, Mardi Gras Merrymen, La Cage aux Folles, and Anubis.

As the aforementioned list suggests, the children of Yuga are many. In 1958, Doug Jones and his friends could not have possibly imagined the phenomenon they started. As John Bogie recalls in *Unveiling the Muse:*

The Lost History of Gay Carnival in New Orleans, "The Yuga Regina was one of the most spectacular sights I've ever seen in my life. When the lights reflected off her royal raiments, the room was filled with explosions and bursts of light like fireworks. Who would have guessed that her children would take up the mantle of Carnival and run with it like they were possessed?"

The following essay takes a closer look at some of the aforementioned krewes, those that have since folded since their founding.

Ambush, February 11, 2022

THE LOST KREWES OF GAY CARNIVAL

IF YOU LIVE IN NEW ORLEANS, THERE'S A CHANCE YOU'VE ATTENDED ONE of the several Gay Carnival balls presented each Carnival season. If you have, you know these balls are highly elaborate productions requiring hundreds of hours of work and thousands of dollars. Perhaps the most amazing thing about the gay balls is that they are produced by relatively few people, depending on the size of the krewe. This year, as the existing krewes show off their hard work, let us take a moment to remember a few krewes that are no longer with us.

Yuga (1958–1962). The Krewe of Yuga, or KY, established the template later krewes would follow, which involved a lot of drag and the naming of royalty. Founded by Doug Jones and his friends, Yuga grew out of an annual house party Jones hosted to view the Krewe of Carrollton parade. The annual Yuga "ball" became so popular it quickly outgrew Jones's home. Yuga's fifth ball, and the krewe itself, ended in 1962 when it was raided by the police. Jones and others believe the police were tipped off by a former member who had been expelled from the krewe.

Ganymede (1968–1974). The Krewe of Ganymede was founded by Vincent Indovina, Scott Hoy, Rivet Hedderel, and Jerry Koplin. Indovina had served as the second King of Amon-Ra in 1967 and his partner, Scott Hoy, had served as Amon-Ra's first Captain in 1966. Indovina was somewhat inflexible, exerting almost dictatorial control over the krewe. After its first ball, titled "The Gods of Mount Olympus," member and costume designer Wendell Stipelcovich left the krewe to cofound the Krewe of Armeinius. Other members left to form the Krewe of Olympus.

Olympus (1971–1990). Lou Bernard, Nick Donovan (a former Captain of Ganymede), and George Wilson founded the Krewe of Olympus in 1970. Their debut ball in 1971, Camelot, is still remembered as one of the most legendary balls a gay krewe has ever produced. Historian Howard P. Smith writes, "The mere mention of the word 'Camelot' within the secretive realm of Gay Carnival still evokes a sense of wonder, magic, awe, and ultimate envy. No tableau ball has excited more passion and praise."[1] The first Captain of Olympus was Jamie Greenleaf, who left Petronius because of internal bickering within the krewe.

Memphis (1976–1983). Of all the former krewes, the least is known about the Krewe of Memphis. As was the case with many krewes, it was probably founded by disgruntled members from another krewe. Memphis is perhaps best remembered for its rivalry with the Krewe of Celestial Knights (both krewes selected a similar ball theme for the 1983 season). We also know it formed a sister krewe in Lafayette.

Celestial Knights (1977–1992). After the 1976 Petronius ball, the captain's election was disputed and caused a split within the krewe led by William Woolley. Woolley and six other members left Petronius to form the Krewe of Celestial Knights, or KOCK. Woolley had been a member of Yuga and a cofounder of Petronius. During his time in those krewes, he learned from the legendary Elmo Avet, the creative spirit behind the first two gay krewes. Woolley absorbed some of Avet's genius, a fact evidenced in the grandeur of KOCK's balls. One innovation Woolley introduced was the introduction of more performers (and hence more costumes) in smaller roles to accompany the main performer.

Ishtar (1981–1986). The Krewe of Ishtar, Gay Carnival's only lesbian krewe, was founded by Diane Dimiceli, Rosemary Pino, and Sue Martin. Dimiceli was a lesbian bar owner who purchased Alice Brady's bar in 1978 and later opened another lesbian bar in Jefferson Parish. Pino owned Club 621 and had raised money for the Krewes of Armeinius and Polyphemus. Martin served as Captain of Ishtar for five of its six balls.

Polyphemus (1983–1992). Close friends Gary Martin, Michael Hickerson, Eugene Fenasci, and David Smith founded the Krewe of Polyphemus in 1982. Hickerson had been the first Black person to join Amon-Ra and would later cofound the all-Black krewes of Somnus and Mwindo. The 1987 Polyphemus ball was especially memorable because it was interrupted by a bomb threat. Many believe the threat was called in by a member of the krewe who was expelled days before the ball because he had fallen so far behind on his costume; Martin feared it would never be completed. The rest of the krewe helped finish the costume, and just when Kevin Keller, a member of Apollo who agreed to pinch-hit wearing the costume at the ball, stepped onto the stage, the auditorium was evacuated. No bomb was found, and the ball went on.

Satyricon (2003–2016). When Mickey Gil was not re-elected Captain of Petronius in 2002, a position he had held for thirteen years, he and his partner, George Patterson, (and sixteen others) left the krewe and founded the Krewe of Satyricon. Early members included Ted Jeansonne, David Boyd, Carl Mack, Joe Brooks, Wedon Brown, Richard Read, and Stephen Rizzo. Also involved in the krewe were longtime French Quarter fixtures like Becky Allen and up-and-coming star Roy Haylock (aka Bianca Del Rio).

The reasons these krewes folded are varied. Sometimes money was a factor. In other cases, the leaders simply grew tired or dispirited. Cofounder and Captain of Polyphemus Gary Martin recalls that by 1992 he had lost so many friends and krewe members to AIDS, he was "ready to call it a day."

As these brief sketches illustrate, the evolution of Gay Carnival krewes is not only a fascinating study in personality conflicts and competitiveness but also of imaginative brilliance. Despite all the drama, the gay krewes and the balls they've produced have provided an important outlet for the creative and artistic talents of the gay community—invitations, posters, set designs, costume designs, etc.

Regardless of why they faded away, however, these lost krewes are an integral part of Gay Carnival history.

Next, we zoom out from Gay Carnival in order to position the gay krewes in a larger context; in so doing, the following essay explores the role of mythology in New Orleans culture generally and Carnival specifically. Moreover, the essay explains, in part, why queer people are so drawn to Carnival.

Ambush, February 18, 2022

NOTE

1. Howard P. Smith, *Unveiling the Muse: The Lost History of Gay Carnival in New Orleans* (Jackson: University Press of Mississippi, 2017).

MARDI GRAS AND MYTHOLOGY

WHEN I WAS A CHILD, I WOULD GET MORE EXCITED ABOUT MARDI GRAS than I would about Christmas Day. Christmas was great—what kid doesn't love toys and candy and all that—but for me, as exciting as Christmas was, it simply meant Mardi Gras was just around the corner.

Mardi Gras is a magical day, unlike any other. Adequate words to describe Fat Tuesday are elusive. Enchanted, mysterious, fun, joyous all seem to miss the mark in that they don't quite capture the merriment of the day. Comus historian Perry Young came close when he wrote, "Carnival is a butterfly of winter, whose last mad flight of Mardi Gras forever ends its glory. Another season is the glory of another butterfly, and the tattered, scattered fragments of rainbow wings are in turn the record of his day."[1]

The Church, of course, claims Shrove Tuesday as a religious holiday, one last chance to party before Ash Wednesday and Lent, but Carnival's pagan roots stretch back to the time before Christ. Besides, New Orleans has never needed an excuse to party.

Carnival is the embodiment of what New Orleans is at its deepest core—a baroque fantasy realm realized, a place of make-believe, a mythical place of transformation. In many ways, Carnival in New Orleans is a reincarnation of the fabled tableaux of King Louis XIV's royal court, a court whose debauchery rivaled pagan Rome at its most depraved. But New Orleans's joie de vivre as exemplified at Mardi Gras is so much more than just drunken revelry.

The extensive folkloric and cultural value of Mardi Gras is lost on those who view it merely as a massive drunken street orgy. Frederick Starr argues correctly the vulgarity of Mardi Gras is superficial, that in substance, Mardi Gras is "a poetic festival steeped in the exquisite high art of allegory."[2]

This insight is reflected in the names of the traditional, mainstream krewes: Comus (god of revelry and excess), Momus (god of satire), Bacchus (god of wine), Proteus (god of the sea and mutability), Orpheus (god of poets and musicians), Morpheus (god of dreams), Endymion (god of shepherds and hunters).

This mythological motif is certainly true of Gay Carnival and is evident in some the names of current gay krewes. Consider:

Amon-Ra—Of all the ancient Egyptian gods, Amon-Ra was the supreme deity
Armeinius—Greek mythological figure whose love of Narcissus went unrequited
Mwindo—Epic hero of the Nyanga people in central Africa
Petronius—Roman satirist who loved luxury
Satyricon—A literary satire written by Petronius
Narcissus—Beautiful young man in Greek mythology who fell in love with his own image

Not all of the gay krewes draw their names from mythology. The Lords of Leather, the Krewe of Queenateenas, and the Krewe de la Rue Royale Revelers all derive their identities from contemporary culture.

Although the Gay Carnival krewes do not parade, they do produce elaborate balls, which have afforded the gay community an opportunity to showcase its creativity and artistry. In decades past, when being in the closet was de rigueur, the gay krewes provided a sense of safety and purpose for gay men as well as an outlet for their gayness to manifest.

The artistry of mythology is a triumph of the imagination. History and imagination are inextricably linked, and New Orleans, a city in love with its history, cannot help, then, but be a wellspring of creativity. Carnival season is the perfect showcase for the city's ingenuity.

At her core, New Orleans (and Carnival itself), is a fascinating study in desire—its pull, its promises, its lies, and its consequences. In New Orleans, this fixation with desire is what fuels Carnival and Mardi Gras, the music and culinary scenes, the city's epic obesity and its rampant alcoholism.

Much like New Orleans herself, Mardi Gras is a wonderfully complex cultural phenomenon, replete with layers of meaning and symbolism. It is revelry, pageantry, and fantasy. It is a chance to wear masks and don different identities—something with which gay men have historically been thoroughly familiar.

The final essay in this section highlights the Krewe of Polyphemus. Polyphemus serves as an exemplar of the gay krewes in that it exemplified not only the competitiveness and drama that characterizes Gay Carnival, but also the devastating effect the HIV/AIDS crisis had on the krewes.

Ambush, February 21, 2017

NOTES

1. Perry Young, *The Mystick Krewe: Chronicles of Comus and His Kin*. New Orleans: Carnival Press, 1931.
2. Frederick S. Starr, *New Orleans Unmasqued*. New Orleans: Dedeaux Publishing, 1985.

REMEMBERING POLYPHEMUS

ONE DAY IN 1982, GARY MARTIN WAS AT VAN GOGH'S EAR[1] CHATTING with his friend Michael "Fish" Hickerson. The two were discussing Carnival and Mardi Gras, and in the course of the conversation, Martin casually remarked, I wouldn't mind starting a krewe. Thus was conceived the fabulous Krewe of Polyphemus.

A New Orleans native, Martin had grown up appreciating Carnival. His father had been heavily involved in straight Mardi Gras, having served as President of Thoth and also been associated with several other krewes, including Iris, Venus, and Freret. When Martin came of age, he inherited his father's appreciation of straight Carnival, but also came to value Gay Carnival as well. He knew and admired Bill Woolley, one of the pioneers of Gay Carnival.

After chatting with Hickerson, Martin gathered some of his friends together and Polyphemus was officially born. Among the charter members were Gary Martin, Michael Hickerson, Eugene Fenasci, and David Smith. After a trip to the library to check out a book on mythology, the small group assembled a list of names and threw them all in a hat. Someone drew the name Polyphemus and that was it. For the record, Polyphemus was the son of Poseidon and the fabled cyclops of Homer's *Odyssey*.

From the beginning, the krewe took immense pride in what they were doing and determined to outshine the older, more established krewes. As Captain, Martin insisted on supervising the costume-making and set a high bar of artistic excellence. Martin's dedication paid off at the krewe's first ball, whose theme was "Gems." Hickerson reigned as Queen Polyphemus I and David Smith reigned as King Polyphemus I.

Polyphemus outdid itself in its third ball, "I Do! I Do!" Carnival historian Howard P. Smith writes the ball "showed incredible attention to detail: each of the tables for special guests had a two-tiered white wedding cake topped with two male grooms."[2] And Rip Naquin remarked in *Ambush*, "It was hard to believe anything could top the festivities thus far but believe us the new royalty did just that. King (Kevin Bergeron) and

Queen Polyphemus III (Gregory Pichon) dazzled the audience with their thousands of plumes and stones, the most breathtaking costumes we have ever seen. The Captain of Polyphemus is certainly to be congratulated on the superb costuming, choreography, and showmanship of this exquisite production."

Martin's attention to detail and high expectations paid off the following year as well. The 1986 "Deco and Design" ball had been inspired by the mysterious art deco designer and artist Erté. After the ball, one of the costumes was displayed in the window at Saks. Erté himself noticed the gown and later complimented Martin on the design.

Polyphemus had established itself as the producer of highly creative and exquisite balls. For the krewe's fifth ball, "The Envelope Please," Martin selected a Broadway theme and was determined to maintain the krewe's reputation for excellence. Martin insisted that all costumes be made at the den, "under my watchful eye," but one member, whose costume upon which the tableau hinged, insisted on making it at his home. As the ball approached, Martin went to the man's home to inspect the costume only to discover it was nowhere near finished. The man was unceremoniously expelled from the krewe and other members worked around the clock in a rush to complete the costume. During the ball, just as member Kevin Keller walked out in the costume, police interrupted the ball because of a bomb threat. The auditorium was cleared as the bomb squad searched the auditorium. Two hours later, after no bomb was detected, the ball resumed. Many attendees remain convinced the expelled member made the anonymous bomb threat phone call.

Three years later, the Polyphemus den was destroyed in a tragic arson on New Year's Eve. Because all the costumes were destroyed, there was no ball in 1990.

But vengeful queens and fires were not the only thing Polyphemus (and the other gay krewes) had to worry about. The AIDS epidemic literally decimated the gay community, including many of the krewes. By 1992, Martin had lost so many friends and krewe members to AIDS, he was ready to call it a day. The 1992 ball, "Holidays," in which Martin served as both Captain and Queen, was the krewe's last and, in the words of Gay Carnival historian Howard P. Smith, "signaled the end of the Golden Age of Gay Carnival."

Ambush, February 11, 2020

NOTES

1. Van Gogh's Ear was a shop located at 907 Bourbon Street.

2. Howard P. Smith, *Unveiling the Muse: The Lost History of Gay Carnival in New Orleans*. Oxford: University Press of Mississippi, 2017.

ʙARS AND GAY SPACES

Societal attitudes toward homosexuality and queerness have undergone a profound paradigm shift in the last twenty years. In the twentieth century, when closet doors were firmly shut, gay and lesbian bars played a crucial role in the LGBT+ community by often being the only place a person could go to meet other like-minded people. It was at the gay or lesbian bar that one could meet other queer friends, pick up a one-night stand, obtain gay-related literature, or just learn what it meant to be queer. In a society devoid of reference points, the gay bar served as a beacon of light in the darkness of the closet. Because New Orleans is a drinking town and because the density of bars in the French Quarter is astronomical, there has never been a shortage of queer bars in New Orleans (although sadly, the last lesbian bar closed in 2012). The essays in this section focus on a number of gay and lesbian bars. "The Queer Quarter: A Moveable Feast" identifies shifting gay zones, clusters of bars and gay-owned businesses, throughout the Quarter over the years. "Bourbon Street Gets Its First Gay Bar" tells the story of Café Lafitte in Exile, the oldest gay bar in the city. "The Glory Days of North Rampart Street" takes a close look at North Rampart Street in the early 1980s. "The Lavender Line: Jerry Menefee, St. Ann, and Bourbon" focuses on the Bourbon Pub and Oz. And "The Phoenix Rises from the Ashes of Smoky Mary" explores the origins of the Phoenix and its connection to Charlene Schneider.

THE QUEER QUARTER: A MOVEABLE FEAST

A RANDOM DAY IN THE 1990S: A BELLIGERENT DRUNK IS BEING OBNOX-
ious and causing problems at The Wild Side, a gay bar on the corner
of Dauphine and St. Louis Streets. The bartender, a trans former prize-
fighter named Miss Do, punches him in the face and knocks him off his
barstool and then yells to no one in particular, "Get him outta here!"
Outside, a group of trans sex workers argue over who is going to pilfer
the drunk's pockets. A car rolls slowly by while the driver makes eye
contact with a young man sitting on a stoop and rubs his thumb against
his index and forefingers.

Welcome to the 1990s version of the "Financial District," a two-block
stretch of St. Louis Street from Bourbon to Burgundy. It borders an area
of the Quarter dubbed the Tango Belt in the Roaring Twenties. After the
famous prostitution district Storyville closed in 1917, brothels had simply scooted sideways a few blocks closer to the river and for many years
thrived in that part of the Vieux Carré.

In the nineties, the Financial District's name was originally derived
from the symbiotic relationship between a shadowy network of bars,
hustlers, johns, drug dealers, and bar regulars. Across from the historic
Hermann-Grima house was Le Round Up, a notorious dive bar frequented
by trans sex workers, ne'er-do-wells, the down-and-out, and what was
known in gay parlance as "rough trade." Up the street at the corner of
Burgundy was the Corner Pocket, a go-go boy bar that catered to gay men.

While that portion of St. Louis Street is still affectionately referred
to as the Financial District by the gay demimonde of the Quarter (and
the thousands of sex tourists who visit each year), the character of the
neighborhood has changed dramatically over the last three decades. Le
Round Up is no more (it's now B-Mac's). The Wild Side became Double
Play and is now Crossing. Only the Corner Pocket survives, still popular
as the place "where the boys are dancin' nightly on the bar!"

But the Financial District is only one of multiple centers of gravity for LGBT+ people that have popped up throughout the Quarter's storied history. These queer nexuses consisted of clusters of bars, restaurants, and other businesses owned and frequented by queer folk. Today one thinks of the intersection of Bourbon and St. Ann and the "Fruit Loop," but in years past there were other gay loci.

In the 1960s and early 1970s, hustlers abounded along Iberville between Royal and Chartres. There were a number of gay bars in that area, including Gertrude's, Wanda's, the Safari Room, the Midship, and the Up Stairs Lounge. The Up Stairs Lounge did not cater to hustlers, although it was burned down by one who was angry for being thrown out of the bar.

Nearby Exchange Place Alley (along with Cabrini Park on the other end of the Quarter) was a popular cruising area among gay men searching for anonymous assignations. In the 1940s, beat writer William S. Burroughs frequented the Alley, although he lived in Algiers. After a drug arrest, he broke bond and made for Mexico.

In the 1950s, St. Peter and Bourbon was the trendy, upscale gay locus. Dixie's Bar of Music and the Bourbon House, a popular eatery among gays and lesbians, dominated the corner, while not far away Pat O'Brien's featured a bar "for bachelors." And next door, behind what would later become Preservation Hall, lived fabled French Quarter eccentric Pops Whitesell, who in addition to his "respectable" photography, also photographed virtually nude men for bodybuilder magazines, the gay porn of the time.

Whitesell, whom Quarterites called the Leprechaun of St. Peter Street because of his diminutive stature, often drank with famed lesbian photographer Frances Benjamin Johnston, who upon retiring moved to New Orleans in 1949 and lived a few blocks away in the 1100 block of Bourbon.

Dixie's and the bachelor room at Pat O'Brien's were reserved for the "upper set"; hustlers were relegated to street corners and parks. In later years they might try to find benefactors at the Chart House, nicknamed the "Wrinkle Room," on the corner of Toulouse and Chartres. And there was also the Caverns, which was notoriously sleazy until Jerry Menefee bought it and opened the Bourbon Pub.

While today there are no lesbian bars in New Orleans, there used to be many of them. Kitty Blackwell, Rosemary Pino, Charlene Schneider, and Diane Dimiceli were all lesbian bar barons. Alice Brady opened her first bar, Mascarade (later Le Round Up), in 1952 and later had Alice Brady's on Ursulines, before opening Mr. D's Hi-da-way and then Brady's at 700 North Rampart.

By the early 1980s, North Rampart was a gay nexus. In addition to bars such as The Grog, Travis's, TT's West, Menefee's, Finale II, and Diane's, there were Restaurant Jonathan and Marti's. Jonathan's was an art deco temple; famed artist and designer Erté graced opening night by showing up in white fur. Up the street, Tennessee Williams was a regular at Marti's, which was across from his home on Dumaine. Around the corner was Daisy Mae's unforgettable junk shop. Farther down just beyond the Quarter were more bars—Les Pierre's, Charlene's, and the Phoenix.

Another gay loop in the 1980s in the lower Quarter consisted of the Golden Lantern, Lucille & Friend's, Mississippi River Bottom, the Great American Refuge, and the notorious Jewel's, which featured a bathtub in a dark room for those into watersports. Not far away, artist George Dureau could be found holding court at Sbisa's.[1]

Today most people would probably say the intersection of St. Ann and Bourbon is the epicenter of gay bar life in the Quarter. Three of the four corners play host to gay bars, with still more bars within a block. This corner is certainly ground zero for Southern Decadence revelers every Labor Day weekend. Oz occupies Pete Fountain's old nightclub, and his name can still be seen on the corner. Historian Richard Campanella notes that St. Ann is often called the lavender line because it separates the straight and gay sections of Bourbon Street.[2]

In a larger sense, the lavender line is starting to blur. As attitudes toward queerness evolve and traditional binary boundaries devolve into something more fluid, the need for gay bars, but not gay spaces, dissipates. In a sense, this is a return to what once was. Before Bienville (who lived into his eighties and never married) renamed Bulbancha Nouvelle Orleans, Indigenous peoples were anything but binary and honored the queer among themselves.

Bars and businesses come and go and it's difficult to predict what gay zones will look like in the decades to come. It is, however, a safe bet the Quarter will always retain a hint of lavender. After all, police chief Provosty Dayries noted in 1958, "Apparently the French Quarter of New Orleans has an atmosphere that appeals to these people."[3]

Yes, Chief Dayries, it certainly does.

The following essay examines the origins of the oldest gay bar in New Orleans; furthermore, it surveys other early gay and lesbian bars in New Orleans and how homophobia shaped the nature of those bars.

French Quarter Journal, June 28, 2020

NOTES

1. Sbisa's was a popular restaurant among gays and lesbians on lower Decatur Street.

2. Richard Campanella, *Bourbon Street: A History*. Baton Rouge: Louisiana State University Press, 2014.

3. Quoted in Frank Perez and Jeffrey Palmquist, *In Exile: The History and Lore Surrounding New Orleans Gay Culture and Its Oldest Gay Bar*. Hurlford, UK: LL Publications, 2012.

BOURBON STREET GETS ITS FIRST GAY BAR

THE OTHER DAY I WAS SITTING IN A BAR CHATTING WITH A FRIEND WHEN several straight women wandered in and sat nearby. My friend, who is somewhat advanced in age, became annoyed and ruefully asked me if I remembered the days when women were not allowed in gay bars. A much younger acquaintance of ours heard the remark and a heated discussion ensued. My old friend (who is in his eighties) insisted that gay bars should be exclusively reserved for gay men while my younger friend (who is in his twenties) countered that such a sentiment violated the spirit of tolerance and acceptance older gays have fought so hard for over the years.

Having heard this debate before in several other bars, I chose to remain silent, but the argument did cause me to ponder the future of gay bars and even if that designation would one day become a thing of the past. It is said that to know where you're going, you have to know where you've come from, so naturally, having an interest in history, the subject also made me consider the history of gay bars.

Gay bars as we know them today in New Orleans did not exist until the early/mid-twentieth century. Prior to that, drinking gays were relegated to a handful of straight bars that did not forbid their patronage but were a little less than welcoming. At the turn of the century in New Orleans, Tony Jackson, the famous gay pianist, used to hang out at a saloon called the Frenchman's (at Bienville and Villere Streets); the bar is also referenced by jazz historians as allowing cross-dressers. There was also the Golden Feather on St. Bernard Avenue and the Dream Castle on Frenchmen Street. And during Prohibition (1920–1933), there was, reputedly, a speakeasy in the lower Pontalba Building. All of these drinking establishments were predominately straight but somewhat gay-almost-friendly.

The oldest gay bar in New Orleans is Café Lafitte in Exile. In 1933, Tommy Caplinger, Harold Barthel, and Mary Collins opened Café Lafitte at the corner of Bourbon and St. Phillip Streets. They were accepting of and welcoming to their gay clientele. (Collins is widely believed to have been a lesbian or bisexual, Caplinger was straight, Bartell's orientation is unknown). Although the bar could not be classified as a gay bar as we think of that term today, it was as gay friendly as the times would permit.

Throughout the 1930s and 1940s, Café Lafitte was a trendy nightspot. Robert Kinney mentions the bar in his classic 1942 book, *The Bachelor in New Orleans*, suggesting, "If the bartender is passed out, go behind the bar and mix your own drink!"[1] In a city known for its bars, Café Lafitte was a must-stop for visitors and a mecca for celebrities, including Lyle Saxon, Tennessee Williams, Frances Benjamin Johnston, Enrique Alferez, and Robert Rouark, among others.

In 1951, the owner of the building that housed Café Lafitte (currently Lafitte's Blacksmith Shop) died. In the process of settling the estate, the building was sold at auction. Caplinger, the sole owner at this point, couldn't afford to purchase the building. Caplinger made the decision to relocate the bar down the street on the next corner. The words "In Exile" were added to Café Lafitte to refer to the bar's gay patrons who were "in exile" from the former location. Café Lafitte in Exile opened its current incarnation at 901 Bourbon in 1953. The grand opening was celebrated with a costume party.

As the 1950s unfolded, Lafitte's became one of a handful of French Quarter "queershops," a derisive term used by police to refer to what we now call gay bars. There was also the Starlet Lounge on Chartres Street and Tony Bacino's on Toulouse Street and a few others. These bars were frequented almost exclusively by gay men—women, even lesbians, were specifically not allowed. A few lesbian bars opened on Tchoupitoulas Street in the Irish Channel in the 1950s but these bars were short-lived. Gays and lesbians finally had bars of their own; the era of gay folk having to "tone it down" in order to drink in straight bars was essentially over, although a few bars managed to successfully blur the line between gay and straight, the most notable being Dixie's Bar of Music, which relocated from the CBD[2] to Bourbon Street in 1949. There was also the My-O-My Club on the Lakefront, which featured female impersonators but essentially catered to a straight clientele.

Before the advent of the internet and the subsequent seismic shift in public attitudes toward homosexuality, the gay bar served for decades not only as refuge and playground for gay men but also as identity giver for those just coming to terms with their gayness. For young and old alike, the gay bar was a safe space as well as a place for answers for those who felt the burgeoning yearnings of the identity that dare not speak its name.

As society and technology have evolved, so has the role of the gay bar. Despite all the progress our community has made and despite how far society has come, it's still not acceptable or safe for a gay couple to go into many straight bars and make public demonstrations of affection. It is, however, becoming increasingly common for straight folk to patronize gay bars in order to show how "tolerant" they are. This is a function of gay bars that my eighty-something-year-old friend probably never imagined. Nevertheless, for good or ill, "straight-friendly" gay bars are the inevitable product of the acceptance for which we as a community have fought for so long. I'll leave it up to you to decide if such a consequence constitutes a case of being careful of what we ask for.

The next essay examines how the queer bar scene had evolved from the 1950s and consolidated on North Rampart Street by the 1980s.

Ambush, October 8, 2013

NOTES

1. Robert Kinney, *The Bachelor in New Orleans*. New Orleans: Bormon House, 1946.

2. Central Business District. Dixie's was originally located in the 200 block of St. Charles Avenue.

THE GLORY DAYS OF NORTH RAMPART STREET

TRAVIS'S. MENEFEE'S. TT'S WEST. FINALE II. ALICE BRADY'S. MARTI'S Restaurant. Restaurant Jonathan. In the early 1980s, all these North Rampart Street haunts were home to a vibrant gay nightlife.

Throughout its history, the French Quarter has given rise to multiple centers of gravity for gay life, but none of these could compare to North Rampart Street in the early 1980s. Circumstances both national and local gave rise to a special moment in time. At the dawn of the Reagan era, when AIDS was but a mere, distant blip on the radar, confidence and hopefulness were in the air. The sexual revolutionaries of the 1970s had emerged victorious and the economic malaise of the country was dissipating.

Locally, the horror of the Up Stairs Lounge arson, a seminal moment in local gay history, was ten years in the past. The hugely successful protest of Anita Bryant's visit to New Orleans was fresh in people's minds, and Gay Carnival was at its zenith.

In the early 1970s, Travis Hickman, Clifford Rednour, and Ron Smith opened Travis's Bar at 834 North Rampart Street, which, after Club My-O-My burned down, became the city's premiere venue for drag, or "female impersonation," as it was still sometimes called. There one could enjoy the likes of Rowena, Alotta Mulotta, Mister Boobie, Ginger Snap, Adrian St. Clair, Gilbertine Livaudais, Sable Starr, Tarrah, and Donnie Jay.

Two blocks up, at 642 North Rampart, was Finale II, the reincarnation of the Finale, which was originally located at Royal and Ursulines Streets in a building owned by Dave and Doris DeVisente. In the 1960s, Dave and Doris ran a restaurant above the bar, which was managed by George Wilson and Nick Donovan. Daisy Mae, a sassy queen who owned a junk shop in the 800 block of North Rampart, was a fixture at the first Finale.

Alice Brady's bar at 700 North Rampart provided lesbians a place of their own, even if gay men were welcome too. If lesbians tired of Brady's, they could easily walk to Ms. Kitty's at 740 Burgundy Street. A little farther away were two more lesbian bars—Charlene's at 940 Elysian Fields and Pino's at 621 Elysian Fields.

Back on North Rampart Street, men could immerse themselves in leather culture at TT's West (820 North Rampart) or enjoy the upscale environment of Menefee's—a "Restaurant-Bar-Health & Swim Club" at 1123 North Rampart.

Menefee's was short-lived but it was the crown jewel of Rampart Street while it lasted. Opened by Jerry Menefee and his partner Tex Knight, both of whom were former bartenders at Café Lafitte in Exile, Menefee's was an attempt to outdo what they had done a decade earlier with the Bourbon Pub (formerly the Caverns).

There was also Jonathan's and Marti's, two restaurants on North Rampart that served as the twin pillars of what Howard P. Smith describes as "gay café society."[1] Restaurant Jonathan was opened by Jack Cosner and Jay Schwab and in addition to serving excellent food also served as a temple of art deco décor. On opening night, the flamboyant queen and fixture in the Quarter's gay demimonde Erté showed up in white fur. Erté, who would become a regular at Jonathan's, was an artist and fashion designer who championed the art deco movement.

Down the street, Tennessee Williams could be found almost every day at Marti's. Williams lived virtually across the street at 1014 Dumaine. Opened in 1971 by Martin Shambra, Marti's foreshadowed the glittering "gay café society" that would characterize the early 1980s.

The glitter, of course, faded. 1984 seems to have been the turning point. Marti's closed in 1984, and Jerry Menefee died that year as well. The Quarter's only bathhouse was raided, and a serial killer was targeting gay men in the Quarter. The specter of AIDS was looming larger and larger.

Jonathan's shuttered its doors in 1986. Travis's eventually became Wolfendale's, which became Starlight by the Park, which became Michael's on the Park, which became Grand Pre's. Brady's would become Dianne's and Fat Jerry's before becoming the Ninth Circle and its current incarnation as the Black Penny. Menefee's, TT's West, and Finale II also faded away.

Other bars would come and go along North Rampart and the strip's fortunes would rise and fall, but nothing can compare to the plethora of gayness that was North Rampart Street in the early 1980s.

The following essay investigates how St. Ann Street became known as "the Lavender Line," separating the gay and straight sections of Bourbon

Street. In the process, it also considers the contributions of flamboyant Jerry Menefee to the French Quarter's gay bar culture.

Ambush, May 8, 2018

NOTE

1. Howard P. Smith, *Unveiling the Muse: The Lost History of Gay Carnival in New Orleans* (Jackson: University Press of Mississippi, 2017).

THE LAVENDER LINE:
JERRY MENEFEE, ST. ANN,
AND BOURBON

In 1958, New Orleans Mayor Chep Morrison famously observed, "Here's to Bourbon Street, where men are men—at least nine times out of ten." At the time, the network of gay life in the French Quarter had a variety of nodes: restaurants, antique shops, cafés, and a number of bars dispersed along several blocks of Bourbon Street. Morrison's wisecrack suggests what everyone knew but rarely talked about—the Quarter had a large, if not quite thriving, gay community.

The "queershops," as the police called gay bars, represented small segments of gay visibility in a very homophobic time. In the same year Mayor Morrison made his infamous joke about Bourbon Street, he appointed his half brother, Jacob Morrison, to lead a "Committee on the Problem of Sex Deviates." This was essentially a public relations stunt to help Morrison's image as a reformer. Nonetheless, the committee was successful in harassing a number of gay bars in the Quarter, most notably the Starlet Lounge and Tony Bacino's.

In his book on the history of Bourbon Street, Richard Campanella writes, "At the nexus of the emerging gay space was the St. Ann Street intersection, and for this reason the so-called 'lavender line' exists along St. Ann today, dividing gay and straight Bourbon with remarkable exactitude."[1]

The "space" Campanella refers to extended from Tony Bacino's bar at the corner of Toulouse and Bourbon to Café Lafitte in Exile at the corner of Bourbon and Dumaine. Beginning in the 1950s, there were a number of bars in that five-block stretch frequented almost exclusively by gay folk. Among these were Tony Bacino's, Dixie's Bar of Music, and Café Lafitte in Exile.

This stretch included four cross streets; so why did St. Ann become the lavender line? Part of the answer lies in zoning. The Bourbon Street

Entertainment District, which was created in 1929, extends from Iberville to St. Ann. In addition to zoning, St. Ann was centrally located between two gay meccas—Lafitte's one block away at Dumaine and Dixie's one block in the other direction at St. Peter. But besides zoning and location, Jerry Menefee, one of the most colorful and flamboyant characters in modern Quarter history, decided to gay it up.

The Bourbon Pub and Parade is housed in a two-story commercial brick building dating back to circa 1829. By the 1960s, the building housed a gay bar called the Caverns. The Caverns was a hustler bar known for cheap drugs and even cheaper sex. A former patron recalls, "It was sleazy. But sleazy in a good way."

Jerry Menefee, who had been a bartender and manager at Café Lafitte in Exile, bought the Caverns in 1974 and renamed it the Bourbon Pub. Menefee and his partner Tex Knight spent a fortune renovating the place, and in the following year, Menefee bought the building for $140,000.

Menefee later opened a bar in Houston called the Parade Disco and would later open the extravagant Menefee's on North Rampart Street. Menefee's was unlike anything New Orleans had seen. Bars, especially dive ones, were everywhere in New Orleans but never had there been a high-end, multipurpose club for gay men. Menefee's housed a restaurant, a gym, a disco, and a pool. The place was filled with custom artwork. "Classy" is the word many old-timers use in remembering Menefee's (although a few say "gaudy").

When Menefee's opened, North Rampart Street had undergone something of a revival and the argument could be made that for a while, North Rampart was the epicenter of gay bar life. North Rampart Street was home to several gay and lesbian bars and gay-owned or gay-friendly businesses. In the early 1970s, the notorious queen known as Daisy Mae owned a gift shop near what was Travis', Wolfendales', Starlight by the Park, Michael's by the Park and current home of Grand Pre's. Other lost bars also on North Rampart included Mabel's Cove, Fat Sam's, Tush, Gigi's, Brady's, Diane's, Mona's, Lindsey's, Applause, North Star, We Are Family, Sundance, Footloose, the Ninth Circle, Finale II, Town Hall, the Bar at Congo Square, the Cabaret, and several others. Next door to Menefee's was the New Orleans Guest House, owned by two former Queens of Petronius, Ray Cronk and Alvin Payne.

Menefee was from a prominent family in North Louisiana and despite being raised in the midst of that cultural desolation, Menefee was a charismatic figure who had panache and a penchant for extravagant living. Pub bartender Don Wentworth recalls sitting at the bar one day in 1984 when Menefee pulled up in his canary yellow Rolls-Royce, scooped him up, and took him to the airport to pick up Grace Jones and her boyfriend, "a young blonde thing," Wentworth recalls. Jones lip-synced a couple of songs that night at the Pub's tenth anniversary party.

In a 1983 *New York Times* interview, Menefee's partner Tex Knight noted, "No one could resist him once he got going. And he was a flamboyant man. He wore tons of jewelry, gold necklaces, rings on every finger, earrings, and enormous hats. You couldn't miss him in a room. No sir!"

Menefee died of a heart attack on October 24, 1984, while recuperating from a battle with cancer. Menefee's on North Rampart Street was idle from 1984 to 1989 and then became the Monster, which, in 1994, became the French Quarter Courtyard Hotel.

After Menefee's death in 1984, Bobby Revere, who was his accountant, became the owner of the Bourbon Pub in 1986. Revere sold the Pub to Sandy Sachs in 2009. Sachs had worked at the bar in the early 1980s while she was attending Tulane University.

When Menefee opened the Pub in 1974, the space that is now Oz was a gay bar called Pete's, the name playing on the fact that famed jazz clarinetist Pete Fountain had a nightclub there in the 1960s.

The building at 800 Bourbon Street was constructed in 1880 and underwent extensive renovations in the 1930s. Pete Fountain opened his club there in 1960, a fact evidenced by the tiles bearing his name on the sidewalk by the front door. Imagine, if you can, Frank Sinatra sitting on the dance floor of Oz and chatting with Jonathan Winters or Robert Goulet while Brenda Lee sings "I'm Sorry." These and many other celebrities made appearances at Pete Fountain's club. Fountain later moved his club to the Riverside Hilton, where he performed regularly until 2003.

After Pete's closed, the space was reincarnated as Le Bistro in 1976. Le Bistro lasted not quite ten years and was the site of the first Miss Gay New Orleans contest. After Le Bistro closed, the space at 800 Bourbon was vacant for a number of years until Oz opened.

But Oz almost never was. The building at 800 Bourbon had been owned by the Panzeca family for over fifty years at the time. In order to maintain the building's nonconforming use (because it was outside the entertainment district boundary), the Panzecas ran a "temporary bar," but the family/business ultimately lost its alcohol permit in 1989, temporarily at least. A lawsuit ensued and the building's nonconforming use was reinstated, despite opposition from the owners of the Pub and Café Lafitte in Exile and the Vieux Carré Property Owners and Residents Association.

Oz opened in 1993 and over the next twenty-one years, Oz became the city's premiere gay dance club. A rivalry developed between Oz and the Bourbon Pub and once, when a small fire broke out at the Pub, the DJ at Oz played the Trammps' classic song "Disco Inferno."

In the early 2000s, Oz was home to a young Bianca del Rio, who performed in a variety of capacities at the club. Del Rio would go on to international fame after winning season six of *RuPaul's Drag Race* in 2014.

Johnny Chisholm, Doyle Yeager, and Bobby Warner, co-owners of Oz, were forced to sell both the building and the business at auction after being unable to pay loans that came due in 2014. In 2015, New Orleans businessman Kishore "Mike" Motwani (T-shirt shops and Willie's Chicken mogul) bought Oz for $8.175 million. Fears that Oz would start selling feather boas and fried chicken have been unfounded. The outside of the club, however, has received a welcome facelift.

More than anything, the Pub and Oz have solidified St. Ann as the "lavender line," a line also reinforced by gay-themed and -owned business on the other two corners of the Bourbon and St. Ann intersection.

The Creole Cottage at the upriver, lakeside corner of the intersection was built circa 1800 and now houses Marie Laveau's House of Voodoo and the gift shop Hit Parade.

Across the street is Napoleon's Itch, a gay bar that occupies a corner of the Bourbon Orleans hotel. This location contains the fabled Orleans Ballroom, which was incorporated into the hotel when it was constructed in 1965. The Orleans Ballroom was opened in 1817, after a fire had destroyed the previous building, by John Davis, who would later open the Orleans theater nearby, thus helping New Orleans become the Opera Capital of North America in the mid-nineteenth century. The ballroom played host to many masquerade, carnival, and quadroon balls throughout the nineteenth century. In 1881, the building became the convent of the Sisters of the Holy Family, a religious order founded by the free woman of color Henriette DeLille. Napoleon's Itch opened in 2004.

I'm not sure what Henriette DeLille would think of a gay bar in her former convent. It is, however, safe to assume that she, like many still are today, would be astounded at the gay presence at St. Ann and Bourbon Streets. The lavender line began to form in the 1950s and became codified by the early 1970s with gay bars occupying both downriver corners. The longevity of both the Bourbon Pub and Oz have helped as well.

In recent years, boundaries such as the "Lavender Line" have begun to blur, and while bars such as the Pub and Oz cater to more straight tourists now than ever before, our next essay focuses on the only leather bar left in New Orleans, and its connection to a beloved lesbian.

Ambush, July 19, 2016

NOTE

1. Richard Campanella, *Bourbon Street: A History* (Baton Rouge: Louisiana State University Press, 2014).

THE PHOENIX RISES FROM THE ASHES OF SMOKY MARY

IN 1982, JAMIE TEMPLE AND GEORGE COSSITT OPENED THE PHOENIX, a leather bar at 941 Elysian Fields Avenue in the Marigny.[1] In the thirty-four years the Phoenix has been open, it has gained an international reputation as one of the nation's premiere leather bars. For much of the twentieth century, the building that houses the Phoenix was a hardware store before it was purchased by pioneering lesbian/women's activist Charlene Schneider, who turned the space into a restaurant called Smoky Mary's. The name was reminiscent of the railroad line that ran from the riverfront down Elysian Fields all the way to the Milneburg area on Lake Pontchartrain. The Pontchartrain Railroad, aka Smoky Mary, operated from 1831 to 1932.

Schneider also owned the bar across the street at 940 Elysian Fields. Charlene's opened in 1977 and over the next twenty-two years would earn a prominent place in the pantheon of legendary New Orleans bars. Bars often take on the personality of their owners, and Charlene's was no exception. Saundra Boudreaux, a regular in the 1980s, recalls, "Charlene cared about her girls, they were family," and "She always made us feel loved and safe." The notion of Charlene's being a "safe space" is a recurrent theme in many women's memories of the bar. At the time, Charlene once recalled, "Women's bars were like boxing rings." The late Toni Pizanie remembered, "She worked toward giving women a better space."

After Smoky Mary's closed, it became a short-lived lesbian bar called Clark's Gable until Temple and Cossitt bought the place in 1982 and redubbed it the Phoenix. In 1991, they remodeled the apartment above the bar and opened the Men's Room Bar, now called the Eagle. In 1995, a leather boutique, COK (Clothing or Kink), was added downstairs. Catering to the leather community, the store offers everything from harnesses to boy butter.

Founding owner Jamie Temple, originally from New Jersey, came to New Orleans to attend the University of New Orleans and after college decided to stay in the city. He is one of the cofounders of the NO/AIDS Task Force (now Crescent Care) and in 1991 served as Southern Decadence Grand Marshal XIX.

Today, reminiscing on those years, Temple says, "My memories of owning the Phoenix are quite positive. I always thought of it as a neighborhood bar first and foremost. A mini community center of sorts you might say. We were at first afraid folks wouldn't follow us across Elysian Fields. Boy, were we ever wrong! We named it after my husband's hometown. We thought it sounded better than the Newark (my Jersey roots)."

Temple and Cossitt sold the bar two weeks before Hurricane Katrina to Bobby Connell. Current owner Clint Taylor bought the bar in 2011.

The Phoenix is strongly associated with Southern Decadence because of its multiple-night street party and other indoor festivities. The Phoenix is home to pigs and pups and bears all year around, but they come out en masse on Labor Day weekend.

On Wednesday, September 2, 1998, the Phoenix became one of the last gay bars in New Orleans to be raided by the police. To kick off Decadence weekend, the bar was hosting "Underwear Night" and many of the patrons had checked their clothes at the door. According to media reports at the time, an unnamed "concerned citizen" had filed a complaint with city officials and the police department citing unsafe sexual activity in the upstairs bar, which according to the complaint, was "extremely out of control on weekends after midnight." A statement issued by the New Orleans Police Department stated undercover vice squad officers "observed males engaging in oral copulation, anal intercourse, digital anal intercourse, as well as mutual masturbation."

Of the fourteen people arrested, thirteen were charged with violating obscenity laws, and the management was booked for "Allowing Sexual Acts on the Premises of [an] Alcohol Beverage Outlet." Witnesses report the police were very rude and made homophobic jokes during the raid. Police spokesman Lieutenant Marlon Defillo issued a public statement describing the raid and releasing the names and addresses of those arrested.

Over the course of its thirty-four-year history, the Phoenix has served as the home bar for a variety of clubs and organizations, a few of which include the Knights d'Orleans, the Lords of Leather, the Renegade Bears, and, more recently, NOLAPAH (New Orleans Pups and Handlers).

Gay male leather culture dates back to the 1940s and evolved out of the motorcycle club movement, which became popular in California in the 1950s.

Ambush, November 8, 2016

NOTE

1. The Marigny is a neighborhood adjacent to the French Quarter.

HIV/AIDS

As the AIDS epidemic unfolded in New Orleans, the LGBT+ community responded in a variety of ways. By the end of the 1980s, New Orleans was a model city for providing AIDS-related services, but at the beginning of the decade, the gay community in New Orleans, as in other cities, was shocked. Ignorance of the disease caused a lot of fear. In addition to political groups like ACT UP and service providers like the NO/AIDS Task Force, living facilities for people living with HIV emerged in the early years of the epidemic. And one lawsuit originating in New Orleans became a landmark case in the growing canon of HIV-insurance law. The essays in this section provide a closer look at New Orleans's response to the AIDS crisis. "How the Greed of an Insurance Company Almost Killed John East" examines a lawsuit that stemmed from Blue Cross / Blue Shield of Louisiana's decision to no longer accept premium payments from third parties such as the Ryan White HIV/AIDS Program. "Acting Up in New Orleans" takes a look at the short-lived New Orleans chapter of ACT UP, the advocacy group founded by Larry Kramer in New York City. "NO/AIDS Task Force" tells the story of how the Task Force came to be and its early growth. "Project Lazarus" and "Belle Reve" describe how the community responded to the crisis by establishing AIDS hospices that gradually evolved into living facilities for those living with AIDS.

HOW THE GREED OF AN INSURANCE COMPANY ALMOST KILLED JOHN EAST

2014 WAS ANOTHER STELLAR YEAR IN THE LONG STRUGGLE FOR LGBT equality. Same-sex marriage became a reality in twenty states, Michael Sam became the first openly gay football player drafted into the NFL, and President Obama expanded federal employment protections to include gender identity. One of the least recognized yet most significant victories involved health insurance for those living with HIV, and it originated in New Orleans.

In January 2014, John East received terrible news. His caseworker at the NO/AIDS Task Force called to inform him that his insurance company, Blue Cross / Blue Shield of Louisiana, would no longer accept payments from third parties.[1] The news devastated East because without insurance, his HIV and other medicines would cost him over $6,000 a month.

East had faithfully paid monthly payments to Blue Cross / Blue Shield of Louisiana since 1985, almost thirty years. In 2009, East's premiums became unaffordable when they were raised to $650 a month. On the day his insurance was set to expire, he qualified for insurance subsidies from the Ryan White HIV/AIDS Program. East breathed a sigh of relief. He was not going to die for lack of medication.

The Ryan White HIV/AIDS Program was established in 1990 and works with local and state governments and community-based organizations, such as the NO/AIDS Task Force, to provide services to an estimated 536,000 people each year who do not have sufficient health care coverage or financial resources to cope with HIV disease. The program is administered by the US Department of Health and Human Services.

Without insurance, East's HIV medicines would have cost over $2,000 per month; combined with his other non-HIV medicines, East would have had to pay out of pocket over $6,000 per month for his medication.

East's financial crisis would not have been as dire if Republican governor Bobby Jindal had not rejected $1.65 billion, funds offered to the state as part of the Medicaid expansion provided for in the Affordable Care Act (Obamacare).

When Blue Cross / Blue Shield of Louisiana announced they would no longer accept third-party payments, Lambda Legal, a national advocacy group for LGBT rights, contacted East and asked him if he would be willing to be the chief litigant in a class action lawsuit against Blue Cross / Blue Shield of Louisiana and two other insurance companies (Louisiana Health Cooperative and Vantage Health Plan). East was reluctant at first but ultimately agreed. Recalling his decision to participate in the lawsuit, East observes, "Health trumps privacy."

Lambda Legal initially sent the three health insurance companies a letter urging them to reverse their policy of not accepting third-party payments. When the three insurance companies ignored the letter, Lambda Legal filed a lawsuit in United States District Court, Middle District of Louisiana on February 20, 2014, against the insurance companies on behalf of East and other low-income Louisianans living with HIV and won an emergency injunction to force the companies to accept the premiums until the case was settled. The Louisiana case caused the federal government to issue a regulation that insurance companies nationwide accept payments from the Ryan White Fund.

When the lawsuit was announced, East said publicly, "No one should be made to choose between medications and keeping a roof over your head and food on the table . . . It is unconscionable, despicable and a humanitarian atrocity that Blue Cross and other insurance companies are dumping policy holders with HIV."

Blue Cross / Blue Shield of Louisiana officials claimed they decided to stop accepting third-party payments in an effort to reduce fraud but could produce no evidence of fraud with regard to the Ryan White Fund payments.

Noel Twilbeck, CEO of the NO/AIDS Task Force, sums up the case's significance by stating, "John's willingness to share his story enabled Lambda Legal to draw great attention to unfair and harmful practices of BC/BS (and possibly other insurance carriers). If the unjust insurance practices had not been challenged, the trickle-down effect of other carriers following them could have meant that hundreds of individuals who needed assistance with premium payments in Louisiana would have been unable to access Marketplace policies."

John East grew up in McComb, Mississippi, and has lived in New Orleans since 1977. He is a US Navy veteran and has worked in the medical industry for thirty years. Michael Callais, his partner of fourteen years, died in 1991 of complications from AIDS, as did East's little brother. East managed the food bank at the NO/AIDS Task Force in 1988 and 1989.

Lambda Legal was founded in 1973. It won the nation's first HIV/AIDS discrimination case in 1983 (*People v. West 12 Tenants Corp.*). Lambda Legal has a long history of forcing insurance companies to cover HIV treatments, and it has also assisted in establishing privacy rights for people living with HIV.

East's landmark case represents a significant, yet largely unacknowledged, contribution from New Orleans to the larger history of HIV/AIDS nationally. The next essay focuses on the role New Orleans played in a major thread of that national history—the activist group ACT UP.

Ambush, December 2, 2014

NOTE

1. In 2014, the NO/AIDS Task Force became Crescent Care and began to offer an expanded range of health and wellness services for anyone and everyone who is seeking health care services in Greater New Orleans and southeastern Louisiana.

ACTING UP IN NEW ORLEANS

As the fiftieth anniversary of Stonewall approaches, my mind is not so much on the gay liberation movement of the 1970s, but rather on the AIDS epidemic of the 1980s. How did the disease affect the movement? How might LGBT+ history have unfolded had there been no epidemic? And what was happening in New Orleans at the time?

In some ways, AIDS had the inadvertent effect of humanizing the gay community. As more and more people became sick, straight people began to have epiphanies—"Oh, I didn't realize my neighbor, coworker, etc. was gay." In this regard, AIDS, to some degree, put a face on—humanized—gay men.

For the truly closed-minded, however, it had the opposite effect. Religious leaders consistently preached that the dreaded disease was God's judgment on a wicked lifestyle. In the minds of many, AIDS reinforced deeply entrenched negative societal stereotypes about gay men, namely that they were promiscuous and sick and perverted and worthy of whatever punishment God or nature might mete out.

By 1988, there was a local chapter of ACT UP (AIDS Coalition to Unleash Power) in New Orleans. ACT UP had been founded in New York City in 1987 as a direct-action group to raise awareness about the epidemic and, more specifically, the lack of adequate funding allocated by the government to fight the disease. The New Orleans chapter of ACT UP met weekly at the NO/AIDS Task Force headquarters. In New Orleans, as elsewhere, there was much about which to act up.

New Orleans ACT UP staged a protest at the Republican National Convention in New Orleans in 1988. Specifically, the group protested the fact that state funding for AZT, the only FDA-approved drug for the treatment of AIDS at the time, was about to run out. Protesters formed what they called a "human billboard" at the entrance to the convention. Protesters held signs and panels from the national AIDS Memorial Quilt and distributed leaflets indignantly questioning why the state and city should spend $800,000 hosting the Republican Convention and not spend a dime on AIDS. ACT UP New York sent a delegation to assist with the protest, but the out-of-towners did not get along well with local ACT UP members. In a 1992 interview, Doug Robertson remembered, "ACT UP New York came down for the Republican convention and destroyed us." The tactics of the New York group turned off the locals and membership dropped dramatically.

The local chapter also called attention to discrimination within the criminal justice system against people living with AIDS. There was a 1991 class action lawsuit against Sherriff Charles Foti alleging maltreatment of inmates in the parish prison, and in 1992, ACT UP held a press conference in front of the criminal courthouse to call attention to police brutality. Specifically, the press conference recounted the case of an incarcerated man who had been beaten by police during an arrest at his home on minor charges. In the course of the beating, the man, who was HIV positive, bled on one of the officer's shirts. The man was charged with attempted murder and booked into Orleans Parish Prison, where he was denied medical treatment.

This homophobic attitude permeated the criminal justice system. The district attorney's office had a policy of charging persons arrested for prostitution with the crime of knowingly transmitting HIV. Attorney Mark Gonzalez, who was a member of ACT UP, testified to the Mayor's Advisory Committee on Lesbian and Gay Issues in 1989 about a client of his who was the victim of this policy. Several police officers had barged into this man's French Quarter apartment, without a warrant, and arrested him on drug possession charges, even though police found no drugs at the scene. During the arrest, the police noticed a bottle of AZT and told him as they were taking him to jail "not to worry about the charges—you'll probably die of AIDS in jail."

In 1990, ACT UP, which then consisted of only half a dozen members, managed to stage a protest at city hall in which five hundred people participated. Several people were arrested, including City Councilman Johnny Jackson. The group was protesting inadequate funding. ACT UP also waged letter-writing and petition campaigns to be sent to Governor Buddy Roemer and Department of Health and Hospitals secretary David Ramsey demanding $3 million worth of funding for Charity Hospital's C-100 Outpatient Clinic. In addition to letters, the group also flooded the governor's office with postcards depicting a coffin with the succinct message: "This is the alternative to C-100 full funding!"

Funding for research and treatment was not the only thing lacking. Ignorance of the disease and the lack of effective treatments created a real need for education and outreach in the early 1980s. Led by Ted Wisniewski, who while doing his residency at Charity Hospital saw the need firsthand, several medical professionals and others in New Orleans began meeting to discuss ways to address the crisis. Some of these people included Rue Morrison, Thomas Norman, Robert Kremitzki, Louise McFarland, Harlee Kutezen, Leonard Doty, Richard Devlin, Craig Henry, Henry Schmidt, Carole Pindaro, Jim Kellogg, Brobson Lutz, Jonathan Clemmer, and Father Bob Pawell. Out of these meetings, the NO/AIDS Task Force was born in 1983.

Eventually, medical research led to the development of effective treatments that no longer rendered a positive diagnosis a death sentence. And gradually, as celebrities like Rock Hudson, Liberace, Greg Louganis, and Magic Johnson were publicly identified as HIV positive, fear and ignorance regarding the disease began to subside. By 1995, New Orleans would have three living facilities for those living with HIV/AIDS: Project Lazarus, Trinity House, and Belle Reve.

Although a cure remains elusive, one wonders not only how HIV/AIDS changed the course of LGBT+ history but also how different the history of HIV/AIDS would have been without ACT UP.

At the forefront of New Orleans's response to the AIDS crisis was the NO/AIDS Task Force, now known as Crescent Care. The following essay explores the origins and humble beginnings of the NO/AIDS Task Force.

Ambush, June 18, 2019

NO/AIDS TASK FORCE

In 1978, C. J. Robichaux and Ernie Wadlington, both medical technicians, attended a medical convention in Lafayette, Louisiana. Part of the convention involved a Quiz Bowl at which Ernie was the moderator and C.J. was a judge. At one point during the game, the two men became embroiled in a dispute over a contestant's answer. C.J. and Ernie continued to get acquainted and when the convention was over, C.J., who lived in New Orleans, found himself driving up to North Louisiana every other weekend to visit Ernie. The pair had fallen in love and before long, Ernie moved to New Orleans, where the two bought a house and settled into a nice domestic life. Neither man had any idea that Ernie was HIV positive.

The virus laid dormant until 1988. C.J. and Ernie were on vacation in Springfield, Missouri, when Ernie became sick. Upon returning home, Ernie's doctor diagnosed him with double pneumonia and also informed him he had AIDS. Ernie struggled for three years and finally succumbed to the disease in May of 1991. Before Ernie's death, C.J. took a leave of absence from his job as a medical technician at Charity Hospital to care for Ernie. By this time, the AIDS epidemic was ravaging not only New Orleans but also cities across the nation. C.J. remembers, "It was like an avalanche. So many people were dying. There was a short period where I could've gone to ten funerals."

In addition to processing his own grief, C.J. also had to deal with the very real possibility that he may have contracted the virus. He assumed he was positive and put off getting tested. Eventually he did get tested and to his surprise he was negative. C.J. recalls, "In the 1980s, before we knew it was a virus, everyone was so scared. The biggest thing back then was fear of the unknown."

C.J. and Ernie's story is typical of thousands of other stories. Ignorance of the disease and the lack of effective treatments created a real need for education and outreach in the early 1980s. Led by Ted Wisniewski, who as a resident at Charity Hospital saw the need firsthand, several medical professionals and others in New Orleans began meeting to discuss ways to address the crisis. Out of these meetings the NO/AIDS Task Force was born in 1983.

The NO/AIDS Task Force has been delivering HIV/AIDS services since its inception. The services offered (followed by the year of initiation in parentheses) include telephone hotline (1983); community outreach (1983); condom distribution (1985); HIV antibody testing and counseling (1985); buddy/companion program (1985); case management (1990); substance abuse and mental health counseling (1990); support groups (1990); early intervention services (TB, Hepatitis B, flu shots, etc.) (1991); home-delivered meals (1992); benefits assistance program (1992); street outreach (1994); changing high-risk environments (1994); food bank (1997); treatment education/adherence counseling (1998); primary medical care (1999); housing coordination (1999); peer support program (1999); case finding (2000); community mobilization project targeting men who have sex with men (2000); liaison nurse home visits (2001); housing case management (2001); medication disbursement (2001); office in Houma/Thibodeaux area (2001); training for allied health care professionals (2002); Exchange House—a transitional residential facility in Houma, Louisiana (2003); awarded CDC grant targeting prevention for MSM—opened Community Awareness Network (CAN) office on Frenchman (2004); awarded CDC grant to tailor and adapt intervention for internet chat rooms (2004); Avita Drugs opened a pharmacy on-site (2004); housing case management program (2005); CareVan arrived as gift from Elizabeth Taylor AIDS Foundation—to be used for medical care and mobile counseling and testing (2006); awarded funding to begin National HIV Behavioral Surveillance site (2006); AIDS Law of Louisiana co-located with the Task Force (2006); primary medical care program expanded with full-time physician and expanded clinic hours (2007); consumer advisory council (2007); medical nutrition therapy (2008); peer suite (computer lab and exercise room) (2008); medical transportation (2008); permanent supportive housing program (2009); awarded Substance Abuse and Mental Health Services Administration funding—began intensive outpatient substance abuse therapy program (2009); CHAT (Curbing HIV/AIDS Transmission) program targeting HIV prevention for youth (2009); awarded Ryan White Part C funding for early intervention services (primary medical care) (2009); Shanti L.I.F.E. (Learning Immune Function Enhancement) (2010); case management program with Orleans Criminal Sheriff's Office (2010); awarded CDC funding for young Black gay/bisexual MSM—opened The Movement program (2012); AIDS Law of Louisiana merged with NO/AIDS Task Force, providing legal services in New Orleans and Baton Rouge (2012); Food For Friends kitchen opened at First Unitarian Universalist Church (2013); counseling and testing program in the Orleans Municipal Court (2013); New Orleans Syringe Access Program moves to NO/AIDS Task Force (2013); awarded Ryan White Part D funding providing resources for women, infants, children, and youth—the Family Advocacy, Care, and Education Services (FACES) program (formerly program of Children's Hospital) joined NO/AIDS upon grant award (2013); awarded funding to become a Federally Qualified Health Center (FQHC) (2013); opened Family Care Service Center at 4640 S. Carrollton Avenue—primary medical care for anyone (2014); and received CARF accreditation (2014)

Today, the agency offers a continuum of services, including prevention education (street and community outreach, venue-based outreach, condom distribution, and community mobilization targeting men who have sex with men), HIV antibody testing and counseling, the statewide HIV/AIDS hotline, case management, case finding, housing coordination, early intervention/primary medical care, mental health, support groups, home-delivered meals, food bank, peer support services, housing case management, and medication disbursement.

NO/AIDS Task Force serves all individuals, regardless of gender, sexual orientation or identity, race, ethnicity, religion, education, or socioeconomic status. The clients served by the agency over the past thirty years have been those individuals and communities most impacted by the HIV/AIDS epidemic. This has included men who have sex with men, women, commercial sex workers, African Americans, Latino/as, and intravenous drug users. Additionally, the agency offers its services in rural areas.

The history of the NO/AIDS Task Force is a brilliant example of a community pulling together to respond to a need. What started as support services has grown into an organization providing comprehensive services. including medical and clinical services, prevention and education, case management, legal assistance, food delivery, behavioral health, and medication assistance. Jean Redmann recalls the agency's early days: "As we realized how daunting the task was, we also realized we were in it for the long haul." Thirty-one years later, the NO/AIDS Task Force is still meeting local needs. Perhaps C. J. Robichaux summed it up best when he said, "The NO/AIDS Task Force has been one of our greatest blessings."

Shortly after this essay was originally published, the NO/AIDS Task Force evolved into a Federally Qualified Health Center offering an expanded range of health and wellness services for anyone and everyone who is seeking health care services in Greater New Orleans and southeastern Louisiana.

In addition to health and information services, housing facilities also emerged in the early years of the epidemic. The first of these was Project Lazarus, which is the subject of the next essay.

Ambush, May 20, 2014

PROJECT LAZARUS

IN 1983, FATHER BOB PAWELL NOTICED A NUMBER OF BLACK WREATHS on doors as he walked through the French Quarter. He soon learned that someone had died of a strange new disease called GRID (Gay Related Immune Deficiency). Alarmed, he turned to prayer and meditation.

Father Bob had arrived in New Orleans in 1976 to found the Tau House, a Franciscan outreach to people alienated by the Church. The ministry was located in a double-shotgun house in the 1000 block of Governor Nicholls Street. He began making his rounds at bars, restaurants, and shops and soon developed a network of friends and acquaintances, and Tau House quickly earned a reputation as a nonjudgmental place where regular sinners could seek spiritual services.

In 1984, a young man known as Robert H. was released from Charity Hospital after a nasty episode from what we now know was AIDS. Robert H. was homeless and penniless and had nowhere to go when a compassionate nurse called the Tau House and pleaded Robert's case. Father Bob gave the young man a place to stay and soon the word spread that someone was willing to care for people with AIDS. This was rather remarkable at the time because most people with AIDS then were completely shunned. Even doctors and nurses treated them tepidly with gloves and masks. Before long the need was obvious and Father Bob along with Father Paul Derossiers of Holy Trinity Church in the Marigny approached Archbishop Hannan about the possibility of providing shelter to homeless AIDS patients. The archbishop immediately agreed it was necessary and right and thus was born Project Lazarus. The home designated to house indigent AIDS patients was just around the corner from Holy Trinity Church in the old convent of the German Benedictine nuns of the nineteenth century. The first residents were Bob T., Leon G., and Ray G. At the time, the location of the house was kept secret for safety reasons. Tau House was the public face of the ministry.

Around this time, Father Bob met Jonathan Clemmer, a nurse at Tulane Medical Center who was getting involved in the emerging AIDS crisis.

Both men joined the newly formed NO/AIDS Task Force, which would collaborate with Project Lazarus in offering AIDS-related services. A support team then came together and included Dr. Ted Wisniewski, nurses Carol Pindaro, Jeanne Dumestre, Mike Callais, Paul Holthaus, and Maurice Geisel, who kept books for the facility. By 1986, Paul Ploche was designated as a fundraiser and Katie Quigley was hired to provide twenty-four-hour assistance to the residents. By the following year, the staff had grown to ten. Other supporters and volunteers in those early years included Armeinius Captain Jon Lee Poche, Arthur Roger, Robert Gordy, Madeleine Kohl, Al McMahon, Robbie Haywood, Don Ezell, and Ginger Snap. Also at this time, the famed Halloween Bal Masque annual fundraiser was founded.

In the early years, Lazarus House (as it has come to be known) essentially functioned as a hospice; it was a place to die. That began to change in 1996 when protease inhibitors became available. These antiviral drugs led to the AIDS cocktails that have enabled those infected with HIV to live much longer than before their advent. Because of this, Project Lazarus is not so much a hospice anymore as it is a transitional living facility. Its mission is to help heal and empower people living with HIV/AIDS by focusing on wellness, providing housing, and offering important support services.

Residents go through an application process and are allowed to stay in the house two years, although most stay six to nine months. During that time, they learn basic life skills that many people take for granted. One beneficial program is the Wellness University, which offers classes on cooking, budgeting, obtaining a GED, coping skills, and living with HIV among others. A nurse is on staff and provides differing levels of medical care according to each patient's need. The staff also features an addiction counselor, which augments a substance abuse program. In addition, Project Lazarus also helps residents find employment if they are able to work.

Overall, Project Lazarus is driven by what executive director Kim Moss describes as "a holistic approach." This is evident in the facility's five serenity gardens and fitness center. There is also a vegetable garden that helps the facility reduce food costs. Residents are taught and encouraged to meditate. Project Lazarus also offers acupuncture, music therapy, and massage therapy. But of all the services and programs Project Lazarus provides, the most important is abstract and intangible according to Moss: "We put our arms around them and love them."

Currently, Project Lazarus has a twenty-three-resident capacity and an annual budget of over $1 million. Sixty percent of its funding comes from the US Department of Housing and Urban Development while the remaining 40 percent comes from private foundations, individual donors, and the Archdiocese of New Orleans. While the archdiocese sponsors it, Project Lazarus is not a part of Catholic Charities. Since its founding in 1985, over 1,200 people have called Project Lazarus home. To learn more about Project Lazarus, visit http://www.projectlazarus.net/index.htm. Volunteers, donations, and tours of the facility are welcome. In addition to Project Lazarus, the HIV/AIDS community in New Orleans is also served by Belle Reve, Home Again, and Trinity House.

While Project Lazarus was successful in meeting a vital need, that need grew exponentially and, eventually, other housing facilities would emerge. The next essay focuses on one of those facilities, Belle Reve.

Ambush, May 28, 2013

BELLE REVE

In 1992, David Mesler, Jan Vick, and Peter Drago were tired of watching their friends die of AIDS. The epidemic was reaching its peak in New Orleans and these three best friends decided to do something about it. One of the major needs at the time was housing. The Lazarus House, which had opened in 1985, was full so they decided to form a nonprofit organization and open another housing facility. Belle Reve was chartered in September of 1992 and opened its doors in March of 1993.

With a federal HOPWA (Housing Opportunity for Persons with AIDS) grant from HUD (Department of Housing and Urban Development), Mesler, Vick, and Drago purchased a modest home in the Bywater and then used their own money to renovate the home to house eight residents. They called the home Belle Reve, French for "beautiful dream," which was also the name of Blanche DuBois's plantation home in Tennessee Williams's *A Streetcar Named Desire*.

In 1994, the home next door to Belle Reve was on the city's blighted property list, and the facility purchased it and renovated it to house four families. They called this home Belle Esprit, or "beautiful spirit." Local interior designer, the late Chet Pourciau, in conjunction with Eric Hess of Hess Marketing, donated time and talents, as well as furniture, to decorate the Belle Esprit community living room. The warehouse behind Belle Esprit was renovated after Hurricane Katrina and is now called Belle Grace. Belle Reve New Orleans can now serve a total of fifteen individuals and four couples or families with children at any one given time. There are usually four to five people on the waiting list to move in. Residents fall into two categories—permanent (primarily people on Social Security disability) and transitional.

In addition to housing, Belle Reve also sponsors support groups and offers programming to help residents transition into independent living. Some of these programs include life skills classes, substance abuse counseling, and psycho-social support. Other services include twenty-four-hour personal care, medication adherence counseling, daily meals, social activities and recreation, and a weekly computer class.

Executive director Vicki Weeks notes, "AIDS doesn't have a face. It affects all nationalities and orientations. And it's not a disease that's going to kill you unless you don't take your meds."

Serving the HIV/AIDS population of New Orleans, Belle Reve was the first nonprofit assisted-living facility of its kind to be licensed in the state of Louisiana. Belle Reve has consistently received superior ratings and honors from monitoring agencies, including a "Certificate of Merit for Outstanding Service" from the City of New Orleans; and the executive director received a "Special Commendation" from the United States Department of State for working with international visitors. Additionally, executive director Vicki Weeks was also honored with an "Acclaim Award" from the Forum for Equality for her tireless work in the HIV/AIDS community. Belle Reve has also won corporate and foundation funding from the MAC AIDS Fund through their MAC Cosmetics, Broadway Cares/Equity Fights AIDS, the Elizabeth Taylor AIDS Foundation, EPNO, Harrah's Casino, BellSouth, Walmart, the Almar Foundation, and from the Friday Night Before Mardi Gras organization, among others.

The majority of funding for Belle Reve comes in the form of three federal grants, including the Ryan White Fund, which subsidizes the facility's psycho-social programming. The Ryan White Comprehensive AIDS Resources Emergency (CARE) Act was enacted by Congress in 1990. Named in honor of Ryan White, a teenager who contracted the disease while receiving hemophilia treatments, the act is the largest federally funded program for people living with HIV/AIDS and seeks to improve the availability of care for low-income, uninsured and underinsured persons with AIDS and their families. Ryan White–funded programs are prioritized by the New Orleans Regional AIDS Planning Council (NORAPC). Founded in 1993, the mission of NORAPC is to develop and maintain a comprehensive system of care for persons living with HIV/AIDS in the New Orleans area that is accessible, responsive, culturally sensitive, and of the highest quality, and to ensure that all persons living with HIV/AIDS live with dignity.

In recent years, the mission of Belle Reve has shifted to providing affordable housing to senior citizens, regardless of HIV status.

Ambush, August 11, 2015

ARTS AND LETTERS

New Orleans has always been a source of inspiration to creative types, whether they be musicians, chefs, artists, photographers, or writers. The Muses of Greek mythology, who ruled over and inspired the arts and sciences, were the offspring of Zeus and Mnemosyne (memory) thereby suggesting that history and imagination are inextricably linked together. New Orleans, a city that embraces its history, cannot help but be a modern-day Mount Parnassus. The essays in this section consider what makes New Orleans such a wellspring of creativity and imagination to queer artists and writers. "Gay Letters and Desire" asks what makes New Orleans so inspirational to writers and artists and concludes it's the same thing that makes the city so appealing to gay folk. "The Gay Lens: Frances Benjamin Johnston and Pops Whitesell" profiles two eccentric photographers who lived in the French Quarter. "The Gentlemanly Last Years of George Dureau" focuses on the legendary artist George Dureau and his friendship with Katie Nachod, who helped him navigate his troubled last years. "Tennessee Williams: Out in the Quarter; In on the Stage" examines not only the playwright's relationship to the French Quarter but also the suppressed queerness in several of his works. "Was John Kennedy Toole Gay?" surveys homosexuality in *A Confederacy of Dunces* and *The Neon Bible* and argues Toole was probably gay.

GAY LETTERS AND DESIRE

A FEW YEARS AGO, AS I WAS CONDUCTING A WALKING TOUR THROUGH the French Quarter, a twenty-ish young man on the tour turned to me and said, "The French Quarter is kind of gay, huh?"

The comment startled me, and my instinct was to be offended, but I wasn't. He smiled when he said it, and I could tell it was more of an observation rather than a condemnation.

"Yes," I replied, "I suppose it is."

I'm not sure what prompted his remark. Was it all the rainbow flags? Was it the frilly cast-iron balconies from which those flags fly? Was it the drag queen who greeted me as she walked by? Perhaps it was the lazy, sauntering sashay of locals in general? Or maybe it was all the mask shops and art galleries and antique stores.

Was it all of the above? Something else?

The more I thought about it in the days that followed, the more convinced I became that the young man had stumbled upon a profound epiphany. This young man had intuitively sensed the density of rainbow history that permeates the Quarter.

"Sensitive" men, especially writers, have always found a sort of subliminal comfort in the Quarter's queer lineage, feeling at home in the Sacred Enclave. Walt Whitman felt it when he cruised sailors and roustabouts along the riverfront. Lyle Saxon felt it at his long-running literary salon in the 1920s and 1930s. John Kennedy Toole certainly felt it when he created the flamboyant character of Dorian Greene.

And Walker Percy, although not gay, felt it as well when he warned, "The occupational hazard of the writer in New Orleans is a variety of the French flu, which might also be called the Vieux Carré syndrome. One is apt to turn fey, potter about a patio, and write *feuilletons* and vignettes or catty *romans à clef*, a pleasant enough life but for me too seductive."[1]

Can the Quarter make a man "turn fey"?

Provosty Dayries, who was chief of police in the 1950s, thought so, once observing, "Apparently the French Quarter has an atmosphere which appeals to these people (gays and lesbians)."[2]

Yes, Mr. Dayries. Yes, indeed.

So, what, precisely, is it that makes the Quarter so appealing to gay folk?

It's the same thing that makes the neighborhood so inspirational to writers. At its core, the Quarter is a fascinating study in desire—its pull, its promises, its lies, and its consequences. The crux of the mutual affinity between queer folk and the Quarter is a fixation with desire. It's what fuels Carnival and Mardi Gras, the neighborhood's music and culinary and bar scenes.

Tennessee Williams came as close as anyone to explaining the phenomenon. It's no mistake Williams set his most famous play on Elysian Fields Avenue. Upon arriving in the city, Blanche DuBois says, "They told me to catch a streetcar named Desire and then transfer to one called Cemeteries."[3] The easy metaphor is that desire leads to death, but Williams, like all gay people, knows reality is not that easy.

Quarterites since Bienville (who lived into his eighties and never married) have been keenly aware of their own mortality, and it is this grim awareness that feeds the urgency of desire. Who knows what dreams may come in that sleep of death, so we better live it up while we have the time.

Elysium is the perfect metaphor for the Quarter. Both are mythical places that defy easy description. For Homer and Pindar, Elysium was the final resting place for tragic heroes. Renaissance poets envisioned Elysium as a paradise filled with joyful indulgences. For Tolkien, Elysium was a realm of gods and elves and other fantastical creatures.

In all these literary depictions, Elysium is positioned on the edge of the underworld, located off-center, on the edge. So it is with New Orleans: on the edge of the continent, on the edge of imagination, on the edge between life and death. To be gay in a homophobic society is to certainly identify with such marginalization.

Which brings us back to the Quarter. For Williams, the Quarter is Elysium. Here, objective reality is adapted to the ideal, not the other way around. Here, the boundary between fantasy and reality is permeable.

In *Streetcar*, Blanche comes to New Orleans to escape her past and begin her gradual descent into madness. Here, madness is not a nightmare but rather a beautiful dream. Whether dining at Galatoire's or musing on the bells of St. Louis Cathedral ("the only clean thing in the Quarter"),

Blanche finds an alternate reality—an Elysium where broken dreams are redeemed, and ghosts no longer haunt.

At one point in the play, Blanche sings "It's Only a Paper Moon," whose lyrics declare if both lovers believe their imagined reality, then it's no longer make-believe. The Quarter and her many gay lovers couldn't agree more.

While New Orleans has inspired scores of writers, the city has also lent itself to the visual arts, especially photography. The following essay examines two queer photographers whose time in the French Quarter briefly overlapped.

French Quarter Journal, November 18, 2019

NOTES

1. Walker Percy, "Why I Live Where I Live," in *Signposts in a Strange Land*, ed. Patrick Samway (New York: Picador, 2000).

2. "Dayries Cites No. 1 Vice Problem," *Times-Picayune*, June 30, 1955.

3. Tennessee Williams, *A Streetcar Named Desire* (1947).

THE GAY LENS: FRANCES BENJAMIN JOHNSTON AND POPS WHITESELL

THE YEAR IS 1946. AN EIGHTY-TWO-YEAR-OLD WOMAN AND A REAL estate agent stand in front of a home on Bourbon Street. The antebellum side-hall American townhouse features a wrought-iron balcony, a neglected courtyard littered with junk, and a former slaves quarters building with no electricity. The architectural details are important to the woman. Unbeknownst to the agent, she is the founder of the Carnegie Survey of the Architecture of the South.

His asking price is right—a steal at $4,600. She signs the papers immediately.

The agent perhaps thought the woman was retiring. And technically she was, but she had no intention of slowing down. At the top of her to-do list was compiling a book of photographs on the architecture of colonial Georgia, and the cataloging of her donation of photographs to the Library of Congress.

Happy to have sold the house, the agent leaves, sauntering down Bourbon with the distinct impression that this elderly, strong-willed woman, with her glass of whiskey, burning cigarette, and no-nonsense attitude, was a force of nature.

He had no idea.

Meet Frances Benjamin Johnston, the most famous lesbian you've never heard of.[1]

Born in 1864 in Washington, DC, Johnston became one of the nation's first photojournalists, an accomplishment in an era when both photography and journalism were decidedly male professions.

After studying art in Paris in the 1880s, Johnston returned home to establish herself as a professional portrait photographer. Among her clients were US presidents Benjamin Harrison, Grover Cleveland, William

McKinley, and Theodore Roosevelt. She is regarded by many as the first unofficial White House photographer.

Later, Johnston turned her camera toward documentary work, photographing day-to-day life in public schools and the working conditions of miners. The architecture and gardens of the post-Reconstruction South fascinated her, an interest that led to her establishing the Carnegie Survey of the Architecture of the South—a sweeping project that pictorially documented over 1,700 sites in nine southern states.

Visiting New Orleans in 1938 for an exhibition of her work, Johnston was easily and utterly captivated by the old-world charm of the Quarter, smitten by its extraordinary architecture and eccentric characters.

The Quarter Johnston discovered had other appeals as well, namely a thriving arts scene and a libertine atmosphere that defied conventional morality. It was during this visit that Johnston probably met Pops Whitesell, a fellow photographer and French Quarter fixture.

Joseph Woodson Whitesell moved to New Orleans from Indiana and quickly became a part of the French Quarter Renaissance of the 1920s. Writing in *64 Parishes*, John H. Lawrence notes, "Whitesell's photography achieved international recognition in professional salon exhibitions. In 1947, he was the ninth most exhibited salon photographer in the world. According to articles published in his lifetime, a charming demeanor and impish appearance made him a universally popular figure among his neighbors in the French Quarter, high society clientele, celebrities from the world of arts and letters, and fellow photographers."[2]

When not photographing Uptown society matrons and Carnival royalty, Whitesell photographed nearly nude, oil-slicked male models for muscle magazines, the closest thing to gay pornography at the time.

Whitesell opened his studio in 1921 at 726 St. Peter Street, behind what is now Preservation Hall. Neighbors affectionately called him the Leprechaun of St. Peter Street because of his diminutive stature and rakish nature.

Not far from Whitesell's studio was the influential Arts and Crafts Club, located on Royal Street in the famed Seignouret-Brulatour house. A few doors down, writer and local bon vivant Lyle Saxon hosted regular cocktail parties and literary salons. The group of bohemians that coalesced in the Quarter in the 1920s included Whitesell and several other gay men, including Lyle Saxon, W. R. Irby, Cicero Odiorne, Weeks Hall, and William Spratling.

By the time Frances Benjamin Johnston settled in New Orleans, Whitesell was the last man standing, a holdover from the glory days of the 1920s. The two became fast friends and lived out their last years in the Quarter—Johnston died in 1952, Whitesell in 1958—and one imagines these two queer photographers passing their days in Johnston's courtyard or perhaps having cocktails at Café Lafitte, the de facto gay bar of the era, located in what is now Lafitte's Blacksmith Shop.

Johnston wrote in a letter to a friend that she lived "in walking distance of the best spots of the Vieux Carré, two blocks from the French Market and the Morning Call, where you can get coffee and donuts at 4am."[3]

It's heartening to envision these two aging nonconformists drinking coffee by the river after a night of carousing, watching the sun rise over Bienville's "beautiful crescent," perhaps reflecting with gratitude on lives well lived and the quirky neighborhood they called home.

The next essay is about a famous New Orleans artist who used photography as a means to capture subjects as studies for his paintings. To his chagrin, George Dureau became just as famous for his photography as for his paintings. In fact, Dureau mentored the late Robert Mapplethorpe.

French Quarter Journal, August 30, 2020

NOTES

1. To learn more about Johnston, read Bettina Berch, *The Woman behind the Lens: The Life and Work of Frances Benjamin Johnston, 1864–1952* (Charlottesville: University of Virginia Press, 2000).

2. John H. Lawrence, "Joseph Woodson Whitesell," *64 Parishes*, 2012.

3. Berch, *The Woman behind the Lens.*

THE GENTLEMANLY LAST YEARS OF GEORGE DUREAU

I RECENTLY HAD AN ESPECIALLY MEMORABLE AND QUITE PERFECT LUNCH with Katie Nachod. Although Katie is a longtime reference librarian with a career's worth of experience at Tulane University and the Louisiana Supreme Court Law Library, and although I serve as president of the LGBT+ Archives Project of Louisiana, and although we both have degrees in English, and although we have several mutual friends, we did not meet to discuss anything regarding library sciences, the glories of literature, or mutual-friend gossip. Rather, our luncheon meeting was all about the late, great George Dureau.

While Friends of Dorothy and Quarterites of a certain age will surely remember Dureau, young readers may not be familiar with him. Dureau died in 2014 after a battle with Alzheimer's disease. Born in 1930 and raised in New Orleans, Dureau was a classically trained artist and photographer who enjoyed international acclaim. He was also a bona fide French Quarter character—an eccentric, larger than life, gay man whose personality radiated charm and quirkiness. He threw fabulous parties. Katie met George near the end of his life. The two became fast friends and ultimately Katie became his caretaker, of sorts.

On a beautiful day, over a leisurely lunch at Café Degas (appropriately enough), Katie regaled me with the enchanting tale of how she became a part of George's life. It is a case study in serendipity.

The lunch was a long time coming. We had met via email over a year earlier through a mutual friend, Peta Mni, who had taken one of my Rainbow Fleur de Lis walking tours on the city's queer history. After the tour, Peta asked a few questions about George Dureau, whom I had mentioned on the tour, and then told me he had a friend I just had to meet—Katie. The plan was for all three of us to have lunch and listen to Katie reminisce about George. Despite several attempts, our schedules never aligned and Peta, to the surprise of all who knew him, died suddenly not long after our failed attempts to get together.

Fast-forward to this summer. Theater critic Brian Sands was having a few people over to watch the fireworks on the Fourth of July, and my partner Chris and I graciously accepted his invitation. Among the eclectic assemblage of guests was Katie, who had brought along George Dureau's half brother, Don. At the conclusion of a brilliant conversation, Katie and I resurrected our lunch plans.

After twenty-something years of working at the Howard-Tilton Memorial Library at Tulane University, Katie took a job at the law library at the Louisiana Supreme Court building in the French Quarter. Each morning, after parking in a lot adjacent to the river, she would walk up Bienville Street before turning on Chartres Street on her way to the courthouse. Each morning, as she walked up Bienville, she noticed George Dureau's studio/residence. Eventually, George introduced himself and the two developed a morning ritual. She would stop at the studio, where George would serve her a pastry. The two would chat for a bit and then, stepping out onto the sidewalk, George would extend his elbow and escort Katie on her one-and-a-half-block walk to work. He did the same in the evening when she finished work.

It was the beginning of a beautiful friendship. George's health gradually declined as he slowly succumbed to Alzheimer's disease. In the beginning stages, he could still function, although he would sometimes get confused or forget to bathe. Katie accompanied him on his wanderings around the Quarter and on regular visits to La Boucherie, one of many French Quarter coffee shops that are no more. Sometimes they would wave toward Canal Street and say hello to Miss Clara, George's mother. And when the police kept giving George tickets for riding his bicycle the wrong way down Royal Street, Katie went to the Eighth District Police Precinct and explained to them who George was and that he didn't understand why he was getting citations and that they should stop harassing him. They did.

When his dementia worsened, Katie organized a group called the "Friends of George," which consisted of over a hundred people whose lives George had touched. When George was no longer able to live by himself, Katie and the "Friends" raised money and had him placed in an assisted living facility, where he lived until his death on April 7, 2014.

After lunch, Katie drove me back to the Quarter. Before she dropped me off, she left me with one last anecdote that seems to sum up George's life. She told me that even at the end, in the days before he died, George would occasionally burst forth into song. His musical selection? Nina Simone's "I Want a Little Sugar in My Bowl."

The next essay turns its attention from art to literature and highlights one of America's greatest playwrights, Tennessee Williams.

Ambush, October 22, 2019

TENNESSEE WILLIAMS:
OUT IN THE QUARTER;
IN ON THE STAGE

THIS WEEK THOUSANDS OF PEOPLE WILL PACK THE HOTEL MONTELEONE and other venues around the French Quarter to celebrate the life and work of Tennessee Williams. The Tennessee Williams / New Orleans Literary Festival is an annual event held each March in honor of the playwright's birthday. The event features readings, lectures, panel discussions, theatrical productions, literary walking tours, and the famous Stella Shouting Contest in Jackson Square.

In addition to being New Orleans's most famous literary resident, Williams also integrated himself well into the gay community in the French Quarter. He rented no fewer than four different apartments throughout the Quarter (429 Royal, 722 Toulouse, 711 Royal, and 632 St. Peter) before buying a Greek Revival townhouse at 1014 Dumaine in 1962. He was a regular at several gay bars, especially Café Lafitte in Exile, and he loved to dine at Marti's—a favorite eatery among gay Quarterites in the 1970s and early 1980s.

Although Williams did not officially come out of the closet until the final years of his life (something for which he was chastised by gay critics), his homosexuality was an open secret and certainly not a surprise to anyone familiar with his works. In fact, a careful reading of Williams's literary canon suggests a man who was deeply conflicted about homosexuality. Alternatively, such a reading may also reveal a profound and disturbing exploration of the closet and all its psychological implications.

In the vast majority of Williams's plays, the gay character is dead before the action begins. In his most famous work, *A Streetcar Named Desire* (1947), Blanche DuBois arrives in New Orleans after the death of her husband and the loss of their plantation; he committed suicide after being caught in bed with another man. This double loss triggers Blanche's eventual commitment to a mental asylum. In the play, not only does the act of being outed lead to suicide, the false reality of the closet and all its consequences leads to insanity.

Suicide is also very much a part of *Cat on a Hot Tin Roof* (1955). The main character, Brick, no longer has sex with his wife and "hasn't been right" since his "good friend" Skipper committed suicide. Brick's implied homosexuality is echoed in his father's backstory: Big Daddy was taken in by two queens as a young man. The play is set on the plantation they bequeathed to him.

Death is also linked with gayness in *Suddenly Last Summer* (1958). In this play, the gay character is cannibalized by a group of young men with whom he paid to have sex. Later, when Sebastian's sister recalls for their mother the bizarre circumstances of his death, the mother tries to have a lobotomy performed on her to remove the memory—clearly an autobiographical reference to Williams's own sister who was subjected to a lobotomy.

While the gay characters are ambiguous and in the background of Williams's plays, they are explicit and in the forefront of his poetry and short stories. For example, the short story "Hard Candy" features an older man who dies of a heart attack as he kneels in front of a young man and performs fellatio on him.

The consistent association of homosexuality with death throughout Williams's work raises the question: was Williams's sexual orientation a source of self-loathing? I tend to think not. Rather, Williams was in a unique position, and possessed the literary talent, to explore the status of homosexuality in the culture in which he lived. In this regard, his work reflected the homophobic attitudes of his time.

That is not to say Williams was not a troubled man. His alcoholism and drug addiction certainly point to that. Albert Carey remembers meeting Williams at Lafitte's in the 1970s: "I saw Tennessee Williams standing by the flame. As I neared him I could see he was very, very drunk but I introduced myself anyway. He gave me a very limp handshake, like a dead fish, and mumbled something incoherently, which kind of grossed me out, and he almost fell down in the process." Dr. John Meyers also recalls meeting Williams at Lafitte's: "I was sitting at the bar, and I knew who he was, but I didn't make a big deal out of it. Then he came over and introduced himself as Tom, which was his given name. We fell into conversation, and he ended up taking me to lunch at Antoine's. I was in medical school at the time and thinking of going into psychiatry. He spoke of his sister's lobotomy—something I don't think he ever recovered from. He seemed more interested in drinking than eating. In fact, I ate most of his food. We had a wonderful conversation and overall, it was a delightful afternoon."

Despite his troubled genius, Williams lived as an openly gay man as much as the times would permit. In 1946, while he was writing *Streetcar* in his apartment on St. Peter Street, his lover Pancho Rodriguez lived with him, and although the romantic relationship did not last, the two remained friends into the 1970s. This brief relationship was followed by a serious fourteen-year commitment to Frank Merlo. After Merlo's death in 1963, Williams's alcoholism and addiction to painkillers became progressively worse until his death in 1983.

In the French Quarter, Williams found a certain freedom that eluded him elsewhere. Upon first arriving in New Orleans, he wrote in his journal that the "town is wide open" and "Here, surely, is the place I was made for."[1] He would eventually call New Orleans his "spiritual home." Such a libertine environment allowed Williams's genius to flourish. It's a shame, and somewhat ironic, that the theater world of Williams's time censored a more frank exploration of homosexuality. Such homophobia may also explain, at least in part, Williams's personal demons.

Williams was, of course, not the only writer troubled by conflicted sexuality. While Williams navigated the closet successfully, such was not the case with John Kennedy Toole, author of the iconic novel *A Confederacy of Dunces*.

Ambush, March 19, 2013

NOTE

1. T. R. Johnson, *New Orleans: A Literary History* (Cambridge: Cambridge University Press, 2019).

WAS JOHN KENNEDY TOOLE GAY?

NEW ORLEANS HAS INSPIRED MANY GAY WRITERS—WALT WHITMAN, Lyle Saxon, Tennessee Williams, Truman Capote, William Burroughs, and John Rechy, to name a few. The sexuality of these writers is unquestioned, but the sexual orientation of John Kennedy Toole, author of *A Confederacy of Dunces*, the iconic and quintessential book about New Orleans, remains unclear.

Speculation concerning Toole's sexuality stems from his depiction of gay characters in his two published novels, *A Confederacy of Dunces* and *The Neon Bible*, both published long after his suicide in 1969. *Confederacy* was written in the early 1960s when Toole was stationed in Puerto Rico after being drafted by the US Army. The book won the Pulitzer Prize in 1981 and since then has sold over two million copies. It is widely regarded as the best (and certainly the funniest) novel ever written about New Orleans.

The subject of homosexuality is prevalent in the novel and manifests overtly in two forms: Myrna Minkoff's concern that Ignatius (the protagonist) is a closet case and in the character of Dorian Greene and the Peace Party rally he hosts. Ignatius resists Myrna's sexual advances, telling us, "My blood failed to rise." In their correspondence, Myrna worries Ignatius is turning into a "screaming queen" and her concern reaches a zenith when he begins "hanging around some queers."[1]

The "queers" all come together at Dorian Greene's apartment in the French Quarter for a private cocktail party at which Ignatius is to speak. Assembled are Timmy the female impersonator, three very butch lesbians (Frieda Club, Betty Bumper, and Liz Steele), a "leather lout" with a riding crop, a young couple having a heated argument in the kitchen (Billy Truehard and Raoul Frayle), and a host of other "elegantly dressed" guests. The description of the party is stunningly insightful:

> Cigarettes and cocktail glasses held like batons flew in the air directing the symphony of chatter, shrieking, singing, and laughing. From the bowels of a huge stereophonic phonograph the voice of Judy Garland

was fighting its way through the din. A small band of young men . . . stood before the phonograph as if it were an altar. "Divine!" "Fantastic!" "So human!" they were saying of the voice from their electronic tabernacle . . . Herringbones and madras and lamb's wool and cashmere flashed past in a blur as hands and arms rent the air in a variety of graceful gestures. Fingernails, cufflinks, pinky rings, teeth, eyes—all glittered.[2]

Of his then unpublished novel, Toole once wrote, "This book is not autobiography; neither is it altogether invention . . . I am not in the book; I've never pretended to be. But I am writing about things that I know, and in recounting these, it's difficult not to feel them."[3]

But the presence of gay characters does not necessarily mean the author is gay. Straight writers have written gay characters before. But the presence of gay characters in a number of works by an author reasonably raises suspicions. Unfortunately, Toole wrote only one other book—*The Neon Bible*, which, like *Confederacy*, was not published until after his death.

The Neon Bible is a bildungsroman set in rural Mississippi—a setting that provides the novel's context and tone, namely a very religious, conservative small town that casts a judgmental eye on anyone who is not a white, straight Christian. The protagonist, a schoolboy named David, admires the way his gay teacher, Mr. Farvy, and his partner transcend the town's disdainful judgment of them. *The Neon Bible* was written while Toole was a junior in high school. The fact a high school junior in the mid-1950s was writing not only gay characters but also about how those characters dealt with homophobia proves that homosexuality was on Toole's mind even as a teenager.

There have been three books written about Toole, two biographies and a memoir written by a friend of his. The most recent biography, *Butterfly in the Typewriter: The Tragic Life of John Kennedy Toole and the Remarkable Story of "A Confederacy of Dunces,"* by Cory MacLauchlin, leaves the question of Toole's sexuality unanswered. *Ignatius Rising: The Life of John Kennedy Toole*, by Rene Pol Nevils and Deborah George Hardy, asserts that Toole was indeed gay and references a male prostitute who claims to have been hired by Toole. But the hustler's name is not given, and he was reputedly drunk during his interview.

Ignatius Rising was soundly panned by the critics when it was released. Esteemed New Orleans literary expert Kenneth Holditch gave the book a one-star rating on Amazon.com and writes, "This pseudo-biography is filled with misinformation, with misquotes (for example, attributing a Poe poem to the wrong story) and to the wildest kind of speculation. It is a scary book, because people who know no better will assume that what these two women write is true—and a good 50 percent of it is either false or based on the wildest speculation."[4]

Ken and Thelma: The Story of "A Confederacy of Dunces" is a memoir by Joel L. Fletcher, who knew Toole and his mother well. The book does not address Toole's sexuality and in interviews recalling their friendship, Fletcher concludes that Toole was asexual, that he was "reticent" when it came to his romantic life and that "he had little or no interest in sex." And yet sex and sexuality permeate Toole's masterpiece, *A Confederacy of Dunces.*

If Toole was in the closet, it is easy to understand Fletcher's conclusion. A closeted man in the 1960s would have cautiously guarded the secret of his sexuality. Considering the rarity of genuine asexuals, along with the presence of gay characters in both Toole's novels, Fletcher's observation may be interpreted as circumstantial evidence of Toole's homosexuality. Any gay man who has spent time in the closet, especially those of a certain age, can certainly understand and probably identify with Toole's reticence when it came to his romantic inclinations.

Such reticence is clearly evident in the extensive John Kennedy Toole papers, which are housed in the Louisiana Research Collection at Tulane University. The papers consist of personal letters, military records, college essays Toole wrote as an undergraduate, photographs, scrapbooks, a few unpublished short stories and poems, and several ticket stubs and playbills from New York theaters, of which Toole was apparently especially fond.

The only references to homosexuality, and indirect ones at that, in the Toole papers are found in a 1958 letter written by Dave Prescott to Toole. In the letter, Prescott provides Toole an update on what was happing at Tulane while Toole was in New York. Describing a party attended by mutual friends, Prescott recalls an exchange between Joe Lyde and Michael Sissons. When Lyde learns Sissons is sharing an apartment with Charles Davis, Lyde jokes, "Oh, trying to recapture your Oxford days?"

Later in the letter, Prescott references the gay bashing murder of Fernando Rios, which had just occurred and then describes another similar attack that occurred a week after the Rios murder: "Shmuel, on his way to some friend's house in the Quarter, was bludgeoned on the skull three times with a lead pipe and robbed." While Prescott's letter mentions the attacks on Rios and Shmuel, he makes no reference to the victims' sexuality.

So, was Toole gay? The short answer is we don't know. There is no hard evidence to draw such a conclusion. The longer answer is "probably." What we do know for sure is that homosexuality was on Toole's mind as a teenager, he wrote gay characters extremely well, he apparently had gay friends and was familiar with the underground gay scene of the French Quarter in the 1960s, he never married, he was depressed and eventually committed suicide. Toole may have answered the question in his suicide note, but his mother destroyed the note shortly after his death.

Does the question of Toole's sexuality even matter? Yes and no. *A Confederacy of Dunces* stands alone as Toole's great legacy as well as a brilliant book of comic genius that has become an integral part of New Orleans's literary history. If Toole was gay, his novel is yet another of many examples of significant contributions by gay folk that have gone unrecognized.

Nine years after this article was first published, I participated in a panel discussion with Dr. Kenneth Holditch on the occasion of Toole's mother's birthday. Holditch knew Thelma Toole well and was considered an expert on *Confederacy* and its history. He even held the rights to Toole's first novel, *The Neon Bible*. Holditch had begun researching Toole's life in order to write a biography of the author. Unfortunately, that work was never completed.

During the panel discussion I raised the issue of Toole's sexuality and asked Holditch if he had any insight or information regarding the topic. Holditch said he did and confirmed Toole was, in fact, gay. We chatted briefly after the program ended and agreed to meet so that he could show me the evidence he had concerning Toole's sexual orientation. Unfortunately, Holditch was in failing health at the time and died before we could meet. I am hoping this evidence will eventually be archived with Holditch's vast collection of personal papers.

Ambush, November 4, 2014

NOTES

1. John Kennedy Toole, *A Confederacy of Dunces* (Baton Rouge: Louisiana State University Press, 1980).

2. Toole, *A Confederacy of Dunces.*

3. Three books about Toole have been published. *Ignatius Rising: The Life of John Kennedy Toole* by Rene Pol Nevils and Deborah George Hardy was published in 2005 and purports to be a biography but was panned by critics and literary scholars for shoddy research. The book caused Toole friend Joel Fletcher to publish *Ken & Thelma: The Story of "A Confederacy of Dunces"* (2005) in response. In 2012, Cory MacLauchlin published *Butterfly in the Typewriter: The Tragic Life of John Kennedy Toole and the Remarkable Story of "A Confederacy of Dunces."*

4. Kenneth Holditch, review of *Ignatius Rising: The Life of John Kennedy Toole*, Amazon.

A CLIMATE OF HOSTILITY

JUDGING BY TODAY, ONE WOULD NEVER GUESS THAT NEW ORLEANS WAS once incredibly homophobic. Today, city hall flies the rainbow flag during Pride Month, the mayor issues proclamations honoring the Southern Decadence Grand Marshals, and the New Orleans Police Department has a liaison to the LGBT+ community. But it wasn't always so. In the years after World War II, as tourism came into its own as a bona fide industry in New Orleans, the city, fearing that queer visibility would scare away tourist dollars, adopted a "climate of hostility" toward the LGBT+ community. In the 1950s, Mayor Morrison even created a "Committee on the Problem of Sex Deviates," whose aim was to rid the French Quarter of homosexuals (spoiler—it didn't work). The essays in this section all describe the efforts and effects of that committee. "Crimes against Nature" analyzes the criminality of queerness in New Orleans, beginning with the first written reference to homosexuality in the city's history—a criminal trial dating to 1724. "Climate of Hostility" casts a critical eye on the chilling effects of the 1950s city-sanctioned "Committee on the Problem of Sex Deviates." "The Persecution of Tony Bacino's Bar" is an in-depth case study of one of the bars targeted by the committee. "The Gay Bashing Murder of Fernando Rios" relates the tragic story of a horrific gay bashing murder and illustrates the violence and lack of justice homophobia engenders. "The Rose Room, the Goldenrod Inn, and Police Raids" reflects on the frequency of police raids on queer bars by focusing on two particular bar raids.

A CLIMATE OF HOSTILITY

CRIMES AGAINST NATURE

In 1724, just six years after New Orleans was founded, a sex scandal involving a ship captain and his cabin boy rocked the fledgling city. Captain Beauchamp of the *Bellone* was discovered to be having a sexual affair with his cabin boy. When word of the romance reached the French Superior Council (the governing authority at the time), the council reprimanded Captain Beauchamp by having the boy reassigned to another ship, *La Loire*. But the amorous captain would not be denied the object of his affection. Beauchamp kidnapped the boy from *La Loire*, brought him back to the *Bellone*, and set sail downriver for the Gulf of Mexico. The Superior Council dispatched a skiff to give chase, but the *Bellone* was the quicker vessel. Beauchamp and his boy escaped as far as Dauphine Island off the coast of Alabama near Mobile, where the *Bellone* sank.

Captain Beauchamp's initial sentence, having the cabin boy reassigned to another ship, constituted little more than a "slap on the wrist." Such a "light" sentence provides a glimpse into the sexual mores and attitudes of French New Orleans. During the American period, Captain Beauchamp and his cabin boy would have faced life imprisonment for their sexual peccadilloes. Although sodomy was technically illegal in seventeenth-century France, the Crown rarely enforced laws against it. Sexual depravity was common in the royal court of Louis XIV and rivaled the most heralded excesses of ancient Rome. The Sun King's brother (who had a fondness for cross-dressing) and at least one of his sons were notorious for their sexual escapades with men. The son even joined what would now be called a gay orgy club. Louisiana, and New Orleans, was born out of this libertine milieu. The Church of course frowned on all of this, but the early colonists in Louisiana generally ignored the moral teachings of Holy Mother Church they found inconvenient.

Sodomy was not officially illegal in Louisiana until 1805, two years after the Louisiana Purchase. Drawing upon English common law, the new American government outlawed "the detestable and abominable crime against nature." But what, precisely, is a crime against nature? The vague wording and lack of a clear definition became the cause for a number of legal challenges as well as efforts by the state legislature to clarify the matter. Despite the legal ambiguities, the general consensus, at least among law enforcement officials, was that any sexual act that did not involve a penis penetrating a vagina was a crime against nature. It was on this pretext that homosexual acts were deemed illegal.

It's important to remember that prior to the mid-twentieth century, homosexuals as a class of people did not exist in the mainstream consciousness. Some people of weak moral character may have committed homosexual acts, but those acts did not constitute a defining identity or orientation. So the thinking went—homosexuality was a verb, not a noun. When gay identities began to emerge and homosexual communities became visible, the straight mainstream became alarmed. The development of gay identities and communities in the 1950s represented a significant, and disturbing, paradigm shift in society.

The existence of gays and lesbians, and more to the point—their visibility, was too much for straight society to bear. Reinforced by the homophobic teachings of Christianity and feeling threatened, the straight power structure that ran the city responded defensively and viciously. Consequently, police harassment of gay folk rose dramatically.

In 1951, the *Times-Picayune* ran a story entitled "Curb Advocated on Homosexuals: Crackdown to Save Young Persons Demanded."[1] In 1955, police superintendent Provosty A. Dayries publicly proclaimed that homosexuals were the city's "Number One vice problem," adding, "They are the ones we want to get rid of most."[2] Jacob Morrison, a prominent citizen and cofounder of the "Vieux Carré Property Owners and Associates" led an effort to have the Starlet Lounge's liquor license revoked because it catered almost exclusively to gay men. In 1958, Morrison was appointed to head a "Committee on the Problem of Sex Deviates." An initial report of the committee proposed a "climate of hostility" be adopted toward homosexuals. In that same year, the manager and staff of Tony Bacino's (another gay bar) were arrested six times. They were charged with violating a city ordinance that prohibited "immoral" people, including "sexual perverts," from working in bars and restaurants. Amazingly, the ordinance was not repealed until 1993. The Krewe of Yuga Carnival Ball was raided in 1962 and resulted in over ninety arrests. Raids of gay bars were common as were payoffs to the police to be left alone. Bar raids continued well into the 1980s. And as recently as the mid-1990s, gay men were often arrested on the old crime against nature statute.

The amount of time, money, and resources the city spent on trying to suppress homosexuality is truly amazing. Consider the case of the short-lived Decatur Street Bookshop. In 1986, Larry Lingle and his partner Bill White opened a gay-themed bookstore on lower Decatur Street in the French Quarter. Although it was a legitimate bookstore (for a while, Lingle also owned the legendary Oscar Wilde Bookshop in New York City and LOBO in Dallas), the Decatur Street Bookshop also sold gay pornography. Almost immediately, the New Orleans Police Department began investigating the bookstore. Undercover agents began frequenting the shop, which was under police surveillance. In addition, the police department rented an apartment across from owner Bill White's residence on Royal Street so they could keep his comings and goings under twenty-four-hour surveillance. White was eventually arrested and struck a plea bargain before the case went to trial. White's lawyer estimated the New Orleans Police Department spent over $100,000 on the whole operation.

The landmark Supreme Court case *Lawrence v. Texas* (2003) invalidated state laws against sodomy eleven years ago. Nevertheless, the Louisiana legislature has consistently refused to repeal the unconstitutional state law. Why? Because doing so might make the knuckle-draggers appear "soft" on homosexuality. The old law is still on the books, and just last year the police in Baton Rouge used it to arrest gay men for merely trying to "hook up." It could happen here too.

So, for your information, here is the complete text of Louisiana Revised Statute 14:89 of the Louisiana Criminal Code:

A. Crime against nature is:

(1) The unnatural carnal copulation by a human being with another of the same sex or opposite sex or with an animal, except that anal sexual intercourse between two human beings shall not be deemed as a crime against nature when done under any of the circumstances described in R.S. 14:41, 14:42, 14:42.1 or 14:43. Emission is not necessary; and, when committed by a human being with another, the use of the genital organ of one of the offenders of whatever sex is sufficient to constitute the crime.

(2) The solicitation by a human being of another with the intent to engage in any unnatural carnal copulation for compensation.

B. Whoever violated the provisions of this Section shall be fined not more than two thousand dollars, or imprisoned, with or without hard labor, for not more than five years, or both.

The following article takes a closer look at the city of New Orleans's attitude toward queer people in the 1950s.

Ambush, May 6, 2014

NOTES

1. "Curb Advocated on Homosexuals: Crackdown to Save Young Persons Demanded," *Times-Picayune*, April 28, 1951.

2. "Dayries Cites No. 1 Vice Problem," *Times-Picayune*, June 30, 1955.

CLIMATE OF HOSTILITY

As THE HOLIDAYS APPROACH AND THE SEASON COMPELS US TO COUNT our blessings and be thankful for them, New Orleans city government is probably the last thing to come to mind. And yet, we as a community do indeed have one thing at least for which to be grateful for as far as city government is concerned. As dysfunctional as it is, we should remember that the city of New Orleans is light-years ahead of the rest of the state in acknowledging our rights.

As *Ambush* readers of a certain age will remember, such was not always the case. In 1958, the New Orleans City Council established a "Committee on the Problem of Sex Deviates." An initial report of the committee proposed a "climate of hostility" be adopted toward homosexuals. As its chairman, the council appointed Jacob Morrison, a prominent citizen and cofounder of the "Vieux Carré Property Owners and Associates."

Morrison had been a thorn in the side of the gay community for years, often attacking gay bars through legal channels. He had a few years earlier led a successful effort to have the Starlet Lounge's (at the corner of Chartres and St. Philip) liquor license revoked and then turned his attention to Tony Bacino's bar on Toulouse. In the summer of 1958, the manager and staff of Tony Bacino's were arrested six times. They were charged with violating a city ordinance that prohibited "immoral" people, including "sexual perverts," from working in bars and restaurants. Amazingly, the ordinance was not repealed until 1993.

Before the city formally resolved to create a "climate of hostility" for gays, the climate was already pretty hostile. A few years earlier, in 1955, police superintendent Provosty A. Dayries publicly proclaimed that homosexuals were the city's "Number One vice problem," adding, "They are the ones we want to get rid of most." Widespread ignorance and familiar stereotypes of gay people were prevalent, especially the notion that homosexuals were predatory and looking to recruit teenagers and children.

In 1951, the *Times-Picayune* ran a story entitled "Curb Advocated on Homosexuals: Crackdown to Save Young Persons Demanded":

A warning that homosexuals in the French Quarter are at work cor-
rupting high school boys and girls was made Friday by Richard R.
Foster, chairman of the Mayor's Committee on the Vieux Carré, in an
address before the Civic Council of New Orleans. For that reason, he
said, the homosexual problem is one of the city's most serious. "In several instances, parents have come to police begging them to save their
children," he asserted. High school boys and girls enticed into places
habituated by homosexuals often see an obscene show or something
of that nature as a starter," he added. The homosexuals are, he said,
"continuously recruiting" and there at least four "places" in the Quarter
which cater to almost no one but homosexuals. "It almost seems as if
youngsters who develop homosexual tendencies in other Southern cities are put on a train and sent to New Orleans," he said.[1]

About a month earlier, the *Times-Picayune* ran another article along the
same lines with a new twist. At a meeting of the mayor's advisory committee, Chairman Foster argued that the city should develop a strategy
for discouraging "perverts" from coming to New Orleans, claiming most
homosexuals in New Orleans were "out-of-towners." That gay people
lived in New Orleans was either incomprehensible or too distasteful to
bear. The level of denial and cluelessness revealed in the article rivals the
level of bigotry and hatred permeating straight society at the time. One
man recently told me, "We never flaunted our sexuality then because we
were so afraid."

In those days New Orleans was much more homophobic than recent
generations can possibly imagine. Despite New Orleans's penchant for
tolerance and its laissez faire attitude, gays in New Orleans have faced a
considerable amount of homophobia, especially from police. Although
police harassment of gay bars now is mainly a thing of the past, it was,
nonetheless, a very ugly past. Many bar owners paid the police to leave
them alone. Such was the case at Café Lafitte in Exile. In the 1960s and
early 1970s, a police officer would come in each week, like clockwork, and
collect an envelope stuffed with cash. Tom Wood stopped making the
payments when he took over the bar and eventually obtained a restraining order against the police because of their harassment. Nevertheless,
the vice squad would, on occasion, either raid bars or send undercover
cops (almost always young and good-looking ones) into the bars to make
arrests. This practice continued well into the 1970s. Bartenders customar-

ily slapped a wooden board on the bar to warn patrons they were getting too touchy-feely. Arrests were often accompanied by a beating and pressure to name other "perverts." Anyone unfortunate enough to be arrested for "crimes against nature" or "committing a lewd act" had his name and picture published in the *Times-Picayune*. This often resulted in family alienation, the loss of a job, and, in some cases, the loss of a place to live.

Times certainly have changed, haven't they? Think about it the next time you walk down the street holding hands with your lover or wear a T-shirt proclaiming your pride or party on the sidewalk outside your favorite gay bar or wear next to nothing for Decadence. There was a time not too terribly long ago when any of those activities would have landed you in jail. Can you imagine being arrested simply for being gay? Thankfully, many of us cannot. Regrettably, some of us can.

While this essay has painted a broad overview of the prevailing heteronormative/homophobic attitude of New Orleans toward queerness in the mid-twentieth century, the following essay focuses narrowly on one particular bar the city targeted.

Ambush, November 20, 2012

NOTE

1. "Curb Advocated on Homosexuals: Crackdown to Save Young Persons Demanded," *Times-Picayune*, 1951.

THE PERSECUTION OF TONY BACINO'S BAR

THE US SUPREME COURT RECENTLY HEARD ORAL ARGUMENTS IN TWO cases that could be landmark decisions for gay rights. As the high court deliberates California's Proposition Eight and the federal Defense of Marriage Act, same-sex marriage rights hang in the balance. Decisions in both cases are expected this summer. In the meantime, a look back at how much public attitudes toward gay rights have shifted over the years offers a good reason to be optimistic. After all, it wasn't that long ago that the legal system was routinely used to persecute gay people. Consider the following case from Orleans Parish Civil District Court.

In 1958, New Orleans Mayor Chep Morrison appointed his half brother, Jacob Morrison, to lead the "Committee on the Problem of Sex Deviates." The committee was the city's way of addressing what many people viewed as a growing problem in the French Quarter—gay visibility. Morrison's self-righteous and homophobic credentials were impeccable. He was a prominent attorney and had a history of leading historical preservation efforts in the French Quarter, and in the early 1950s, he led a citizens' crusade against the Starlet Lounge, a gay bar at the corner of Chartres and St. Philip Streets. Morrison was eventually successful in having the Starlet Lounge's liquor license revoked in 1953.

The committee's first order of business was to turn its disapproving eye on Tony Bacino's Bar, a known "queershop" at 738 Toulouse Street. During the first week of its existence, the committee had the manager and two bartenders at Tony Bacino's arrested five times. They were charged with violating this extraordinary city ordinance: "No person of known lewd, immoral or dissolute character, sexual pervert, inmate of a brothel or house of prostitution or assignation, B-drinker, person who gambles illegally, as defined by law, lottery operator, lottery collector, lottery vendor or seller or user of narcotics, either paid or unpaid, shall be employed in such a place of business as a singer, dancer, beer carrier, waiter, bartender, waitress, girl bartender, or barmaid. Nor shall such persons be allowed to congregate or frequent such place of business."[1] Amazingly, this ordinance was not repealed until 1993.

In the 1950s, it was common for gay bars to routinely pay off the police to leave them alone. But Roy Maggio, the manager of Tony Bacino's, was apparently not so inclined. Instead of making the customary "protection" payments or folding under the pressure of police harassment, Maggio and the two bartenders, Louis Robichaux and Amos McFarlane, both of whom had previously worked at the Starlet Lounge, applied for, and were awarded, a temporary restraining order against the police.

The city attorney responded by arguing the plaintiffs had obtained the temporary restraining order under false pretenses. In a brief arguing the temporary restraining order should be dissolved, the city argued the bartenders had committed the following "lewd acts": they "kissed," "embraced," and "fondled" patrons of the bar, they addressed male patrons as "Darling," Sweetheart," and "Doll," they proposed "unnatural sexual intercourse" to Navy sailors, and they encouraged patrons to "conduct themselves in a lewd and preverted [sic] manner."

Transcripts from the subsequent legal proceedings reveal a McCarthy-like investigation into the lives and characters of the bartenders. Here is a sampling of some of the questions Assistant City Attorney Raoul Sere peppered the plaintiffs with: "Have you at any time kissed or embraced other males in the place known as Tony Bacino's?" "Have you ever kissed them on the mouth?" "Now when attending bar at Tony Bacino's how are you attired?" "Do you use false eyelashes?" "Do you wear earrings?" Do you wear bracelets?"[2]

And on it goes just like that for over one hundred pages of court proceeding transcripts. Such an inquisition seems incomprehensible to us now. Can you imagine being interrogated in court about what you wore and what you said and what you did at a bar last weekend? Thankfully, such witch hunts are a thing of the past, but in 1958 prosecutions like this were de rigueur, not just in New Orleans, but all over the country. Police raids of gay bars in New Orleans continued well into the 1970s, and it would be another fifteen years before the American Psychiatric Association removed homosexuality from its list of mental disorders.

Roy Maggio, Louis Robichaux, and Amos McFarlane eventually lost their case and abandoned their fight on appeal. The case of Tony Bacino's is significant not only in that it was an early attempt to have discriminatory laws based on homophobia ruled unconstitutional but also in that it was a perfect example of the "climate of hostility" toward the LGBT+ community the city of New Orleans actively encouraged. In such an atmosphere, the staff and patrons of Tony Bacino's could not have possibly fathomed the fact that the US Supreme Court would one day seriously consider the constitutionality of same-sex marriage. And yet that day is here, thanks in no small part to the courage of gay people who were and are willing to fight unjust laws in the courts; people like Roy Maggio, Louis Robichaux, and Amos McFarlane.

In the same year Tony Bacino's bar was raided, a gay bashing murder occurred in the French Quarter that resulted in a sensational trial, which is discussed in detail in the following essay.

Ambush, April 16, 2013

NOTES

1. Ordinance Number 18537, section 6.

2. Civil District Court for the Parish of Orleans, Division F, No. 364–219, "Roy Maggio et al. v. City of New Orleans."

THE GAY BASHING MURDER
OF FERNANDO RIOS

A FEW WEEKS AGO, GAY COMMUNITIES ACROSS THE NATION COMMEMO-
rated the fourteenth anniversary of the murder of Matthew Shepard.
Shepard, you may recall, was a college student who was brutally beaten,
tied to a fence post, tortured, and left to die on October 12, 1998, in
Laramie, Wyoming. Shepard was killed simply for being gay, and his
murder galvanized gays everywhere to speak out against homophobia.
As a result, legislation was introduced to include sexual orientation in the
federal hate crimes law. After a ten-year struggle against social conserva-
tives who opposed the measure, Congress finally passed the Matthew
Shepard Act in 2009. President Barack Obama signed the bill into law
on October 28, 2009.

While Matthew Shepard's murder was a touchstone in our national
fight for equality, he was not the first gay person killed just for being gay.
In fact, the gay community in New Orleans also has a martyr who pre-
dates Shepard by forty years. In 1958, Fernando Rios was savagely attacked
and murdered by three homophobes in the heart of the French Quarter.

It was September and the fall semester at colleges and universities was
underway. At that time, a common recreational activity among undergraduate men at college campuses across the nation was to "roll a queer."
This homophobic ritual essentially consisted of two to five guys going to
the "gay" section of town, or a gay bar if the town had one, and beating
up someone they perceived to be gay.

In New Orleans, that meant the French Quarter and Café Lafitte in
Exile, the oldest gay bar in the city. And so, one night, three undergradu-
ates from Tulane University (John Farrell, Alberto A. Calvo, and David P.
Drennan) decided to "roll a queer." The three men went to the Quarter
for a night of carousing. Early in the evening, Farrell suggested they "roll
a queer," but Calvo and Drennan dismissed the idea. Later, after drink-

ing for several hours, Farrell brought up the idea again, this time with no resistance.

Farrell went to Café Lafitte in Exile about 1:30 in the morning and settled on Fernando Rios, a twenty-six-year-old tour guide visiting from Mexico. The two sat next to each other in the bar and chatted for a while before they decided to leave together. As Rios and Farrell were walking through the Quarter, they entered an alley adjacent to St. Louis Cathedral, where Calvo and Drennan were lying in wait. The three undergrads then attacked Rios, beating him repeatedly in the head and kicking him in the stomach several times.

After the attack, the three gay bashers returned to campus bragging about the assault and showing off Rios's wallet, which they had stolen. Rios, barely conscious and unable to move, was not discovered until the next morning. His face bloody and swollen, he was rushed to Charity Hospital, where he subsequently died.

During a routine autopsy, the city coroner discovered Rios had an unusually thin cranium, and this revelation played a key factor in the subsequent murder trial. Farrell, Calvo, and Drennan were arrested and went to trial on murder charges on January 21, 1959. The defendants admitted to the beating but argued Rios died because of his feminine "eggshell cranium," not because of their attack. Tortured logic aside, this defense made perfect sense to a homophobic, all-male, all-white jury in 1959, and the three students were easily acquitted by the jury after deliberating a mere two hours and fifteen minutes.

The acquittal and press coverage of the trial provide a glimpse into the highly homophobic public attitudes of the time. When the "not guilty" verdict was announced, the courtroom erupted in cheers and applause. The New Orleans *States-Item* pictured on its front page a picture of the defendants smiling broadly next to a boxed joke entitled "Today's Chuckle," which read, "Overheard in a nightclub: ordinarily I never chase a man, but this one was getting away."[1] Also, a deluge of letters poured into the editorial offices of the city's newspapers, the overwhelming majority of them supporting the homophobic defendants and urging the city to "clean up the Quarter." The few letters in support of Rios were often backhanded. One incensed reader argued the police should leave the gay bars alone so the "perverts" wouldn't feel compelled to mingle with "normal" people.

This hateful reaction was the polar opposite of the public outcry after Matthew Shepard's murder. I don't know whatever happened to John

Farrell, Alberto Calvo, and David Drennan, but sometimes I wonder. If they are still alive, they would be in their sixties. Did they ever regret killing Fernando Rios? Were they self-loathing closet cases? If so, did they ever come out? Did any of them bear gay children or grandchildren? Were they alive when Matthew Shepard was murdered? If they were, what was their reaction? Did they, like the larger society in which they lived, evolve and become more open-minded and tolerant? Or did they, like far too many still among us, cling to their prejudice and fear?

What does it matter, you may ask? Maybe not much. What does matter, though, is that we live our lives openly and never fail to speak out against homophobia. The recent spike in bullying suicides among gay teens proves there is still much to do. If the gay community in New Orleans had risen up in outrage after the murder of Fernando Rios, then perhaps Matthew Shepard and countless other victims like him wouldn't have had to die by the bloody hand of homophobia.

In 2016, I received an email from Sean Farrell, the son of John Farrell. He was writing to inform me that his father had recently passed away and, in the course of going through his father's papers, he learned for the first time his father had been a defendant in a murder trial while he was a student at Tulane. He had performed a Google search and found the original version of this article. I put him in touch with Clayton Delery, who was writing a book on the Rios murder at the time. Delery interviewed Sean Farrell, and the transcript of that interview is included in his book, *Out for Queer Blood: The Murder of Fernando Rios and the Failure of New Orleans Justice* (2017).[2]

The homophobic climate and rhetoric that gave rise to the violence that claimed Rios's life was reinforced and underscored by constant police raids of gay bars. That is the subject of the next essay.

Ambush, November 6, 2012

NOTES

1. "Today's Chuckle," *States-Item*, January 22, 1959.

2. Clayton Delery, *Out for Queer Blood: The Murder of Fernando Rios and the Failure of New Orleans Justice* (Jefferson, NC: Exposit, 2017).

THE ROSE ROOM, THE GOLDENROD INN, AND POLICE RAIDS

THERE HAVE ALWAYS BEEN QUEER PEOPLE IN NEW ORLEANS, AND WHILE the city currently looks favorably upon us, it wasn't always so. It wasn't too long ago that rainbow flags on Rampart Street and mayoral proclamations for Pride and Southern Decadence would have been inconceivable. The New Orleans Police Department was still raiding gay bars as recently as the 1980s.

It was really bad in the 1950s. Just as the tourism industry began to blossom in the years after World War II, many business leaders and politicians at city hall felt that gay visibility would frighten away straight tourist dollars. Back then, the tourist market was primarily white, straight male conventioneers. The queer tourist market was still in the closet. The attitude among the powers-that-be toward our community was to encourage them to "tone it down." To make sure the queer community got the message, police raids of gay and lesbian bars were common.

One of the most sweeping police raids occurred in 1953 when officers descended upon several gay and lesbian bars throughout the French Quarter and Marigny. Forty-three women were arrested at the Goldenrod Inn on Frenchmen Street alone. Historian James Sears notes, "Then there was also the Goldenrod—whose front area for straight men served as a cover for a back-room lesbian bar—where one Saturday night in 1953 forty-three women were booked for disturbing the peace and being 'loud and boisterous.'"[1]

John D'Emilio, who made passing reference to this particular raid in *Sexual Politics, Sexual Communities*, writes, "In New Orleans in 1953, vice officers packed Doris Lunden and sixty-three other women into vans after clearing them from a lesbian bar in the French Quarter. The next day, Lunden found the court overflowing with men and women brought in from other bars in the city."[2]

Chris Straayer in *Deviant Eyes, Deviant Bodies* quotes Lunden's reaction to being arrested: "That night we had to go to court and I discovered then that they had raided every gay bar in New Orleans. It was like a big cleanup. I had never seen so many gay people in my life. It was really exciting. I almost forgot to be scared about whether I would be convicted or not. My case was dismissed, but I think that set me free in some way."[3]

Police raids of gay and lesbian bars continued for decades. Consider this headline in the *Times-Picayune* on September 9, 1962: "18 Arrested on Morals Charge."

The article stated: "Eleven women and seven men were arrested late Saturday night in an Uptown cocktail lounge and booked in the Second District station with vagrancy by loitering in a place where homosexuals congregate. The place was identified by Sgt. Frederick Soule, commander of the special headquarters (vice) squad as the Rose Room, 4520 Magazine."[4]

The article then lists the names, ages, and addresses of those arrested. The Rose Room eventually became the iconic Brothers Three Lounge, which closed earlier this year when the last of the three brothers, eighty-six-year-old Mr. Johnny, died.

Thankfully, the days of police raids are gone now. Sadly, so are the days of lesbian bars. The last lesbian bar in New Orleans, Rubyfruit Jungle, closed in 2012.

Ambush, November 19, 2019

NOTES

1. James Sears, Rebels, Rubyfruit, and Rhinestones: Queering Space in the Stonewall South (New Brunswick, NJ: Rutgers University Press, 2001).

2. John D'Emilio, *Sexual Politics, Sexual Communities* (Chicago: University of Chicago Press, 1998).

3. Chris Straayer, Deviant Eyes, Deviant Bodies: Sexual Re-Orientation in Film and Video (New York: Columbia University Press, 1996).

4. "18 Arrested on Morals Charge," *Times-Picayune*, September 9, 1962.

ACTIVISM

The essays in this section explore early advocacy efforts in New Orleans, beginning with the local chapter of the Gay Liberation Front. Despite a few attempts at organizing in the early and mid-1970s, especially after the horrific Up Stairs Lounge arson, sustained activism began with the Gertrude Stein Society, which helped stage a hugely successful protest against Anita Bryant's visit to New Orleans in 1977 and eventually evolved into the Louisiana Lesbian and Gay Political Action Caucus (LAGPAC), which operated from 1980 to 2005. A common theme in these articles is the presence and effect of prejudice and bias within the movement. "Activism and Ink" surveys the history of gay journalism in New Orleans and its genesis in early efforts at political organizing. "The Gay Liberation Front Marches on City Hall" looks at the short-lived Gay Liberation Front, one of the earliest activist organizations in the city, and examines why it folded. "Anita Bryant Comes to New Orleans" recalls the nation's leading homophobe's visit to New Orleans and the first significant public demonstration on behalf of LGBT+ rights in Louisiana. "The Southeastern Conference of Lesbians and Gay Men" reviews the 1981 conference, which was held in Baton Rouge, and evaluates the conference program as a lens to gain insight on activism in the early 1980s. "Gay Bars, Gender Discrimination, and Boycotts—1980s Style" illustrates how misogyny and racism almost destroyed LAGPAC (the first sustained LGBT+ political action group in the state) from within.

ACTIVISM AND INK

GAY JOURNALISM TRACES ITS ROOTS TO THE 1960S AND ORIGINALLY
manifested itself in the form of bar bulletins and organizational newsletters. In those pre-internet, pre-Stonewall, highly homophobic years, the notion of a gay media was an alien concept because gay communities, if we can even call them that (perhaps gay subcultures is a better description) were essentially rendered invisible by the monolithic heterosexual society. *The Advocate* was founded in 1967 in Los Angeles as a local publication but soon thereafter went national. As gays, lesbians, and feminists began claiming a stake in the cultural revolution of the 1970s, gay political organizations proliferated across the nation and, with them, organizational newsletters and local newspapers.

In New Orleans, the earliest gay-identified publication was a newsletter entitled *Sunflower*, which was published in 1971 by the recently formed local chapter of the Gay Liberation Front. The first edition featured testimonials from several men, one of whom was straight, who were harassed, beaten, and arrested while in or near Cabrini Park (now commonly called the Dog Park), which was, apparently, quite the cruising ground, in the lower French Quarter. The New Orleans chapter of the Gay Liberation Front was formed in 1970. In January of 1971, the group (roughly seventy-five people) marched on city hall and staged a demonstration protesting police harassment.

The Gay People's Coalition, which was formed in 1973 after the Up Stairs Lounge fire, launched another publication called *Causeway* and established the Gay Crisis Phone Line. *Causeway* was edited anonymously by a Tulane student named Bill Rushton, who also edited the *Vieux Carré Courier*. An editorial from the January 1974 edition of *Causeway* declared, "There are enough gay men and women in New Orleans who are able to do anything they wish—be it swinging an election or electing a gay city councilman."[1] This clarion call, while certainly true, fell on deaf ears. As the embers of the Up Stairs Lounge fire cooled, so did the ire of the gay community. In what was to become the dominant pattern of gay activism in New Orleans, the Gay People's Coalition and *Causeway*, like the Gay Liberation Front and *Sunflower* before them, eventually faded away.

In 1974, former Baptist minister Mike Stark formed the Gay Services Center, which was located on Burgundy Street in the Marigny. Initially, the group enjoyed a flurry of activity, including the publication of a newsletter, the *Closet Door*. But the group's promise was never fulfilled. In a familiar pattern, the newsletter and the group were soon moribund.

In 1975, the Gertrude Stein Society was formed by Bill Rushton, Alan Robinson, and Ann Gallmeyer. The Gertrude Stein Society succeeded in assembling a mailing list, publishing a newsletter, and hosting a variety of social and political events, the most amazing of which was a gay-themed television talk show called *Gertrude Stein Presents*. In one episode, Rushton interviewed Christine Jorgensen, whose sex change in 1951 had shocked the world. Her appearance galvanized the slumbering political consciousness of the local gay community, and soon businesses and politicians began to court the gay community. Gay activism in New Orleans had finally produced some results, meager for sure, but results nonetheless.

In 1977, Roy Letson and Gary Martin founded *Impact*. *Impact* differed from the aforementioned publications in that it was not an organizational newsletter but rather a general newspaper. Throughout its twenty-two-year run, *Impact* went through several phases. In 1998, Kyle Scafide sold *Impact* to Window Media, a publishing concern based in Atlanta. A year and a half after the sale, the paper folded. Shortly after the sale, longtime writer and former editor of *Impact* Jon Newlin wrote, "Nevertheless, LimpAct has reinvented itself before and may well do so more than once again—reinvention usually had to do with what time Miss Letson had gotten up that particular day, thus the paper had its highbrow periods and its hard news periods and its arts-and-leisure periods and its scandal-sheet-tabloid periods, sometimes more than one at once."[2] Newlin would go on to write a column for *Ambush* for eight years. Newlin's writing was sassy and tongue in cheek and tinged with streaks of brilliance.[3]

Ambush was founded in 1982 by Rip Naquin and Marsha Delain. Originally, the magazine covered Baton Rouge and North Louisiana but was expanded to include New Orleans when Naquin and Delain moved to the city in 1985. *Ambush* now serves the Gulf Coast from Houston to Pensacola.[4]

Reflecting on the history of the paper, Rip Naquin-Delain recalls, "Our first publication was *The Zipper*, distributed in Baton Rouge and lasted a year. The following publication was the *Alternative*, distributed in Baton

Rouge, Lafayette, Lake Charles, Alexandria, Monroe, Shreveport, and Houma, Louisiana, which was going into its sixth anniversary when we sold it to go into a straight bar business in Hammond. The person we sold it to ran it into the ground and it closed within a year."

Naquin-Delain continues, "When we left the straight bar business, we decided to do a publication reaching the whole state, including New Orleans. A group of our friends from across Louisiana came to our home in Baton Rouge to brainstorm for the publication. On the last night, we got cocktailed and tried to come up with a catchy name, and our dear friend Victoria Windsor, a famous drag queen from Monroe (weighing in at over four hundred pounds) better known as Queen Victoria, said 'Ambush,' and we all agreed, it'd catch attention."

Thirty-one years later, *Ambush* is one of the oldest remaining LGBT+ themed print publication in the United States. The long tenures of both *Ambush* and *Impact*, especially in contrast to the short-lived organizational newsletters of earlier years, suggest that for gay publications to succeed, they must emanate from a business model rather than a strictly political or ideological orientation, which is to say that while some people may want "hard news," they also want lighter fare such as entertainment, gossip, and party pictures. In this regard, the gay media is not much different than the straight media.

After Rip Naquin died in 2017, Marsha sold the paper to local attorney Tomy Acosta. *Ambush* remained in print until the COVID-19 pandemic of 2020, at which time it became exclusively digital.

The following essay highlights the first queer political action group in New Orleans, the local chapter of the Gay Liberation Front.

Ambush, January 14, 2014

NOTES

1. Bill Rushton, "Editorial," *Causeway*, January 1974.

2. Jon Newlin, "Madame John Dodt's Legacy #24," *Impact*, date unknown.

3. Back issues of *Impact* are available at a number of archival repositories in New Orleans and on the LGBT+ Archives Project website.

4. Back issues of *Ambush* are available at a number of archival repositories in New Orleans and on the LGBT+ Archives Project website.

THE GAY LIBERATION FRONT
MARCHES ON CITY HALL

GAY PRIDE HAS COME AND GONE FOR ANOTHER YEAR AND THE GAY COMmunity in New Orleans now looks forward to another Southern Decadence. Despite a thriving LGBT+ community in New Orleans, Pride has never really generated the excitement and activity here that it does in other major metropolitan areas. New Orleans is not a radical city and our gay forefathers always preferred to organize socially rather than politically. This is evident in the storied history of the Gay Carnival krewes and the enormous popularity of Southern Decadence. This is not to say, however, that New Orleans is entirely without a history of gay activism; indeed, there were many attempts at organizing politically, especially after the Up Stairs Lounge fire in 1973 and when antigay crusader Anita Bryant came to town in 1977. But many of these attempts were short-lived.

One of the earliest efforts at gay political activism in New Orleans occurred in 1971 when the Gay Liberation Front marched on city hall. The national Gay Liberation Front had been founded in New York in 1969 a few weeks after the rebellion at the Stonewall Inn. At that time, the major voice for gay rights was the conservative Mattachine Society, whose response to the Stonewall riot was a call for gays to settle down and work within the system to bring about change. This conservative, measured response angered some within the Mattachine Society who felt the time had come to give up on traditional and gradual reform. When the leadership of the Mattachine Society denounced the group's public support of a Black Panther rally, several members abandoned the Mattachine Society to form the Gay Liberation Front. This break represented a new way of thinking about gay rights. Instead of slowly gaining acceptance within the existing society, the radicals who formed the Gay Liberation Front called for the creation of a new society.

The New Orleans chapter of the Gay Liberation Front was formed in 1970 by Lynn Miller and David Solomon. In January of 1971, the group (roughly seventy-five people) marched on city hall and staged a demonstration protesting police harassment. The group made three demands:

1. An immediate end of all hostility, brutality, entrapment, and harassment by the New Orleans Police of gay men and women and of their places of gathering.
2. Formation of a Governor's Panel empowered to conduct a complete and thorough investigation of the police methods and actions against gay people. On this panel shall sit one gay man and one gay woman.
3. The immediate suspension from duty of Police Superintendent Clarence Giarusso and vice squad head Souler, until the Governor's Panel has completed its investigation. Should the panel find against these men, they shall be terminated immediately.[1]

The demonstration and the protestors' demands received some coverage in the *Times-Picayune* but were, for the most part, generally disregarded. They did not go unnoticed, however. Straight New Orleans was shocked not only at the visibility of gay people but also, perhaps more so, at the alarming fact they were demanding things.

The New Orleans chapter of the Gay Liberation Front disbanded a few months later. Soon after the group fizzled out, some members went on to found the local Metropolitan Community Church and a local Daughters of Bilitis chapter.

The seeds planted by the New Orleans GLF lay dormant for several years but would fully bloom in 1977 with the largest queer rights rally in New Orleans's history. The impetus was Anita Bryant.

Ambush, July 9, 2013

NOTE

1. "Gay Liberation Group Marches," *Times-Picayune*, January 24, 1971.

ANITA BRYANT COMES TO NEW ORLEANS

WHEN IT WAS ANNOUNCED IN 1977 THAT ANITA BRYANT, THE NATION'S leading homophobe, would be coming to New Orleans to perform two concerts, local gay activists Alan Robinson and Bill Rushton must have thought to themselves, "Oh, hell no!"

The popular homophobic singer, and former Miss Oklahoma, had made quite a splash in Miami earlier in the year when she led a campaign to repeal Dade County's recently passed antidiscrimination ordinance that granted legal protection to gays and lesbians. She called her campaign "Save Our Children" and argued, "What these people really want, hidden behind obscure legal phrases, is the legal right to propose to our children that theirs is an acceptable alternate way of life. I will lead such a crusade to stop it as this country has not seen before." She was also quoted as saying, "As a mother, I know that homosexuals cannot biologically reproduce children; therefore, they must recruit our children," and "If gays are granted rights, next we'll have to give rights to prostitutes and to people who sleep with St. Bernards and to nail biters."[1] Bryant went on to found Anita Bryant Ministries, which claimed to "cure" homosexuals by "deprogramming" them.

Robinson, who was a gay activist while studying at the University of Illinois, had arrived in New Orleans two years earlier. He met Rushton while volunteering at the Gay Services Center, a community outreach facility in the Marigny that had been founded in 1974 by Mike Stark. Rushton, a student at Tulane University at the time, had been involved with the Gay People's Coalition (GPC) and edited the organization's publication *Causeway*. The two activists began dating, and one night over dinner, they, along with Ann Gallmeyer, founded the Gertrude Stein Democratic Club, which eventually became the Gertrude Stein Society.

Upon learning that Bryant would be coming to town, the Gertrude Stein Society reached out to several local gay organizations and progressive groups and formed HERE (Human Equal Rights for Everyone). The group's purpose was to plan a protest against Bryant's concerts. HERE eventually grew into a coalition of fifteen different groups.

In response to Bryant's upcoming visit, HERE contacted Rod Wagner, a board member of the New Orleans chapter of the American Federation of Television and Radio Artists, and impressed upon him Bryant's virulent opposition to gay rights. The New Orleans Board of AFTRA then unanimously passed a resolution asking its members to not air the Bryant concerts.

Wagner is quoted as saying, "They were afraid, and our board agreed, that her appearance could set up even more of a climate for violence here than we're already experiencing. And we are having our troubles. For instance, several older gay men have been stabbed to death in the French Quarter in the past few weeks, and I understand the suspect has said, 'Jesus doesn't like gay people.' What also concerns us are the reports of violence in the Miami area." He goes on to cite a bumper sticker popular in Miami at the time that read, "Kill a Queen for Christ."

The second prong of HERE's attack was a rally to be held at Jackson Square followed by a march through the French Quarter to the Municipal Auditorium, where Bryant was scheduled to perform. In the weeks before that rally, Robinson and Rushton flooded the French Quarter with flyers announcing the rally. Because Byrant was the official spokesperson for the Florida Citrus Commission, many gay bars in the French Quarter stopped serving Florida orange juice.

On the day of the rally, June 18, Robinson, Rushton, and the other organizers were astonished and delighted by the turnout. They had hoped for a couple of hundred people to show up. Crowd estimates at the time peg the attendance at 2,500 to 3,000 people. After the speechmaking, the crowd sang "We Shall Overcome" and began marching from the square along St. Ann Street before turning right onto Bourbon and left onto Dumaine.

In his landmark book on southern gayness, *Rebels, Rubyfruit, and Rhinestones*, James Sears describes the march: "Supporters on wrought iron balconies wrapped with banners cheered. The march extended four blocks from sidewalk to sidewalk . . . Marking one of the largest civil rights demonstrations in the city's history, thousands of protestors arrived at the North Rampart Street Municipal Auditorium Entrance. [The] Gertrude Stein [Society] was elated: 'The reaction within the ranks was explosive, euphoric, and pure; the silence of the past is ended.'"[2]

The success of the rally energized the LGBT+ community in New Orleans and also served as a harbinger of the shift in public attitudes toward homosexuality. Similar protests were held in other cities where Bryant performed, and the backlash against Bryant's bigotry caused the Florida Citrus Commission to drop her as its spokesperson. Her popularity among fundamentalist Christians further plummeted in 1980 when she divorced her husband, Bob Green. She married her second husband, Charlie Hobson Dry, in 1990 and attempted to resurrect her singing career, but in 1997, the couple filed for bankruptcy in Arkansas. They would do the same in Tennessee in 2001.

The Gertrude Stein Society gradually morphed into the Louisiana Lesbian and Gay Political Action Caucus (LAGPAC), which was greatly influenced by the Southeastern Conference of Lesbians and Gay Men.

Ambush, December 3, 2013

NOTES

1. Anita Bryant and Bob Green, *At Any Cost* (Grand Rapids, MI: Fleming H. Revell, 1978).
2. James Sears, Rebels, *Rubyfruit, and Rhinestones: Queering Space in the Stonewall South* (New Brunswick, NJ: Rutgers University Press, 2001).

THE SOUTHEASTERN CONFERENCE OF LESBIANS AND GAY MEN

IN 1975, TOM CARR WAS A GRADUATE STUDENT AT THE UNIVERSITY OF North Carolina at Chapel Hill. At a time when gay rights was a fairly new concept, Carr persuaded the city of Chapel Hill to pass an ordinance that protected gays and lesbians from discrimination. Carr was very active in the Carolina Gay Association (CGA), which had been founded by Dan Leonard, Michael Grissom, and others at UNC in 1974 to increase gay awareness on the campus. Carr, Leonard, Grissom, and the other early members of the CGA probably had no idea how influential their efforts would become, but they did have a vision, and that vision has positively impacted millions of LGBT+ folk over the last forty years, especially in the South.

In 1976, Carr, working through the CGA, coordinated the first Southeastern Gay Conference (the name was later changed to the Southeastern Conference of Lesbians and Gay Men). Held at Chapel Hill, that first conference attracted hundreds of attendees from all over the South. The annual conference, held in cities across the South (including New Orleans in 1986), grew not only in numbers, but also in stature, relevance, and influence.

In 1981, the conference was held in Baton Rouge on the LSU campus. A glance at the conference program from that year offers an insightful look at the issues gay folk were dealing with at the time. Consider the following workshop titles: "Gay Switchboards: Forming and Operating a Referral, Information and Crisis Line," "Suicide Prevention," "Hidden People: Social History of Gay People," "Gay Health Issues," "Establishing a State Organization and Lobbying Office," and "Using Political Systems: The Time Is Now" (which was conducted by longtime New Orleans gay activist Roberts Batson).

The conference program is also telling in what topics were not included. HIV/AIDS was not yet a blip on the gay radar screen; marriage equality and, to a lesser extent, gays serving openly in the military were inconceivable. In an era before the widespread use of personal computers, much less the internet, the primary focus was on sharing information—very basic, fundamental information that we often take for granted today. Gay political organizing was in its nascent stage then and its chief obstacle was rampant homophobia—both externally throughout society and internally for the untold millions still in the closet.

The 1981 conference in Baton Rouge was the first of several South-eastern Conferences New Orleans activist Stewart Butler attended. Reflecting on the experience, Butler recalls, "It established the seed for the Louisiana State Conference, which was held at the Country Club in the Bywater later that same year (1981)." The Louisiana State Confer-ence was organized and sponsored by the Louisiana Lesbian and Gay Political Action Caucus (LAGPAC), which had been founded in 1980 by Roberts Batson and Alan Robinson.

The second Louisiana State Conference was held in Baton Rouge at George's bar. Although heavy rains dampened attendance, the conference did feature the first public appearance of the New Orleans Gay Men's Chorus. Glenn O' Berry, a member of the chorus, suggested to conference organizers that since the conference was sponsored by LAGPAC some people may have thought the conference was exclusively political and therefore stayed away. The organizers agreed and began to reach out to other nonpolitical gay groups to participate in the conference.

Thus, the Louisiana State Conference morphed into Celebration in 1983 and was held at Armstrong Park in that year. The Celebration gatherings, which lasted into the early 1990s, featured workshops, keynote speakers, musical entertainment, and food.

Celebration is just one example of the conferences and efforts that were spawned by the SECLGM. Ron Joullian, an activist in Alabama who had helped establish AIDS outreaches and a Gay Center in Birmingham, met Stewart Butler at the 1983 Southeastern Conference in Atlanta. Reminiscing on the conference thirty-two years later, Joullian observes, "It was quite an eye-opener for this little group of country bumpkins from Birmingham." Joullian and his partner, Tim Angle, became friends with Butler and his partner, the late Alfred Doolittle, and eventually moved to New Orleans.

Considering the social milieu in which the Southeastern Conference was founded, the phenomenal success of the SECLGM was inevitable. Butler, Joullian, and others who attended the Southeastern Conferences recall them fondly, often using adjectives like "energizing," electrifying," and "inspiring." When asked why the SECLGM was so significant, Butler looked at me as though I had just checked in from another planet and said, "The dispensation of sorely needed information." When asked the same question, Joullian responded, "We gays from rural areas got to meet other gays and afterward we didn't feel so alone."

As gays and lesbians began to organize politically, the issue of gender discrimination reared its head. Political organizations were divided in how to address the issue. The next essay is a case study in how divisive the topic was, especially for LAGPAC.

Ambush, March 10, 2015

GAY BARS, GENDER DISCRIMINATION, AND BOYCOTTS—1980s STYLE

THE RECENT CONTROVERSY SURROUNDING WOOD ENTERPRISES SEEMS to have quieted down. For those readers who have been in a coma or may not otherwise know, Tom Wood aroused the anger of a significant portion of the leather community earlier this year when it was revealed that he was responsible for the closure of the Phoenix's upstairs darkroom. A boycott of Wood-owned bars was organized, and T-shirts were even printed that admonished, "Stay Out of the Woods."

Lost in the public outcry over one bar owner turning in a rival bar for state code violations was a much more serious issue—gender discrimination. There was a time when gay male bars did not want female patrons and the reverse was true for lesbian bars. Many gay bar owners required multiple forms of identification from women trying to enter and/or invoked obscure dress code requirements as a deterrent. There were exceptions, of course—Dixie's, Up Stairs, Safari Lounge, for example—but gender discrimination was the norm even as recently as the 1980s.

Boycotting gay bars because of gender discrimination is nothing new. One such boycott occurred in 1980—and it nearly destroyed a brand-new political organization created to fight for equality, the Louisiana Lesbian and Gay Political Action Caucus. LAGPAC would go on to achieve great things over the course of its twenty-five-plus-year history, chiefly the creation of a statewide conference, the demonstration of the LGBT+ voting bloc, and the passage of a nondiscrimination ordinance in New Orleans in 1991. But shortly after LAGPAC was formed, it faced a crisis that threatened its very nascent existence.

The issue of what we would now call cis-gay male privilege reared its head when Rich Sacher and Henry Schmidt, representing Dignity (a gay Catholic organization) and another group called GLAD (Gays and Lesbians Against Discrimination) proposed to the LAGPAC board that it boycott Café Lafitte in Exile and the Bourbon Pub for their policies of not allowing women and African Americans into their bars.

The board rejected the proposal, citing that its mission statement only covered sexual orientation. But this was only a guise; the real reason was more nuanced. Some members of LAGPAC felt that at this embryonic and fragile stage of its existence, LAGPAC should not wander into the controversy. Complicating the matter was the fact that the bar owners, Tom Wood (Café Lafitte in Exile) and Jerry Menefee (the Bourbon Pub), were members of LAGPAC (Menefee served on the development committee). The board's decision not to join the boycott almost destroyed LAGPAC. Years later, in a 1990 workshop at the Celebration Conference, Stewart Butler, a charter member of LAGPAC and board member, acknowledged the decision was a mistake.

The vote caused a backlash among the general membership and some of the board of directors. Melanie Miranda and Pat Denton abruptly departed the meeting and subsequently resigned from the board. In her resignation letter, Denton chastised the board for its hypocrisy:

Having thought that this organization opposed and would stand against discrimination based on sex as well as that based on sexual preference . . . And being further led to believe that LAGPAC stood for full access to public accommodations as stated in its recently set goals, but finding that in actuality (by virtue of its refusing to take a stand against existing and blatant sexual discrimination being practiced by some gay bars—one in particular going so far as to publicly display a "Men Only" sign—it gives tacit approval to discrimination based on sex, I must conclude that the majority of this Board does not stand for full equality for all people.[1]

Denton's seat was filled by the appointment of Liz Simon to the board, but before Simon accepted, she had a few concerns of her own. Simon had earned an MA in social work from Tulane University and worked in private practice as a therapist for a primarily gay and lesbian clientele. Simon was not new to activism; she had previously served as chair of Women Against Violence Against Women and on the board of the YWCA Battered Women's Program. She had also been involved in the Gertrude Stein Society and was a founding member of LAGPAC. Simon agreed to join the board on the condition it conduct a workshop on "Oppression Dynamics." Simon also formed a Lesbian-Feminist Caucus within the auspices of LAGPAC.

Despite the Board's efforts to contain the damage from its controversial decision, several LAGPAC members quit the organization over the issue, some writing excoriating letters. As chair of the membership committee, Stewart Butler attempted to do damage control by reaching out to several disgruntled members with limited success. One wrote to him,

> Dear Stew, Thanks but NO thanks, and believe me I've "carefully considered" LAGPAC—and discover each time I have only feelings of CONTEMPT for it. I see its members running around changing everyone else's house—but nothing is done at home. I sincerely hope our rich and powerful Bar Owners support LAGPAC in every way—for staying out of their way . . . If your membership is down, I feel good. Try C.C.C.—that's what I tell people—especially if they are black or female. Sorry Stew, but like I said I have nothing but CONTEMPT for LAGPAC—PLEASE remove my name from your mailing list—and be thankful I stay away."[2]

LAGPAC received letters not only from its own members but also from other organizations encouraging it to examine its own prejudices and privilege. One such letter came from Louisiana Sissies in Struggle: "By setting goals that will predominantly benefit people of European origins and holding events in gay establishments that are openly racist (Bourbon Pub / Parade Disco) LAGPAC is endorsing the institutions of white supremacists and white racism in America—if not in rhetoric, certainly in practice."[3]

In retrospect, LAGPAC's decision not to join the boycott was a mistake. Nevertheless, it survived that mistake by learning from it and, ultimately, did manage to become an extremely effective political organization.

So, if you're still "Staying Out of the Woods," you're not the first.

Ambush, July 30, 2019

NOTES

1. Letter from Pat Denton to LAGPAC cochairs Jean Carr and Roberts Batson, February 21, 1981, Stewart Butler Papers, Louisiana Research Collection, Tulane University, Box 1.

2. Letter from Ed Frost to Stewart Butler, August 2, 1982, Stewart Butler Papers, Louisiana Research Collection, Tulane University, Box 1, Folder 17.

3. Letter in the Stewart Butler Collection, Louisiana Research Collection, Tulane University, Box 1, Folder 17.

ACTIVISTS

The essays in this section highlight the lives and work of five activists: Stewart Butler, Courtney Sharp, Skip Ward, Charlene Schneider, and Barbara Scott. "Lion in Winter: A Tribute to Stewart Butler" was published not long after Butler died in 2020 and recalls Butler's fascinating journey from closeted ex-army, straitlaced married man to radical marijuana-smoking hippie activist. Butler was a latecomer to the queer rights movement and began his work as an activist at the age of fifty. He would become heavily involved with the Louisiana Lesbian and Gay Political Action Caucus (LAGPAC) and PFLAG. Butler, along with Courtney Sharp, was also an early trans activist. Sharp began her career fighting workplace discrimination and eventually led an eight-year crusade to have the national PFLAG organization include trans people in its mission statement. "Courtney Sharp: Unsung Trans Hero" describes that crusade. "Queer Pioneer Skip Ward" profiles Radical Faery and back-to-the-land advocate Skip Ward, an early voice for LGBT+ rights in rural central Louisiana. "Remembering Charlene Schneider" recalls the life of legendary bar owner Charlene Schneider. "Go Your Own Way: The Life of Barbara Scott" looks back on the life and work of feminist Barbara Scott. Scott founded *Distaff*, an early and long-running feminist publication, and also became the first openly gay political candidate in Louisiana in 1971 when she ran for the State House of Representatives.

LION IN WINTER:
A TRIBUTE TO STEWART BUTLER

IN 2010 I FOUND MYSELF STANDING ON ESPLANADE AVENUE BEFORE A Creole Cottage with red hearts on its reddish front facade. A rainbow flag graced the roof along with a sign that read "Peace on earth." A banner declared, "End the War." On the front of the house, a historical marker reads:

> The Faerie Playhouse
> 1308 Esplanade Ave.
> This Creole Cottage became the home of Stewart Butler and Alfred Doolittle in 1979 and was the site of many organizational meetings in the lesbian, gay, bisexual, and transsexual civil rights movement during the late 20th Century and early 21st Century. The garden behind this home contains the remains of many significant leaders in that struggle for equality, including Charlene Schneider, John Ognibene, and Cliff Howard, as well as artist J. B. Harter.
> The Bienville Foundation
> 2007

The scent of marijuana drifted onto the sidewalk from the alley leading to the back courtyard as the alley gate opened. I was about to meet Stewart Butler. He materialized out of a thick haze of cannabis smoke, as if conjured by some strange magic.

The old gay wizard, eighty at the time, stood before me with his two dogs—Putz, an English Springer Spaniel, and Holly, a mix. All three smiled at me warmly.

He was not tall but had a commanding presence. Think Benjamin Franklin as a hippy. His shoulder-length hair draped from a purple and gold fishing cap. His eyes were a piercing, yet gentle, blue. His T-shirt read,

"Use me, Dump me, Crush me, Melt me, Use me again. Glass recycles." Around his neck were a cross, the Rastafarian colors, and a marijuana leaf. He invited me inside and, as he poured my coffee, said, "There are many spirits in this house."

I believed him.

He then told me about Alfred, his lover and soulmate of thirty-five years. The two had met in 1973 during Carnival season. Stewart and a friend were barhopping in the Quarter when they ran into Alfred, who had just arrived in town. At Café Lafitte in Exile, the venerable old watering hole located at the corner of Bourbon and Dumaine, Alfred whispered sweet obscene nothings in Stewart's ear. Stewart was smitten.

"He looked just like Prince Valiant," Butler recalled.

The two left Lafitte's and made their way back to Stewart's home. Alfred told him, "You'll probably throw me out in the morning like the rest of them." But Stewart didn't throw him out. Alfred and Stewart remained together until Alfred's death in 2008.

Theirs was a relationship that would shape the course of LGBT+ history.

Alfred hailed from a prominent San Francisco family. When Alfred was diagnosed with schizophrenia as a young man, his family put him in an institution. Alfred had other plans and escaped. He had always loved to travel. A few years earlier, in Paris, he lived briefly in the fabled Beat Hotel, where he met Allen Ginsberg, Peter Orlovsky, Brion Gysin, Ian Sommerville, Gregory Corso, Harold Norse, and William S. Burroughs. He had an affair with Norse, who gifted Alfred with a few of his famous acid drawings. Alfred's period as a global flaneur ended when he came to New Orleans and met Stewart.

A few months after connecting, Stewart and Alfred were at the Up Stairs Lounge at the corner of Iberville and Chartres Streets the night an arsonist set fire to it. Butler was a regular at the bar and often took his dog, Jocko, to the Up Stairs. The dog, much to the delight of the other patrons, liked to drink vodka and milk out of a bowl. On the fateful night of the fire, Stewart and Alfred left the bar just minutes before flames erupted.

A few doors down, at Wanda's bar, Stewart and Alfred had not even settled in when they heard the sirens. The scene they encountered outside was horrific. Word of the fire had spread quickly, and a throng of people gathered in the streets as mayhem ensued.

Years later, Stewart recalled that one of the most difficult things was going to work the next day and pretending to be unaware or unconcerned with the tragedy. Most workplaces at the time doubled as closets and while the demimonde of the French Quarter knew Stewart was gay, his boss and coworkers did not.

Surviving the fire that night was just one of a lifetime of remarkable moments in Stewart Butler's life. Butler, with Alfred's help, would go on to become one of the most consequential LGBT+ activists in New Orleans history.

Born in 1930, Butler grew up in New Orleans and at the age of twelve moved to Carville, Louisiana, where his father took a job at a leprosarium. Coming of age in a colony of Hansen's disease patients gave Stewart a unique understanding of marginalized communities and helped shape an abiding compassion for the less fortunate.

After a stint at Louisiana State University, Butler served in the army before moving to Alaska, where he finished his education and became involved in labor politics. He was elected to the Alaskan Territorial Senate, but Alaska's admission to the union nullified his election before he could take office.

Upon returning to New Orleans in 1964, Stewart lived from pillar to post for a few years. From 1965 to 1968, he lived in a total of twelve different places, including five in the French Quarter, four along Esplanade Avenue. Several roommates came and went. During this time, he worked various odd jobs as a busboy, a waiter, and a draftsperson for three land surveyors.

When Alfred inherited his fortune, Stewart retired and became a full-time activist. He joined the Gertrude Stein Society, which served as a forerunner of sorts to LAGPAC (Louisiana Lesbian and Gay Political Action Caucus). Butler was a charter member of LAGPAC and played a key role in the 1991 passage of a New Orleans City Council nondiscrimination ordinance. LAGPAC was the first gay rights group in Louisiana and Stewart was at its heart.

He was also at the forefront of the transgender rights movement long before it became fashionable. Through his involvement with PFLAG (Parents and Friends of Lesbians and Gays), he and Courtney Sharp led a successful campaign to have transgender people included in the national PFLAG mission statement.

Stewart also participated in HIV/AIDS activism, criminal justice reform, voter registration drives, and a dozen other causes. In 1987, he led a protest against the pope's visit, and the following year, he helped organize a protest against the Republican National Convention.

More recently, in 2012, he called a number of people together and expressed his desire to do something about preserving local queer history. Thus, the LGBT+ Archives Project of Louisiana was born. A statewide collective, the LGBT+ Archives Project collaborates with universities, libraries, museums, and archival repositories around the state to preserve materials that chronicle the LGBT+ community in Louisiana.

Stewart died in his sleep at the Faerie Playhouse on March 5, 2020. I had a chance to visit with him a few hours before he passed. I was struck by the weight of history this man shaped and the countless lives he touched. He truly was a lion in winter.

R.I.P., Stewart. And tell Alfred hello.

One of Butler's close friends and fellow activists was Courtney Sharp. Together, Butler and Sharp made a significant, yet often unrecognized, contribution to trans history. That story is the focus of the next essay.

French Quarter Journal, August 1, 2020

COURTNEY SHARP: UNSUNG TRANS HERO

LIKE SO MANY TRANS PEOPLE, COURTNEY SHARP'S JOURNEY TO SELF-realization was a long one. Growing up she knew she was different but couldn't quite put her finger on it. All she knew for sure was that she had better keep that difference secret. Her family was religious, and this was North Louisiana, after all. When her "difference" began to manifest, her family, which was Roman Catholic, steered her into traditional gender roles.

Sharp was born in New Orleans but had moved away as a child when her father took a job near Vidalia, Louisiana. While attending college at Louisiana Tech in Ruston (near the Arkansas border), she attended a talk on campus given by Christine Jorgensen—the first widely recognized trans woman in the US (she transitioned in the early 1950s). Most of the attendees came out of curiosity, but it was more than that for Sharp. Sharp was looking for answers, a reference point, hope.

Sharp had dealt with her internal struggle by turning to academics as a coping mechanism. Incredibly bright, in 1976, she earned two degrees in chemical and biomedical engineering. She then landed a job with a chemical company in Lake Charles, where she worked for seven years before being hired by another company.

When she anonymously asked the human resources department what the company policy on being transsexual was, she received no response. She then asked a lawyer to assist her in obtaining information, but still no response was forthcoming. Sharp kept working because she really enjoyed her job, but after a few years the struggle had become too intense to deny. When Sharp personally approached the HR department, she was told that she would be fired if she began transitioning. The excuse the company gave her was that it would create a "hostile work environment."

She then began seeing a psychiatrist at a gender clinic in Galveston in 1985. She kept working but gradually became depressed to the point of being hospitalized in 1992. Sharp eventually sued her employer in federal court, but her case was dismissed. She was eventually terminated from her job for long-term disability. Unemployed and on disability, she then began spending countless hours researching and educating herself on trans legal issues. She regularly attended transgender conferences in Houston.

In 1993, Sharp moved to New Orleans. She had lost her career as well as her family, who rejected her when she began transitioning. She was lost, lonely, broke, and depressed. She considered suicide. But a nagging thought kept her from ending it all. She had learned of a statistic that haunted her. In her own words, Sharp recalls, "Forty percent of the kids in my community are killing themselves and I know exactly why. What am I going to do about it?"

The answer was to get involved with PFLAG and the community. She volunteered at the LGBT Community Center, which was then located on North Rampart Street, and also worked with LAGPAC (Louisiana Lesbian and Gay Political Action Caucus).

She became close friends with Stewart Butler, who had been a charter member of LAGPAC since 1980 and was now heavily involved in PFLAG. Butler had been instrumental in the passage of the 1991 nondiscrimination ordinance in New Orleans and was the veteran of numerous political campaigns. Both Butler and Sharp recognized the need for transgender rights, protections, and inclusion. At that time, the idea of gay and lesbian rights was so radical that trans rights was "beyond the pale," which is to say inconceivable to most people, even those within the LGBT+ community. Sharp and Butler were ahead of their time.

One of the flaws of the 1991 nondiscrimination ordinance was that it did not include protections for transgender persons. Sharp and Butler led a quiet campaign to correct that injustice by including transgender language in the 1995 Home Rule Charter. Because the charter was so grand in scope, no one was really paying attention to Sharp and Butler's efforts, and they were ultimately successful in slipping in the phrase "gender identification." People were so focused on the big picture they didn't notice the details.

At the time, Sharp was serving as the first transgender person on the mayor's advisory committee (MAC) and the following year joined the board of directors of LAGPAC. In 1998, Sharp and LAGPAC turned their attention to the state legislature. MAC and LAGPAC worked together to file a nondiscrimination bill that included transgender protections. Simultaneously, the Forum for Equality, another political action group based in New Orleans, had a similar bill filed that did not include transgender language.

The two bills confused the New Orleans delegation to the state House of Representatives. The delegation was generally sympathetic to LGBT+ causes, but the two bills revealed a frustrating lack of communication and coordination. The delegation called a meeting of both LAGPAC and Forum for Equality officials and chastised them for "not having their shit together."

During the meeting, Tony Clesi, an attorney for the Forum, angrily asked, "Why in the hell are we talking about including transsexual people when we need to protect gays and lesbians?" He did not know that Sharp, who was in the room, was transgender. Sharp was shocked at the remark and left the room to calm down and collect her thoughts. Upon returning to the meeting, she referenced Clesi's question and said, "This is why . . ." and then, after coming out as trans, excoriated the Forum for Equality for its hypocrisy.

The aforementioned episode foreshadowed the national controversy in 2007 when House Speaker Nancy Pelosi and Representative Barney Frank removed transgender language from ENDA (the Employment Non-Discrimination Act).

In 2000, when a Louisiana Winn-Dixie grocery store fired Peter Oiler for cross-dressing when he wasn't working, Sharp helped organize a protest campaign. While a lawsuit was working its way through the federal court system, Sharp said, "The transgender community had demanded that Winn-Dixie institute a non-discrimination policy for gender identity & expression and sexual orientation. We also asked them to institute sensitivity training. Those demands have not been withdrawn and were not dependent upon the legal case."[1]

In addition to battling politicians and corporations, Sharp also waged a subtler campaign within the LGBT+ community to foster greater understanding and inclusion of transgender people. When she joined PFLAG, she asked why the group did not include transgender young people in its mission. The question caught the attention of the local chapter's leadership (Sandra Pailet, Julie Thompson, and Randy Trahan), and they took Sharp to dinner to discuss the matter further. They were receptive.

Sharp had put transgender youth on the local PFLAG chapter's radar but there was still much to do, namely convincing the local PFLAG's board of directors that the trans issue was something the national organization needed to address. Her strongest ally was, again, Stewart Butler. Together they gradually persuaded the local chapter to lead the fight for transgender inclusion in the national PFLAG mission statement.

The New Orleans chapter of PFLAG formally proposed that the national organization vote to include the word transgender in its mission statement. The resolution would be voted on by the national board at the national conference in San Francisco in 1998. The board required written arguments both for and against the resolution before they voted. Sharp wrote the argument for trans inclusion. The resolution passed, and PFLAG became the first national LGBT+ organization to include trans people in its mission statement.

In 2000, Courtney Sharp became the first transgender member of the national PFLAG board of directors.

While Sharp was leading the charge in the fight for trans rights, another activist was working in and fighting for another marginalized group— rural gay men. Skip Ward is the subject of the following essay.

Ambush, October 8, 2019

NOTE

1. "Shame on Winne-Dixie: 3rd Anniversary of Peter Oiler's Firing," document in the personal collection of Courtney Sharp.

QUEER PIONEER SKIP WARD

GROWING UP GAY IN THE SOUTH HAS NEVER BEEN EASY, WHICH IS WHY New Orleans has historically been a mecca for LGBT+ folk wishing to escape small-town closets all across the rural South. North Louisiana is about as Deep South as it gets—land of Baptists and Pentecostals: a desolate cultural hellscape of ignorance, racism, and homophobia. It was, and, to some extent, still is, a very lonely place for LGBT+ people. Until recently, virtually all closet doors were cemented shut and life behind them was hopeless and dark. But in 1971, a man in Alexandria, Louisiana, came out of the closet and in so doing raised a beacon of light and hope to untold thousands.

Blanchard "Skip" Ward was born on September 17, 1920. After growing up in Alexandria, Ward joined the US Navy and graduated from NSU in 1950. After coming out as a gay man in 1971, he became an advocate for gay rights. In the 1980s, Ward became very involved in LAGPAC (Louisiana Lesbian and Gay Political Action Caucus), a political activist organization.

Ward and his partner, Gene Barnes, began publishing a gay-themed newsletter and formed Le Beau Monde in 1981. Le Beau Monde was an informal social group of gay people who met regularly to "explore the humanistic and spiritual aspects of being gay."

Spirituality had always been an integral part of Ward's life. As a child, his grandmother instilled in him a strong mistrust of organized religion, especially Christianity. Ward eventually became a lifelong Unitarian Universalist and went on to cofound the Unitarian/Universalist Church's Gay Caucus. Ward became associated with the Radical Faeries (a national organization for rural-based gender and sexual nonconforming spiritualists), and in 1994, he and Barnes acquired twelve acres of land in North Louisiana and called it Manitou Woods. It became a retreat space for spiritual communion and meditation.

In 1987, Ward wrote, "I'm not sure where we should be going with our new-found spiritual consciousness. We are walking forth upon new ground, watered by streams of paganism, faerie spirituality, shamanism, and a revival of *berdache* spirituality."[1]

The aforementioned quote is from a letter Ward wrote in response to a letter he received from a gay man in New Mexico who was curious about gay spirituality. This was just one of dozens of gay men who wrote Ward seeking advice. Ward took the time to respond to all of them, and his letters are beautiful expressions of wisdom and courage.

A few excerpts. To a closeted man: "Still trying with women, you wrote. If it had worked for me, just screwing women, I'd not be gay today. Many have tried this. Sure, you can get married, have kids, etc., but you'll never cease to look longingly at certain people of your own sex."[2]

"I learned long ago that for me it is thoughtful, considerate, and kind to leave women alone. Why involve one of them in a hopeless relationship, doomed to incompleteness. Women deserve someone who can love them unreservedly, unconditionally. And so do men!"[3]

To a man who had just come out of the closet in 1983 and was fearful of the consequences: "How can ignorant, but maybe well-meaning people threaten or hurt us anymore? Together we have no fear to tangle with wildcats. And we can climb Everest too, because we are learning the rewards of courage with its concomitant of prudence."[4]

In all these letters of hope and encouragement, there are undertones of quiet confidence and profound wisdom delivered in a gentle fraternal spirit. In other letters, letters to politicians, Ward adopts a tone of moral indignation and challenges the bigotry and prejudice of US senators and congressmen.

Skip Ward was a voice—often the only voice—for thousands of gay people in the South who had chosen silence and invisibility. In speaking on their behalf, he also challenged them to find their own voices. In this regard, Skip Ward was a visionary who offered courage to a people that desperately needed it. He was ahead of his time.

Skip Ward died in 2009. Part of his remains are buried in the Memorial Garden behind the Faerie Playhouse, the longtime home of Stewart Butler and his late partner Alfred Doolittle.

The next essay focuses on beloved lesbian bar owner and activist Charlene Schneider.

NOTES

1. Letter in the Blanchard "Skip" Ward papers at the Louisiana Research Collection, Tulane University.

2. Letter in the Blanchard "Skip" Ward papers at the Louisiana Research Collection, Tulane University.

3. Letter in the Blanchard "Skip" Ward papers at the Louisiana Research Collection, Tulane University.

4. Letter in the Blanchard "Skip" Ward papers at the Louisiana Research Collection, Tulane University.

REMEMBERING CHARLENE SCHNEIDER

UPON GRADUATING FROM HIGH SCHOOL, CHARLENE SCHNEIDER LANDED a job as a cryptographer with a private company that subcontracted with NASA. Charlene worked at Michoud Assembly Facility, in New Orleans East, where she had a top-level security clearance. It was a great job, and she was devastated when she was fired for being a lesbian. She had been arrested in a lesbian bar, and in the early 1960s, this was grounds for dismissal in most jobs. The injustice of it all had a profound impact on Charlene, who resolved to fight for gay and lesbian equality. The consequences of that decision reverberate still today.

Being arrested in a gay bar usually meant the person's name and picture would appear in the next day's newspaper, which, in turn, often resulted in the person being fired or evicted or generally ostracized by friends and family. Charlene went on to be arrested in bar raids six more times. Typically, women in a lesbian bar would be charged with "lewd behavior" or sometimes even prostitution. Charlene later recalled, "You didn't get arrested if you had a purse, though."

After leaving Michoud, Charlene took a number of jobs, including stints at Western Union and the *Times-Picayune*. She was working as the social director at the country club when Susan Landrum and Doddie Finley encouraged her to open a bar for lesbians. Charlene, always fearless, decided to take a chance. Having no experience in the bar business, Charlene called upon Kitty Blackwell, who had opened The Grog on North Rampart Street in 1969, to help her set up the bar. (Blackwell would go on to own Ms. Kitty's on Burgundy Street, Mississippi River Bottom on St. Philip Street, and Kathryn's Upstairs-Downstairs in Metairie.)

Charlene's, located at 940 Elysian Fields, opened in 1977. Open only twenty-two years, Charlene's would make its mark on the New Orleans bar-scape.

Bars often take on the personality of their owners, and Charlene's was no exception. Saundra Boudreaux, a regular in the 1980s, recalls, "Charlene cared about her girls, they were family," and "She always made us feel loved and safe." The notion of Charlene's being a "safe space" is a recurrent theme in many women's memories of the bar. At the time, Charlene once recalled, "Women's bars were like boxing rings." The late Toni Pizanie remembered, "She worked toward giving women a better space." Charlene would often accompany patrons to their cars upon leaving the bar.

Her charisma was underscored by the care and concern she had for her guests. She would often sit with women at the bar and ask them about their lives and offer them encouragement or advice. "She genuinely cared about us," one regular recalls. And whenever a new girl would come into the bar, Charlene went out of the way to make her feel welcome.

On such occasions, Charlene probably remembered her first time at a lesbian bar. In 1957, while still in high school, Charlene went to the Tiger Lounge (originally on Tchoupitoulas Street but later on Burgundy Street), which was owned by a former nun named Jo Jo. In an interview with *Curve Magazine*, Charlene once described going to the Tiger Lounge that night: "I felt at home, because finally, I knew where I belonged. It was wonderful seeing people like myself. I saw eight of the butchest women you've ever seen in your life. I fell in love with each and every one of them."[1]

In addition to providing a warm, safe space for lesbians, Charlene's was also a hotbed of political activity. Charlene fought tirelessly for equal rights and often held voter registration drives at her bar. She often invited LGBT-friendly politicians to come to the bar to address patrons. Charlene was instrumental in working with LAGPAC (Louisiana Lesbian and Gay Political Action Caucus), which often held meetings at her bar, and Councilman Johnny Jackson in getting the New Orleans City Council to pass a nondiscrimination ordinance in 1991. She was one of the first members of the New Orleans chapter of PFLAG (Parents and Friends of Lesbians and Gays) and she helped start Pride Fest. She had a leading role in the protest rally and march against Anita Bryant in 1977 when the homophobic singer came to New Orleans, and she participated in the National March on Washington for Gay and Lesbian Rights in 1979.

It was not uncommon for Charlene to grab the microphone at events at her bar and lecture the crowd on the importance of voting and being politically active. On closing night at Charlene's in 1999, Loretta Mims recalled, "I wouldn't have voted if it wasn't for Charlene." Another regular, Bridgette, observed, "Charlene showed us how to get into politics." And Rebecca Stilley described the closing of Charlene's as "the end of an era for women in the city."

For her work on behalf of equal rights, Charlene Schneider was the recipient of the Human Rights Campaign Equality Award, the Forum for Equality Community Service Award, and the Gay Appreciation Award for Lifetime Achievement. Her bar also received the first Gay Appreciation Award for Bar of the Year.

Linda Tucker, Charlene's longtime partner whom she met at the bar one Sunday afternoon in 1987, remembers, "A lot of grass roots came out of her club. She would be amazed today by how far we've come." After Charlene's closed in 1999, Charlene and Linda enjoyed a quiet life in Bay St. Louis on the Mississippi Gulf Coast until Charlene's death in 2006.

Reminiscing on their time together, Linda Tucker told me, "We had such a wonderful life together. She was a wonderful soul, and our relationship was just magical."

The following essay focuses on another remarkable lesbian whose influence in the French Quarter lingers still today, the fascinating Barbara Scott.

Ambush, October 13, 2015

NOTE

1. *Curve Magazine*, date unknown.

GO YOUR OWN WAY: THE LIFE OF BARBARA SCOTT

IT'S ELECTION SEASON, AND THE POPULAR RESTAURANT-OWNER-TURNED-political-candidate is fielding questions from reporters while drawing beer for thirsty patrons in her St. Peter Street establishment.

The Republican is running to represent the French Quarter and the surrounding area in the state legislature.

She is also a feminist lesbian with a platform of legalizing marijuana and ending legal discrimination against Blacks, gays, and women.

The candidate is Barbara Scott. The year is 1971.

Barbara Scott was ahead of her time, and she left an indelible mark on the French Quarter.

I had the pleasure of meeting Scott recently. Although I had known about her for years, I was not prepared for the charm and warmth she exudes. I had researched her life and work, especially in the context of second-wave feminism. I'm not sure what I expected. An angry old crone ready to burn her bra and eager to size me up with distrust?

Barbara Scott was not that. She drove in from her Mississippi coast home and parked in front of my office on St. Ann Street. Diminutive in stature but with enormous charisma, her smile immediately disarmed me.

A Mississippi Delta accent, still thick as cane syrup, humanized the legend. She took my arm, and we began walking slowly to a coffee shop. As we strolled, she looked around with childlike wonder, remarking with satisfaction: "The Quarter looks good."

She was born in Memphis in 1936 and raised in rural Mississippi. Scott's love affair with New Orleans dates back to her childhood when she visited with her family. One of her earliest memories is meeting Jack Benny in the Roosevelt Hotel elevator in 1945. Compared to humdrum life in the Mississippi Delta, New Orleans was all glamour, she says.

And sin.

She discovered the French Quarter underbelly a few years later when she returned for her high school senior trip. Wandering into the Dungeon, she was astonished to see men engaging in oral sex in a dark corner.

At Pat O'Brien's she witnessed a lesbian couple enjoying an evening together when an alpha male approached uninvited and started hitting on them. The more butch of the two "read him" and then threw him against the wall.

This was not rural Mississippi.

After high school, Scott studied art at Millsaps College before transferring to the Newcomb College Institute at Tulane. Along the way she spent a year in Japan studying with renowned artist Hiroshi Kado. While studying in Japan, she was arrested for espionage.

While attending Newcomb, Scott married, and the couple moved to California, where they had three sons. In San Francisco, Scott was an account executive with a prominent public relations firm before returning to New Orleans.

In 1967, Scott bought an old Creole townhouse at 719 St. Peter and had it rezoned so she could open a restaurant. The Fatted Calf quickly became a favorite among Quarterites and was named one of America's most unique cafés by *Venture Magazine*.

Scott's attention and repairs to the building garnered her a second Vieux Carré Restoration Award. She had been recognized by the Vieux Carré Commission with the same award two years earlier for her restoration of 509–11 Burgundy.

In addition to delicious food and historical preservation, Barbara Scott was also serving up feminist literature. As part of her campaign for the state house in 1971, Scott issued an eight-page manifesto outlining her feminist platform called Distaff.

The following year Scott and a coalition of feminist activists founded *Distaff*, the longest-running feminist newspaper in America. Edited by Mary Gehman, the paper featured writers such as Pat Denton, Clay Lattimer, Phyllis Parun, Suzanne Pharr, Darlene Olivo, Donna Swanson, and several others who constituted a key flank in the second-wave feminist movement.

Scott remained in Arkansas for six years before returning briefly to the Mississippi Gulf Coast and living in Paris for six months. She then returned to New Orleans to pursue an education.

In 1984, she earned a BA from Tulane with majors in studio art, English literature, and Latin American studies. She then earned two master's degrees from Tulane in social work and gerontology before being awarded a PhD in gerontological education from the University of Southern Mississippi in 1992. Her dissertation was titled "Carl Jung's Developmental Tasks for the Second Half of Life."

In recent years, Scott has settled into a quiet, peaceful life in Pass Christian, on the Mississippi Gulf Coast. She has revisited her art, creating a series of sculptures called "Goddesses," which have appeared in a number of shows.

So, what about the Republican angle? That was the result of Scott's pragmatism. There was essentially only one party in Louisiana at the time and the Democrats already had several candidates in Scott's race. She didn't have a chance in the Democratic primary, but the Republican race was wide open.

Commenting on her practical approach to party politics, Scott later said, "I had been elected to the Republican state committee because it gave me pardon powers for anyone in the New Orleans district. There were no female judges at all. I wanted to pardon every woman in Orleans Parish Prison."

After our interview I was reminded of Faulkner's famous description of New Orleans: "A courtesan whose hold is strong upon the mature, to whose charm the young must respond."[1]

Like the French Quarter itself, Barbara Scott has repeatedly reinvented herself. And like Faulkner's courtesan, she is still "smiling across her languid fan."

French Quarter Journal, September 12, 2019

NOTE

1. William Faulkner, "New Orleans," *New Orleans Sketches*, ed. Carvel Collins (Jackson: University Press of Mississippi, 2010).

ORGANIZATIONS

THE ORGANIZATIONS FEATURED IN THIS SECTION REPRESENT A CROSS section of the New Orleans LGBT+ community. As of this writing, four of the five groups are still active. Based on personal interviews with the founders and early members of five key LGBT+ organizations in New Orleans, these essays trace the origins and early years of those organizations. "For the Love of Song—The New Orleans Gay Men's Chorus" explains how the chorus grew out of Jerry Zachary's frustration with the party image and negative connotations of the gay community and his desire to put a respectable face on it. "Jeanne Manford and New Orleans PFLAG" recalls the birth of the New Orleans PFLAG chapter and its subsequent impact on the national PFLAG organization, namely the inclusion of trans people in the PFLAG mission statement and the establishment of the local scholarship fund, which became a model for other chapters. "Metropolitan Community Church" details the congregation's founding, both locally and nationally, and delves into the tragic role it played in the 1973 fire at the Up Stairs Lounge. "LGBT Community Center of New Orleans" probes the rocky history of the center by focusing on a financial scandal concerning the group's building fund. "The LGBT+ Archives Project of Louisiana Turns a Year Old" charts the infancy of the Archives Project, which works to preserve local queer history, by chronicling its founding and early achievements.

FOR THE LOVE OF SONG—
THE NEW ORLEANS
GAY MEN'S CHORUS

THE YEAR IS 1982. IT'S CHRISTMASTIME IN NEW ORLEANS AND YOU'RE celebrating the season by visiting with friends at your favorite gay watering hole in the French Quarter. Your conversation is suddenly, pleasantly, interrupted by an angelic chorus of voices singing Christmas carols outside the bar. Surprised, you wonder if the carolers realize they are at a gay bar. Curious, you peek outside only to see a group of handsome gay men singing. Meet the New Orleans Gay Men's Chorus.

The chorus had been founded earlier in the year by Louisiana native Jerry Zachary. Zachary earned a BA in music from Louisiana Tech University in 1971 and an MA in music from LSU in 1973 before moving to Chicago. Inspired by the success of the Windy City Gay Men's Chorus, Zachary decided to start a similar group in New Orleans after he moved to the city in 1981.

Also playing a role in the formation of the New Orleans Gay Men's Chorus was Zachary's social and political conscience. The lack of interest in the local Gay Pride Festival coupled with the arrest of about a dozen men in front of Jewel's Tavern (a notorious gay bar) for obstructing the sidewalk motivated Zachary to take action. He was also fed up with what he describes as "the Mardi Gras mentality"—the notion that Mardi Gras was the only thing that mattered in New Orleans. Noting the apathy of the gay community and the negative connotations that were often associated with it, Zachary says, "The chorus was always about putting a face on the community that wasn't drag or sleaze." And for thirty-one years, that is just what the NOGMC has done.

Singing carols at the bars that first Christmas proved to be a great promotion and recruiting tool. Membership and interest grew, and within a year, the chorus traveled to New York, where it performed at Lincoln

Center with nine other gay choruses in what was the nation's first festival of gay choruses. These choruses evolved into the Gay and Lesbian Association of Choruses, of which NOGMC is a founding member. The NOGMC has performed at every subsequent GALA festival—Minneapolis (1986), Seattle (1989), Denver (1992), Tampa (1996), Montreal (2004), Miami (2008), and Denver (2012).

The chorus performed its first Gay Pride Concert in 1983 at St. Mark's Church in the French Quarter. The group also held regular rehearsals at the church, which did not charge the group in exchange for one performance a month. Several other area churches had denied the chorus the use of their facilities for rehearsals. But St. Mark's has always been very supportive of the chorus.

When the chorus performed at Le Petit Theatre for the first time in 1983, Le Petit's board of directors wouldn't allow the use of the word "gay." Zachary cleverly sidestepped that restriction by including the symbols for the musical notes "g," "a," and "e" on the poster that read "New Orleans Men's Chorus." Reflecting on the controversy, Zachary recalls naming the group, "I wanted Gay in the title because you didn't see that word in print back then."

Reviewing the performance, critic Frank Gagnard wrote, "It was black-tie-full dress before intermission and preppie khakis and rolled up sleeves afterwards . . . The amateur group, directed (with baton) by its founder, Jerry Zachary, applied itself seriously to a varied program, ranging from Lassus's 'Echo Song,' Purcell and Haydn—but not a scheduled Bach selection—to contemporary concert-hall names and show tunes as fresh as 'Memory,' from 'Cats.'"

The NOGMC performed again at Le Petit in 1988 in what was billed as "Showtime at Le Petit." This time the NOGMC hosted groups from Washington, DC, Los Angeles, Madison, Wisconsin, Denver, and Seattle. Other joint concerts have been with choruses from Houston, St. Louis, Philadelphia, and Chicago.

In addition to collaborating with other gay choruses from around the country, the NOGMC has also worked with international choruses, most notably the gay men's chorus from Berlin, Manner Minne, and the Stockholm Gay Men's Chorus. Yet despite its international reach, the NOGMC's heart remains close to home.

The chorus has always tried to support southeast Louisiana's gay and lesbian community throughout its history. A short list of the events they have participated in include caroling from bar to bar in the early years; caroling at C100, C600, Belle Reve, PFLAG, and at Lazarus House; performing for the Lazarus Remembrance Service, AIDS Memorial Dedication, MCC's Spirit Awards, NO/AIDS Task Force "Art Against AIDS," World AIDS Day services, HAART, Pride Parades in both Baton Rouge and New Orleans, Mr. Louisiana Leather contest, and at the Mardi Gras balls of Petronius, Lords of Leather and Armeinius.

Although their primary purpose has been to serve the gay community, the chorus also serves as a model of gay pride to the straight world. The chorus has performed with the New Orleans Opera Chorus in *Aida* in 1989, with the Louisiana Philharmonic Orchestra in Mahler's Symphony No. 2 entitled "Resurrection" in 2008, and has appeared on news programs on both the local CBS and NBC affiliates. They also sang for the New Orleans World's Fair in 1984 and have caroled at the Riverwalk along the Mississippi River.

An exhibit of memorabilia from the early years of the New Orleans Gay Men's Chorus will be on display at a meeting of the LGBT+ Archives Project of Louisiana on Friday, November 8, at the Marigny Opera House, 725 St. Ferdinand Street at 6:30 p.m. The exhibit and meeting are free and open to the public. The chorus will perform its thirty-first annual holiday concert on December 13 in New Orleans and on December 14 in Baton Rouge. For more information, visit http://www.nogmc.com/.

In the same year the New Orleans Gay Men's Chorus was founded, the New Orleans chapter of PFLAG was also founded. The next essay details not only how the local PFLAG chapter was formed, but also how it influenced the national organization.

Ambush, November 5, 2013

JEANNE MANFORD AND NEW ORLEANS PFLAG

Two weeks ago, PFLAG (Parents, Family and Friends of Lesbians and Gays) founder Jeanne Manford passed away at age ninety-two at her home in Daly City, California. In 1972, Manford's son Morty was physically attacked during a Gay Activist Alliance demonstration in New York. After the attack, Jeanne Manford wrote a letter to the *New York Post* declaring, "I have a homosexual son and I love him." She then marched with her son in the Christopher Street Liberation Day Parade (predecessor to New York City's Pride Parade). During the march, she proudly held a sign that said, "Parents of Gays: Unite in Support of Our Children." The message resonated, and soon thereafter POG (Parents of Gays) held its first meeting at the NYC Metropolitan Church. POG evolved into PFLAG, which now boasts over 200,000 members in over five hundred chapters across the United States.

The phenomenal success of PFLAG has been nothing short of remarkable, and its contributions to our collective fight for tolerance and equality are immeasurable. PFLAG's national history is well documented but what is not as well known is the New Orleans chapter's pivotal role in influencing the national organization. Specifically, the New Orleans chapter pioneered the effort to have transgender persons included in the national PFLAG mission statement. In addition, the local chapter's scholarship program became the model for the national organization's scholarship program.

The New Orleans chapter of PFLAG was founded in 1982 by Niki Kearby and Betty Caldwell.[1] Cofounder Niki Kearby says the chapter grew out of her dissatisfaction with her church's intolerance of homosexuality. One of Kearby's friends who had worked in the church's administrative offices was fired when she admitted to being gay. Kearby had grown up a devout Methodist and was a member of the Rayne Methodist Church on St. Charles Avenue. After her friend's dismissal, Kearby began attending the more gay-friendly St. Mark's United Methodist Church in the French Quarter.

The earliest New Orleans PFLAG meetings were held at a Catholic community center on Barracks Street in a very small room. About twenty people attended the first meeting, half of whom had to sit on the floor. The *Times-Picayune* initially refused to run an ad for the meeting but after some string pulling, the paper's owner acquiesced and ran the ad. Attendance steadily increased and the meetings were eventually moved to Mercy Hospital.

The New Orleans PFLAG scholarship program began with a generous donation from Rich Sacher and his partner. The first scholarship was awarded in 1991. Since that time, the local chapter has dispensed over $500,000 to over 450 LGBT+ students. Currently the program offers scholarships ranging from $1,000 to $10,000 to eligible students. The scholarship program is funded by the contributions of businesses, foundations, and private individuals. For more information on the scholarship program, visit the New Orleans PFLAG website at http://pflagno.org/scholarship_general.asp.

In 1998, PFLAG became the first national gay rights organization to include transgender people in its mission statement. This bold move was made at the insistence of the New Orleans chapter. Local PFLAG president Julie Thompson recalls the group first writing letters to the national office urging the inclusion of transgender people in their mission statement and not receiving a reply. Then the national group had a meeting New Orleans.

The local chapter seized this opportunity to personally impress on the national leadership the need for transgender inclusion. They were successful and now PFLAG has a national transgender network called TNET. (Many members of the local PFLAG chapter and LGBT+ community were pioneers in the struggle for transgender rights, a struggle spearheaded by local activists Stewart Butler and Courtney Sharp.)

By establishing a model scholarship program and leading the fight for transgender inclusion, the New Orleans chapter of PFLAG played a large role in shaping the national organization and contributing to its extraordinary success. In this way, the gay community in New Orleans has made a significant contribution to the national struggle for gay rights. By helping create a more tolerant and understanding society, it has also improved the lives of thousands of gay youth. As a community, we owe our local PFLAG chapter an enormous debt of gratitude.

And that goes for Jeanne Manford too. In addition to demonstrating that one voice can indeed change the world, Manford's life was also a testament to the power of love to overcome hate. Manford was honored by President Barack Obama in his 2009 address to the Human Rights Campaign. Describing Manford and her work, the president said the story of PFLAG was "the story of America . . . of ordinary citizens organizing, agitating, educating for change, of hope stronger than hate, of love more powerful than any insult or injury." Jeanne Manford, Mother of the Straight Ally Movement, may you rest in peace.

While PFLAG was meeting the needs of parents, the Metropolitan Community Church was meeting the needs of queer people who still felt a connection to Christianity but were alienated from mainline, traditional churches. The New Orleans Metropolitan Community Church is the subject of the next article.

Ambush, January 22, 2013

NOTE

1. For a fuller discussion of the New Orleans chapter of PFLAG, see chapter 9 of Frank Perez's *Political Animal: The Life and Times of Stewart Butler* (Jackson: University Press of Mississippi, 2022).

METROPOLITAN COMMUNITY CHURCH

IN THE 1960S, A YOUNG MAN IN CALIFORNIA STRUGGLED TO RECONCILE his homosexuality with his Pentecostal faith. To make matters even more complicated, he was an ordained minister who had recently been defrocked. Nothing so unusual about that; nor was his suicide attempt uncommon. What makes Troy Perry's story unique is that despite the psychological horrors of the closet and the profound self-loathing engendered by Christianity, Perry never doubted that God loved him.

On October 6, 1968, in Huntington Park, California, a dozen people gathered in Perry's living room for a worship service, and thus was born the Metropolitan Community Church. Today, the Metropolitan Community Church (MCC) boasts over 45,000 members and adherents in over three hundred congregations spanning twenty-two countries.

The New Orleans chapter of the MCC was founded on Sunday, April 18, 1971, at the First Unitarian Church. On that day, Reverend David E. Solomon presided over an organizational meeting of interested people. The group's first worship service occurred on May 9, 1971. Originally organized as the Elysian Fields MCC, it was officially chartered as the MCC of Greater New Orleans in March of 1972.

After a year and a half, Reverend Solomon moved on and his assistant, Deacon Bill Larson, became the pastor. Needing a place to meet, Larson approached Phil Esteve, who had just opened the Up Stairs Lounge, about meeting in a spare room attached to the bar. Esteve agreed, and for a few months, the MCC met in the bar. The congregation then met for about six months in St. George's Episcopal Church in Uptown New Orleans. The congregation then began to meet in the home of Reverend Bill Larson.

After services, most of the congregants would go to the Up Stairs Lounge for fellowship at the Sunday Beer Bust. Many were there on Sunday, June 24, 1973, when an arsonist set fire to the bar and killed thirty-two people. Among the dead were Pastor Larson and the assistant pastor George Mitchell, along with several members of the church.

In the aftermath of the fire, the Reverend Troy Perry and other church officials came to New Orleans to rally the community and help the devastated church. Father Bill Richardson of St. George's Episcopal Church held a small memorial service, an act of Christian kindness for which he caught not-so-holy hell. His congregation reacted with such hatred that he threatened to resign if they didn't forsake their homophobia. Roman Catholic Archbishop Hannan issued an order that the fire victims could not be buried in the Catholic Church. Other mainline denominations also refused their facilities for memorial services. The notable exception was Dr. Kennedy of St. Mark's United Methodist Church.

The church began rebuilding in the fall of 1973 and rented a storefront at 3127 Magazine Street. MCC New Orleans was rechartered on Easter Sunday 1974. The altar used at the church contained a gold plaque with the names of the congregants lost in the Up Stairs Lounge fire and for a while held the cremated remains of Reverend Bill Larson. Larson, along with a few others, was eventually interred at St. Roch Cemetery in space donated by Roland Mace and Vic Scaliese.

From the time of the fire (1973) to the early 1990s, the MCC was in a state of constant change, in terms of its official name, meeting places, and pastors. Nevertheless, the church did produce some fruit. In 1977, it helped organize the protest against Anita Bryant. Reverend Ron Pannell, who served from 1976 to 1980, raised the church's awareness by doing a number of radio and television interviews and conducting a successful "bath-house ministry." And in 1978, the church took a public stand against California's Proposition 6, also known as the Briggs Initiative, which would have banned gays and lesbians from working in public schools.

From 1994 to 2006, the local MCC was led by the Reverend Dexter Brecht. The church finally found what was supposed to be a permanent home when it purchased a facility at 1228 St. Roch (at Marais). This building was sold in 2001 with the hopes of purchasing a facility on Canal Street, but that deal never materialized. After Hurricane Katrina in 2005, membership dropped from thirty-three to twenty.

After the departure of Reverend Brecht in 2006, eighteen members of the church resigned their membership, leaving the church with only thirteen members. In 2007, Reverend Clinton Crawshaw became pastor and began a concentrated outreach to the transgender and other marginalized communities. Under Pastor Crawshaw's leadership, weekly attendance grew to around one hundred.

In 2013, the MCC adopted a new mission statement: "The mission of MCC New Orleans is to offer a safe and holy place where everyone—with particular outreach to the gay, lesbian, bisexual, transgender, queer/questioning and marginalized communities—can worship, receive affirmation, and celebrate God's love."

In addition to religious needs, there were other, more practical needs in the queer community, which in the early 1990s gave rise to the LGBT Community Center of New Orleans.

Ambush, April 26, 2016

LGBT COMMUNITY CENTER OF NEW ORLEANS

The Lesbian and Gay Community Center of New Orleans turns twenty-two years old this year, and a look back at its history is a fascinating study in the age-old dichotomy of the ideal versus the reality. From its inception, the community center has embraced the noble vision of unifying the various subgroups of New Orleans's LGBT+ community; conversely, the reality is that the center's history has been marked by sharp division stemming from a lack of leadership, general dysfunction, and unrealized potential. Historically, the center's board of directors has been prone to coups d'état from within, and in its twenty-two-year history, the center has seemingly gone through numerous directors. And yet the center is still here, which is something of a miracle considering all the challenges it has faced.

In 1992, the Lesbian and Gay Community Center of New Orleans was founded by a group of friends who believed the local LGBT community needed a central organization/location to dispense information and provide resources. Founding members included Stewart Butler, Betty Caldwell, Alfred Doolittle, Mark Harper, Nikki Kearby, Rip and Marsha Naquin-Delain, Toni Pizanie, Dianne Ranna, Alan Robinson, J. Michael Tetty, Leo Watermeier, and others.

Originally, the center was located at 816 North Rampart Street on the first floor of a property owned by former state representative and mayoral candidate Leo Watermeier. By the mid-1990s, the center's board began considering the possibility of a permanent home. In 1996, cochairs Rip Naquin and Rene Parks led a fundraising campaign that helped the community center raise $30,000 for a building fund. These funds were placed in two CDs.

In 1999, Nikki Kearby and Betty Caldwell, who had cofounded the New Orleans chapter of PFLAG in 1982, graciously offered the community center the use of a building they owned on Decatur Street in the heart of the Marigny neighborhood. Kearby and Caldwell renovated the space and charged the center a very modest rent with the understanding that as the center grew, the rent would gradually increase to offset the cost of the renovations. Kearby and Caldwell even expressed their intention to bequeath the building to the community center on the condition that the center demonstrate it was stable and sustainable. None of this was in writing; Kearby and Caldwell made the arrangement in good faith. Various boards throughout the 2000s squandered that good faith as well as the good faith of members of the community. The money raised for the building fund began to be diverted and used for operational expenses.

In 2009, the center was on the verge of closing due to lack of adequate funding, a sad note *Ambush* columnist Toni Pizanie (and center founder and former board member) recognized in her column, "Sappho's Psalm." Citing the board's arrogance, Pizanie wrote, "The blame falls directly on the Center Board, and the non-business like or non-organized attitude that has caused the Center to fail . . . they have been unwilling to take advice or direction from anyone." This criticism hit a nerve and as a result, the entire board (Mary Griggs, Dave Haynik, Shawn Johnson, and Charlotte Klasson), with the exception of Crystal Little, resigned in protest. Little, a longtime volunteer, pleaded with them to not resign and argued that Pizanie's criticism was constructive, but they didn't want to hear it, thus proving Pizanie's point.

When the building housing the center suffered extensive water damage during Hurricane Isaac in 2012, Kearby and Caldwell's adopted daughter (who had assumed management of the property) told the community center board that it would have to pay increased rent to cover the repairs. The board (which never paid the increased rent they agreed to in 1999 to cover the initial renovations to the building) decided it could no longer stay there. The center has been homeless since then.

All this is not to say the center has not done some good. In 2000, the center received a federal grant and launched the Hate Crimes Project, which tracked hate-based crimes against LGBT+ and other groups targeted by discrimination. In 2003, the center began hosting an annual Trans Day of Remembrance to commemorate the lives of transgender people murdered every year. After Hurricane Katrina, the center hosted a meeting of the Community Coalition, a collective of LGBT+ and allied organizations that met to share information and collaborate during the initial recovery period. And in 2011, the center established a program called Safe Space for LGBT+ and questioning youth.

The Community Center is currently in a transitional phase. Last year the center moved into a small administrative space in the Art Egg Studios on South Broad Street and established a new mission statement. The current mission of the community center is to provide resources and advocacy that foster community development and social and economic justice efforts to strengthen the collective power of gender and sexual minorities and their allies in the GNO area. The vision of the center is to create a greater New Orleans area where gender and sexual minorities are equitable and empowered.

Concerning the future of the Center, current director Sebastian Rey says,

> We want to provide the things we can—information, referrals, advocacy, and communication. In fact, our online community resource directory will provide accessible information about LGBT and allied doctors, lawyers, and other services in our area. Moving forward, we will focus especially on issues of economic and racial injustice, which we know disproportionately affect the LGBT community. In New Orleans, the income gap is severe, and LGBT people feel the effects through un- or underemployment—and we know that economic instability is a risk factor for HIV and suicide, which already ravage our community. Most importantly, we want to balance the trend of creating top-down programming with community-driven projects. We will support individuals in our community to pursue their own visions for LGBT equality, offering the tools for one person to create the veterans' support program and another an LGBT youth book club. Nothing will move this community forward faster than enabling the individuals within it to realize their own power and their own ability to organize and make change.

Although the center's future is uncertain, one thing can be said about its history: it's a prolonged study in untapped potential. In that regard, the center is truer reflection of our local LGBT+ community than the center's critics would like to admit. Then again, Rey wryly observes, "Asking for LGBT unity is like asking for world peace." Nevertheless, it's still a good question, certainly one worth asking.

The community center eventually lost its lease at the Art Egg Studios building and shuttered its doors for good in 2023. In its place, a new organization, the New Orleans Pride Center, was created.

The following essay examines the first year of an organization founded to preserve local queer history—the LGBT+ Archives Project of Louisiana.

Ambush, March 25, 2014

THE LGBT+ ARCHIVES PROJECT OF LOUISIANA TURNS A YEAR OLD

THIS MONTH THE LGBT+ ARCHIVES PROJECT OF LOUISIANA TURNS A year old. The idea of preserving our local history was on the minds of Stewart Butler, Otis Fennell, and Mark Gonzales in 2012. In that year, they founded the Legacy Project with the aim of compiling oral histories. After completing one interview (with Stewart Butler), they realized that the time, logistics, and money involved was somewhat overwhelming, and the Legacy Project eventually fell by the wayside. However, the need and desire to preserve local gay history was still strong, and from the ashes of the project rose the LGBT+ Archives Project of Louisiana.

In June of 2013, a handful of people interested in local gay history began meeting to discuss the need to preserve our history and ways in which such an endeavor might be undertaken. It was decided early on that an organization was needed to provide information and resources to those interested in local gay history. One of the first steps was to survey what LGBT+ holdings currently existed in local libraries and collections. Questionnaires were sent to archivists at several local institutions. In addition, on-site visits were made to several local repositories. In October of 2013, the Society of American Archivists held their national conference in New Orleans and several members of that group's LGBT Roundtable met with members of the LGBT+ Archive Project of Louisiana. In November, a community meeting was held in order to gather input from the public.

After several months of information gathering, the LGBT+ Archives Project of Louisiana adopted the following mission statement: "The mission of the LGBT+ Archives Project of Louisiana is to promote and encourage the protection and preservation of materials that chronicle the culture and history of the Lesbian, Gay, Bisexual, and Transgender community in Louisiana." In June of 2014, the LGBT+ Archives Project of Louisiana was officially born at a public meeting where a set of bylaws was adopted, and officers were elected.

The Archives Project aims to educate the public about the importance of historical preservation and how individuals can safely entrust local archives with the care of the historical treasures they possess. The project also plans to help make these materials more accessible to researchers and the public at large by maintaining a catalog of LGBT+-related collections in archives around the state. It is important to note that this project does not contemplate setting up an archive of its own. Rather, it aims to educate the public about the resources and attributes of existing archives in Louisiana.

The project's first year has been incredibly successful. In addition to raising awareness of the importance of preserving LGBT+ history, the project has facilitated the donation of archival materials and conducted public events that promote the project's mission. These events include a personal archiving workshop in which three local archivists taught those in attendance how to properly care for their personal collections and the Generations Forum (cosponsored with New Orleans Advocates for LGBTQ+ Elders), which featured a lecture on local queer history followed by a panel discussion. The project's website, especially its extensive bibliography of local gay history sources, has proven extremely useful to researchers and journalists. Also, two fundraising events were conducted at Grand Pre's and Café Lafitte in Exile. The project currently boasts over one hundred members.

On June 19, the Archives Project held its annual membership meeting, which was attended by roughly sixty people. The keynote speaker was LSU professor Alecia Long, who spoke about "Saving the City from Sex Deviates: Preservationists, Homosexuals, and Reformers in the French Quarter 1950–1962." Officer elections were also held at the meeting.

It was also announced that a major event is planned for November 14—the Oracle Gala. The event will be hosted by Varla Jean Merman and Michael Sullivan and feature live entertainment as well as a silent auction. The highlight of the evening will be a tribute to Alan Robinson and Father Bill Richardson and an announcement of where their personal papers are being donated. Alan Robinson was a longtime gay activist and one-time owner of the FAB bookstore on Frenchmen Street. Father Bill Richardson was the pastor of St. George's Episcopal Church at the time of the Up Stairs Lounge fire and graciously allowed the use of St. George's for a memorial service for the victims of the fire.

The Archives Project chose the name "Oracle Gala" because an oracle is defined as "a person through whom a deity is believed to speak, or a shrine in which a deity reveals hidden knowledge." The name speaks directly to the mission of the Archives Project because our history is, indeed, sacred. Gay history is a treasure that has for too long been hidden. The LGBT+ Archives Project of Louisiana is working hard to get that history out of the closet.

Ambush, June 30, 2015

THE UP STAIRS LOUNGE FIRE

THE UP STAIRS LOUNGE FIRE IN 1973 WAS A SEMINAL MOMENT IN NEW Orleans LGBT+ history. The fire claimed thirty-two lives, making it the deadliest fire in New Orleans history and the deadliest crime against queer folk in twentieth-century America. The public reaction to the fire reflected the homophobia of the time and served only to keep closet doors shut. Some have described the fire as a southern version of Stonewall, but that comparison doesn't exactly work. Whereas Stonewall led to tangible effects—the creation of the Gay Liberation Front and the Christopher Street Liberation March (forerunner to Pride parades)—the Up Stairs Lounge arson compelled many in New Orleans to retreat deeper into the closet. The essays in this section highlight three individuals, two of whom died in the fire, and also survey how interest in the fire has grown in recent years. "Remembering the Up Stairs Lounge Fire" provides an overview of the event and the city's reaction to it. "The Saga of Ferris LeBlanc's Mortal Remains" tells the sad tale of fire victim Ferris LeBlanc, whose body was never claimed because his family did not learn of his fate until decades after his death. "Recently Discovered Document Sheds Light on the Aftermath of the Up Stairs Lounge Fire" focuses on the closeted Reverend Bill Richardson, who caught hell for holding a memorial service for the victims. "Remembering the Rev. Bill Larson" recalls the troubled life of the MCC pastor who perished in the flames. And "Interest in the Up Stairs Lounge Fire at an All-Time High" recounts the growing interest in the fire after its fortieth anniversary.

REMEMBERING THE
UP STAIRS LOUNGE FIRE

On Sunday evening, June 24, 1973, the deadliest crime against gays and lesbians in the history of the United States up to that point occurred at the Up Stairs Lounge in the French Quarter. On that night, an arsonist set the bar on fire, killing thirty-two people and injuring still more. Many people, then and now, mistakenly believe the fire was a hate crime motivated by homophobia. But it wasn't. Rather, the crime was motivated by anger and revenge.

On that fateful evening, an unruly hustler, Rodger Dale Nunez, was physically thrown out of the bar for badgering and fighting with a regular customer, Mike Scarborough. Scarborough was in the bathroom when Nunez, who was in the next stall, started harassing him. Scarborough complained to the bartender. As he was being escorted out of the bar, Nunez threatened to "burn you all out." About thirty minutes later, a fire broke out on the stairwell. Then the buzzer in the bar rang, which usually meant a cab had arrived. Luther Boggs, a regular at the lounge, opened the door to the stairwell to be greeted by roaring flames. As the fire spread, panic ensued. Bartender Buddy Rasmussen led about twenty people through a rear fire exit, which was not clearly marked. Many dashed for the windows, but the windows had iron bars. A few were skinny enough to squeeze through, but the others were doomed.

Katherine Kirsch was on her way to buy cigarettes around 7:45 p.m. when she smelled smoke at the corner of Iberville and Chartres. She opened the stairwell, saw the flames, and immediately ran to the Midship Bar next door to call the police. Fire trucks arrived about two minutes later. They were met by a grizzly, horrific scene. The lifeless body of Bill Larson, pastor of the local Metropolitan Community Church, was wedged in the window, his face and right arm protruding stiffly over the street. Buddy Rasmussen saw his boyfriend, Adam Fontenot, knocked off his feet with a blast from a fire hose while he flailed around on fire. George

Mitchell escaped the fire but ran back in to rescue his boyfriend, Louis Broussard; their bodies were found intertwined, thereby occupying in death a position they so often occupied in life. Many of the dead were burned beyond recognition but were ultimately identified through the dental records of local dentist Perry Waters, who also perished in the fire.

Nunez committed suicide the following year. Some believe Nunez killed himself because he was so filled with remorse. Initial media reports and the police response to the fire were less than sympathetic. Some family members of the deceased refused to claim the ashes of their "loved" ones. Radio commentators joked the remains should be buried in fruit jars. The *States-Item* described the aftermath of the fire in graphic language: "Workers stood knee deep in bodies . . . the heat had been so intense, many were cooked together."[1] On the issue of identifying the victims, Major Henry Morris, a detective with the New Orleans Police Department, said, "We don't even know these papers belonged to the people we found them on. Some thieves hung out there, and you know this was a queer bar."[2]

While the media reaction was cruel and the police were nonchalant, the religious establishment's reaction was downright hateful. Church after church refused the use of their facilities for a memorial service. Father Bill Richardson (himself a closeted gay man) of St. George's Episcopal Church, however, believed the dead should have a service and graciously allowed, over the protest of many parishioners, the use of St. George's sanctuary for a prayer service on Monday night, which was attended by roughly eighty people. He was subsequently chastised by his bishop and received no small amount of hate mail. Days later, a Unitarian church also held a small memorial service. A larger service was held on July 1 at St. Mark's United Methodist Church on the edge of the French Quarter. Reverend Troy Perry, founder of the Metropolitan Community Church, officiated the service at St. Mark's along with Methodist Bishop Finis Crutchfield, who would die fourteen years later from AIDS. After the service, Reverend Perry pointed out a side entrance for those who wished to avoid the television cameras that waited outside the main entrance. Of the estimated 250 people in attendance, no one took his offer.

The Up Stairs arson attracted gay activists from all over the country to New Orleans. Reverend Troy Perry and others criticized the gay community of New Orleans for its apathetic attitude and general lethargy regarding the gay liberation movement so much in vogue in other American cities at the time. Local bar owners concerned about how all the attention might affect their businesses and prominent gay men who had grown comfortable with their place in the order of things responded by calling Perry and the other activists "carpetbaggers" and "outside agitators."

Despite these objections, the fire motivated a flurry of activism, but these efforts were short-lived. The Up Stairs Lounge fire was a seminal moment in the history of gay New Orleans, the significance of which was even noticed by the arch-conservative *Times-Picayune*. A month and a half after the fire, the paper published a weeklong series of six articles, all written by Joan Treadway, concerning homosexuality, the first of which was titled "Gay Community Surfaces in Tragedy of N.O. Fire." The tone of the article is surprisingly objective, and Treadway even quotes local gay activists who succinctly summarized the multitude of dilemmas facing gay New Orleanians: police harassment, job and housing discrimination, and general societal alienation.

In addition to forcing straight New Orleans to acknowledge its gay community, the fire also forced the gay community in New Orleans to confront itself. In this regard, the fire should have been a southern Stonewall—a wake-up call that sparked a movement. But it wasn't. Now, forty years later, our community is planning to commemorate the victims of the fire.

The commemoration ceremonies are scheduled for June 24 and are designed to remember this significant event in our history and to afford the thirty-two victims of the fire the dignity and respect they were denied at the time. Commemoration events are as follows.

The ceremony begins at 3:00 p.m. at the Williams Research Center of The Historic New Orleans Collection (410 Chartres Street). Artist Skylar Fein will give a brief lecture accompanied by a slideshow on the fire. Fein's presentation will be followed by a viewing of the Research Center's archival material concerning the fire, including the original police report as well as an original manuscript of Johnny Townsend's 2011 book about the fire entitled *Let the Faggots Burn: The Up Stairs Lounge Fire*. In 2008, the Up Stairs Lounge tragedy was memorialized with an art exhibit by Skylar Fein at the Contemporary Arts Center as part of the first annual Prospect 1, a citywide collection of art exhibits. It was restaged in 2010 in New York by No Longer Empty.

The Historic New Orleans Collection event will be followed by a jazz funeral procession from the Williams Research Center to the site of the fire at the corner of Iberville and Chartres Streets. There a solemn reading of the victims' names will take place. After the ceremony, there will be a second line parade to a cocktail party at Café Lafitte in Exile.

The commemoration ceremonies will be capped off at Café Istanbul with the New Orleans premiere of *Upstairs*, a new musical by Wayne Self. Wayne Self is an activist playwright and composer whose theater, music, advocacy, and writings have inspired, educated, and entertained thousands. He is a GLAAD media spokesman and a *Huffington Post* blogger, whose own website provides a needed platform for thoughtful, compassionate LGBT+ voices. *Upstairs*, Self's third musical, was inspired by his time as a music director for a Metropolitan Community Church—a gay-affirming denomination whose New Orleans congregation lost many members to the Up Stairs Lounge Fire. Self has an MFA in musical theater performance with an emphasis in composition from Notre Dame de Namur University and is a candidate for an MTS from Pacific School of Religion in Berkeley.

Ten years after this article was first published, the LGBT+ Archives Project of Louisiana spearheaded a coalition of several local organizations in planning a fiftieth anniversary commemoration conference. Participating in the weekend of commemoration events were the family members of some of the fire's victims, including Ferris LeBlanc. LeBlanc's tragic story is the subject of the next essay.

Ambush, April 2, 2013

NOTES

1. Lanny Thomas, "Fun . . . Drinks . . . Song . . . with Death at the Piano," *States-Item*, June 25, 1973.

2. Lind, "Fire Bares," *States-Item*, June 25, 1973.

THE SAGA OF FERRIS LEBLANC'S MORTAL REMAINS

ON JUNE 24, 1973, MARILYN DOWNEY WENT TO BED IN HER SAN JOSE, California, home and had a dream. In it, her doorbell rang and when she answered the door she saw standing there her brother, Ferris LeBlanc, whom she had not seen or heard from in years. Forty-two years after the dream, she has still not seen or heard from Ferris and until a few months ago she had no idea whatever became of her brother.

Originally from Michigan, Marilyn and Ferris grew up in a tight-knit family of thirteen siblings in California. Ferris fought for his country in World War II in the D-Day invasion and at the Battle of the Bulge. The family loved Ferris very much and never minded that he was gay. In fact, Ferris would often bring his lover Robert, and later Rod, to family gatherings. Such acceptance was highly unusual in the 1950s and 1960s.

But then, in 1970, Ferris suddenly disappeared and seemed to drop off the face of the earth. His partner at the time, a man named Rod, was controlling and abusive and the couple had incurred no small amount of financial debt. In 1973, Rod's murdered body was found in a ditch in Oakland, California. When Ferris's family learned of the murder, they theorized that perhaps Ferris had gone into hiding for fear of his own life. His nephew Skip Bailey also suspected he may have been embarrassed about his relationship with Rod and how he was manipulated into borrowing money from the family.

But these were merely guesses and suppositions. Marilyn and Skip and the rest of the family just didn't know what happened to Ferris. They would wonder often about his fate for decades. Then, in January 2015, just before Marilyn went to Tucson, Arizona, to visit her son Skip, she received a call from her brother, who told her he had learned on the internet that Ferris died in a fire in New Orleans in 1973.

Upon arriving in Tucson, Marilyn informed her son Skip of what she had just learned, and Skip began scouring the internet and discovered the horrible tragedy of the Up Stairs Lounge arson. On June 24, 1973, an arsonist had set a fire at the Up Stairs Lounge, a gay bar in the French Quarter. As a result of the fire, thirty-two people died, including Ferris LeBlanc. An arrest was never made, and the case remains officially unsolved.

The bodies of three of the victims were never identified, and several of the bodies were never claimed, most notably the Reverend Bill Larson of the local Metropolitan Community Church, whose family was ashamed of his sexuality and released his body to the MCC. Ferris LeBlanc was identified by a ring he was wearing, but his body was never claimed. His and the other three unclaimed bodies were buried by the City of New Orleans in a potter's field.

Skip continued gathering information. He ordered the only two books ever written about the fire—Johnny Townsend's *Let the Faggots Burn* (2011) and Clayton Delery-Edwards's *The Up Stairs Lounge Arson: Thirty-Two Deaths in a New Orleans Gay Bar, June 24, 1973* (2014), and he ordered a copy of Royd Anderson's short documentary film *The Up Stairs Lounge Fire* (2013). He also reached out to other filmmakers who are working on documentaries about the fire, Robert Camina and Sheri Wright.

As soon as Marilyn and her son Skip and his wife Lori learned of this, they immediately planned to claim Ferris's body and bring him home. They had already planned a trip to New Orleans to celebrate Marilyn's eighty-fifth birthday. For decades, it has been assumed that Ferris's family didn't claim his body because they were ashamed of his sexuality, but this is not the case; they simply did not know what happened to him.

Their first order of business was determining exactly where Ferris was buried. This was difficult because the graves are unmarked. It has long been assumed that he and the other unclaimed bodies were buried at Holt Cemetery, but this assumption was wrong. Anderson's documentary includes footage of the burial, and after visiting Holt Cemetery, Skip, his wife Lori, and Marilyn began to suspect the burial took place in a different cemetery.

Skip began contacting city hall to find out more information and immediately hit a brick wall.[1] The bureaucrats were initially nonresponsive and unhelpful. The City Cemetery Office told him they have no record of indigents, but the coroner's office did keep such a record—but those records were destroyed by Hurricane Katrina. Skip persisted in his search and eventually learned that Ferris and the others were buried at Resthaven Cemetery. Skip recalls, "Finding out where he was buried was the biggest challenge."

Upon visiting Resthaven, the family discovered that the six-acre area where indigents were buried was closed in with a fence, which was locked with a padlock. Lori said, "It looked like a cow pasture."

Skip contacted the city again to request the gate be unlocked so they could enter the area, but again he met resistance. And again, his persistence paid off. Mayor Landrieu's chief of staff, Ms. Brooke Smith, agreed to have the gate unlocked and the grass mowed so the family could visit the burial site.

Although they will not be bringing Ferris home to California, his family was at least able to visit the cemetery and thereby gain some closure. Marilyn, Skip, and Lori want people to know that Ferris was loved deeply and had they known of the tragic events that took his life, they would have claimed his body when he died. They are also looking for any information about Ferris's life. If you knew Ferris, or have any information about him, please contact me and I will put you in touch with his family.

As I concluded my interview with Marilyn Downey, I asked her if there was anything else she wanted to add. She replied, "I've been waiting forty-two years for my doorbell to ring and I'm glad I finally now know Ferris won't be ringing my doorbell."

Nearly ten years later, the exact location of LeBlanc's burial remains a mystery, but his family has not given up hope of recovering his body. Another figure associated with the story of the Up Stairs Lounge is Reverend Bill Richardson. His role in the story of the arson is the focus of the next essay.

Ambush, June 2, 2015

NOTE

1. In 2022, on the forty-ninth anniversary of the fire, the New Orleans City Council passed a resolution acknowledging the fire and the city's homophobic response to it. The resolution also offered an apology and recognized the thirty-two victims of the fire.

RECENTLY DISCOVERED DOCUMENT SHEDS LIGHT ON THE AFTERMATH OF THE UP STAIRS LOUNGE FIRE

LAST MONTH THE REVEREND RICHARD EASTERLING WAS CLEANING OUT a closet at St. George's Episcopal Church on St. Charles Avenue where he serves as rector when he found a letter that had not surfaced in nearly forty years. The letter was from the late Reverend Bill Richardson, former rector of the church in the early 1970s, to his vestry (church committee) defending his controversial decision to allow the use of St. George's Church for a memorial service for the victims of the Up Stairs Lounge fire. The letter is an eloquent plea for tolerance and a beautiful expression of inclusiveness, as well as a succinct statement of frustration that unfortunately still rings true for many religious members of the LGBT+ community.

Many of the thirty-two victims of the fire were members of the newly formed Metropolitan Community Church, which gathered regularly at the Up Stairs Lounge. Reverend Bill Larson, pastor of the New Orleans MCC, perished in the fire. Despite the religious devotion of the group, the fact that they were gay was too much for the mainline religious denominations to handle. The traditional religious establishment's reaction to the fire was downright hateful. Church after church refused the use of their facilities for a memorial service. Father Bill Richardson of St. George's Episcopal Church, still in the closet at the time, allowed the use of St. George's sanctuary for a prayer service on Monday night, which was attended by roughly eighty people.

Father Richardson's decision to host a memorial service at St. George's caused an immediate backlash, so much so that he felt compelled to issue the following statement, which is reproduced here in its entirety:

June 28, 1973

AN IMPORTANT STATEMENT FROM THE RECTOR

In view of the uproar caused by the Memorial Service at St. George's Monday night for the Rev. "Bill" Larson and others who died in New Orleans worst fire last Sunday night, I wish to point out the following:

1. St. George's is not a private club but the House of God.

2. The Rector is given authority by the canons of the church to arrange services at all times.

3. The group asked me for permission to hold their memorial service at St. George's. In good conscience I could not turn them away. Do you think Jesus would have?

4. Bill Larson, a fine humble, devoted Christian, and minister of that group was trying to exercise his pastoral ministry that evening at the bar.

5. The group asked us not to give the service any publicity and we in turn asked the press not to publicize this, but since they are always looking for stories for the public they paid scant heed to our request.

6. The small chapel on Magazine Street used by this group could not begin to hold the 50 or 75 or more persons who attended the service.

7. God's Church exists to help all people, regardless of who they are or what they do.

8. While there has been considerable criticism from some of our own members, and from a few outsiders, most of which has been relayed not to me but to several of the ladies of our parish (who are not the authority), there is a mounting number of people in the community, both clergy and lay persons, who are voicing their entire agreement that the memorial service was a very Christian thing for St. George's to permit, and the question again comes up, "Would Jesus have barred these grief-stricken people from His Church, or would He have welcomed them?"

9. Therefore: If any considerable number of St. George's members still feel that our Church is to minister only to the select few, and not to the whole community, then I shall seriously consider resigning as your Rector in the near future, so the Bishop and the Vestry can look for someone else.

(signed) William P. Richardson, Jr.

P.S. I love you all, even if you violently disagree with me. But remember, we must try not to be Pharisees, thinking we are better than others. At all times I try to follow what I believe to be the Lord's Will, and the

Christian attitude. Upon returning from India the last of July, I shall decide what course of action to take.

Ultimately, Reverend Richardson did not resign over the uproar and eventually retired in 1976. He became very involved with Integrity, an outreach ministry of the Episcopal Church aimed at LGBT+ people. Later, he would also become involved in the New Orleans chapter of PFLAG. He is remembered today by those who knew him as brilliant, compassionate, and courageous.

Richardson was not the only clergyman affected by the fire. The next essay outlines the heartbreaking life of the Reverend Bill Larson, who perished in the flames at the Up Stairs.

Ambush, September 10, 2013

REMEMBERING THE REV. BILL LARSON

BILL LARSON IS PERHAPS MOST OFTEN REMEMBERED AS THE FIGURE trapped in the window of the Up Stairs Lounge in a ghastly photograph taken moments after the infamous fire an arsonist set there in 1973 was extinguished.

Those familiar with the tragic story of the Up Stairs Lounge know that Reverend Larson was the pastor of the local Metropolitan Community Church in New Orleans, but many do not know much more about this man whose tragic death marked the end of an almost just as tragic life.

Born William Roscoe Lairson in Kentucky in 1926, he was the youngest of six children born to a mother who married at the age of sixteen. His father died of alcoholism before Bill was born. After being widowed, his mother, Anna, packed up the six children and moved to a small town in Ohio.

When Bill was not quite a year old, Anna became ill and lost custody of her children temporarily until she could recover and reassemble her life. Bill was sent to a state-sponsored nursery. When the family was reunited, the kids often had to fend for themselves while Anna worked as a waitress.

One of Bill's earliest memories was that of his six-year-old sister Dorothy being killed by an oncoming car when she ran into the street. Mother Anna received an insurance settlement but squandered the money on fast living. Once again, the state intervened and the Lairson children became wards of the state.

Anna's downward spiral continued until it reached a nadir when she was almost arrested for living with a man to whom she was not married. To avoid criminal charges, the two married. Bill's stepfather was less than supportive of Anna's children.

At this time, Bill was living in an orphanage—the Butler County Children's Home. Here young Bill was often chastised for what one report calls a "sex problem." It was evident to his caretakers that Bill was, in the words of one notetaker, "a sissy." In addition to being interested in other boys, Bill also had a passion for music, especially playing the piano and singing. And his devotion to the Bible led one staff member to conclude he would grow up to do "religious work."

When he was a junior in high school, Bill enlisted in the army and fought in Europe during World War II. Upon returning from the war, he married his high school sweetheart and had a son. The marriage, however, did not last. When Bill decided to enter the ministry, his wife left him. When the divorce was final, Bill's mother disowned him.

The pain of Bill's childhood drove him to religion and the loss of his wife and son seemed only to strengthen his faith. For a brief time after the divorce, he moved to Chicago and began calling himself Ros Larison as he worked as a nightclub singer. He eventually made his way to New Orleans and began attending St. George's Episcopal Church, which at the time was pastored by the closeted Reverend Bill Richardson.

Although he never attended seminary or received any formal theological training, Bill became the pastor of the Metropolitan Community Church (MCC). The New Orleans MCC had been founded in 1971 by David Solomon, a former Pentecostal minister. Larson became his assistant, and when Solomon left, Bill became the de facto leader of the church.

The fledgling church needed a place to meet and, for a while, conducted services at the Up Stairs Lounge before Larson, a carpenter by trade, converted a small home on Magazine Street into a sanctuary with a parsonage in the rear. This was the home of the MCC in 1973. By this time, Bill had slightly modified his last name by dropping the "i" from Lairson.

In 1972, he made one last effort to connect with his family. He traveled to Jacksonville, Florida, where his older brother Arthur and his wife Virginia were living. As they were visiting, he mentioned to Virginia that he was pastoring a gay church in New Orleans. Her response was to throw him out of the house. It was the last contact he ever had with his family. Despite the persistent rejection of his family, Larson never wavered in his faith.

Sunday, June 24, 1973, started out like any other Sunday—with Larson welcoming worshippers to his home and leading them in a church service. In the afternoon, as was customary, many of the congregants gathered at the Up Stairs Lounge for the weekly beer bust.

Although the day started like any other Sunday, it would end in tragedy. Larson and twenty-eight others died that night in the bar when an arsonist set fire to the stairwell (three more would die from their injuries in the days that followed).

Bill's mother Anna was contacted after his death, but she refused to claim the body and released it to the MCC, which maintained his cremains until he was interred in St. Roch Cemetery in 1981.

Through the efforts of researcher and author Robert Fieseler, a military plaque was placed at Larson's grave in 2018.

The next essay examines scholarly interest in the fire in 2014.

Ambush, June 5, 2018

INTEREST IN
THE UP STAIRS LOUNGE FIRE
AT AN ALL-TIME HIGH

UNTIL TODAY I HAD NEVER ACTUALLY BEEN INSIDE THE SPACE THAT ONCE housed the Up Stairs Lounge.

Ascending the stairs, where the arsonist started the fire, I thought of the thirty-two people who climbed that stairwell on Sunday evening, June 24, 1973, and it occurred to me that probably none of them thought it would be the last time they would make that climb. Then I thought of the stairwell at my apartment on Royal Street and also of the stairwells at some of my favorite bars and it occurred to me how climbing those stairs always made me happy because at their top was a place of refuge and rest, of safety and sanctuary, of good times and happy memories. Upon reaching the last few steps, I noticed the coal-black char marks on the walls and ceiling. Part of the wood had rotted away and left a gaping hole, still there after forty years.

Upon entering the space, which is now used as a storage area for Jimani, the bar downstairs, I was greeted by Sheri Wright, Clayton Delery, Jimmy Masacci, and a survivor of the fire, who was visiting the site for the first time since that fateful night. They were all there to be interviewed by Wright for a documentary film she is making.

As the interviewing commenced, Delery and I stepped outside the building and began chatting about the upcoming release of a book he has written about the fire, *The Up Stairs Lounge Arson: Thirty-two Dead in a New Orleans Gay Bar, June 24, 1973*. He pointed out to me the window where Luther Boggs and Eddie Gillis jumped to the sidewalk while they were on fire. A bartender from the neighboring Midship bar ran out and poured pitchers of ice water on them. Boggs would later die in the hospital. Delery also informed me that Jean Gosnell, who escaped with Boggs and Gillis through the same window, and who lived across the street, had to move after the fire because seeing the burnt building everyday was so painful.

There were other stories like that, and I quickly concluded that Delery's book promises to be the most detailed account of the tragedy and perhaps the definitive treatment on the subject, though not the first. In 2011, Johnny Townsend published *Let the Faggots Burn: The Up Stairs Lounge Fire*, the bulk of which was written in 1989–1990. Consisting primarily of biographical sketches of the victims of the fire, Townsend's book is an invaluable resource for anyone interested in the Up Stairs Lounge fire.[1]

In addition to both Townsend's and Delery's books, two documentary films about the tragedy are currently in production. Both films, by Robert Camina and Sheri Wright, are scheduled to be released later this year. Camina's last film, a documentary about a police raid on a gay bar in Fort Worth, Texas, called *Raid of the Rainbow Lounge*, opened to rave reviews, and won multiple awards at film festivals around the country. Wright's film will be her first.

Both books and both documentaries are indications that popular and academic interest in the fire is on the rise. *Time* magazine ran an article on the fire last year that coincided with fortieth anniversary of the tragedy. Also last year, playwright Wayne Self produced a dramatic musical based on the fire. And the local commemoration ceremony last summer garnered much press in both the print and television media.

All this historical interest is a good thing, of course, even if it has come a little late. The Up Stairs Lounge fire was, after all, the deadliest crime against gays and lesbians in our nation's history. Yet the fire remains largely ignored in LGBT+ historical narratives. To my knowledge, *The Advocate* has never run a story on the fire. Even many locals don't know about it.

But along with this flurry of interest in the fire come questions. What is the fire's significance in our collective history? Why has it been neglected in the media for so long? Why is it important to remember the fire? And what can we learn from it?

There are some who say the fire was our Stonewall. It's an interesting comparison but not entirely accurate. Whereas Stonewall caused people to raise their voices and spurred them to action, the Up Stairs Lounge fire did not spark a movement of gay activism in New Orleans. In fact, the silence after the fire yields an important insight about the mentality of gay folk in New Orleans in 1973. When the Reverend Troy Perry and others came down after the fire to chastise the gay community for its apathy, they were called carpetbaggers and told to mind their own business. Those Friends of Dorothy had grown so accustomed to their status as second-class citizens, and invisible at that, that they settled for the closet. They didn't want to come out and, even if they did, they clearly weren't ready to.

In retrospect, it's easy to say the fire and the pathetic public response to it should have caused more outrage, more action. The real question is why it didn't. I'm hoping Delery, Wright, and Camina explore that question in their upcoming work.

As of this writing, three documentary films and three books about the Up Stairs Lounge fire have been released, along with a number of podcasts. The Fiftieth Anniversary Commemoration Conference in 2023 also generated a lot of media coverage, including sixty-one media placements, some in national publications, reaching an estimated 173 million readers.

Ambush, January 28, 2014

NOTE

1. In addition to these two books, Robert Fieseler's *Tinderbox: The Untold Story of the Up Stairs Lounge Fire and the Rise of Gay Liberation* was published by Liveright in 2018. In 2023, Johnny Townsend updated *Let the Faggots Burn* and reissued the book with a different title, *Inferno in the French Quarter*.

SOUTHERN DECADENCE

EVERY LABOR DAY WEEKEND, 250,000 LGBT+ PEOPLE (MOSTLY GAY men) arrive in New Orleans to celebrate what has come to be known as Southern Decadence. While most gay bars have their own programming during the five-day extravaganza and private parties abound, the real party is on the street. The highlight of the weekend is the Grand Marshal's Parade, which is always on Sunday afternoon. But Southern Decadence did not start out as a big event; in fact, in the early years it wasn't even a primarily gay event. Historically, Southern Decadence is significant because it demonstrated to the city the spending power of the LGBT+ community. By opening the city's eyes to the potential of the queer tourist market, Southern Decadence facilitated and enabled shifting public attitudes about queerness. Money may not buy acceptance, but it does buy a lot of tolerance. The essays in this section trace the humble origins and growth of Southern Decadence in 1972 as a house party among friends to the third-largest event in the city's annual calendar. "How Labor Day Weekend Became Decadent" identifies the founders of Southern Decadence and describes its early years. "The Two Sides of Decadence" examines how the enormous economic impact of Decadence has affected the essential spirit of the festival. "Grand Marshal Observations" reflects on the office of Southern Decadence Grand Marshal and explores how different Grand Marshals have modified the traditions they inherited. "Tiffany Alexander and Southern Decadence 2011" provides an in-depth look at two Grand Marshals and their parade. And "Southern Decadence 2020 Update: The Southern Decadence That Wasn't" contextualizes Southern Decadence in light of the COVID-19 pandemic.

HOW LABOR DAY WEEKEND BECAME DECADENT

SOUTHERN DECADENCE BEGAN IN 1972 WITH A GROUP OF FRIENDS WHO playfully called themselves the "Decadents." This core group included Michael Evers, his boyfriend David Randolph, Frederick Wright, Maureen and Charlie Block, Robert Laurent, Tom Tippin, Robert King, Robert Gore, Preston Hemmings, Bruce Harris, Kathleen Kavanaugh, David Red, Ed Seale, Judy Shapiro, and Jerome Williams, among others. All were young, mostly in college or recently graduated, and counted among themselves male and female, Black and white, and gay and straight.

Many people are aware Southern Decadence began as a going away party for Michael Evers and a welcome party of sorts for Maureen, but what is not as well known is that there were actually two parties. The "Decadents" met regularly at Randolph and Evers's home in the Treme, which they dubbed "Bell Reve," after the plantation Blanche DuBois lost in Tennessee Williams's *A Streetcar Named Desire*. Sunday Night Bourre (a popular card game in south Louisiana) and croquet games were a staple of the Decadents' social life, as was gathering at Matassa's bar to begin a night of carousing in the Quarter.

As Labor Day approached, Randolph, who was roughly ten years older than Evers, had to leave town on family business. Wright was returning from Chicago to visit his good friend Evers. Maureen kept complaining there was nothing to do. School would be starting soon, and an end-of-summer party was in order.

The Decadents planned a costume party on the Sunday before Labor Day. It was a fun party marked by spiked punch and a lot of drug use, especially marijuana and LSD. A few weeks later, Evers left to join Randolph in Michigan. Robert Laurent designed and sent out invitations that encouraged all to come dressed as their favorite Decadents to another party to say goodbye to Evers. About fifty people attended the party.

In 1973, the Decadents decided to have another party on the Sunday before Labor Day. Laurent suggested they all meet at Matassa's and "parade" back to Belle Reve. This was the second Southern Decadence but the first parade. The party continued in 1974 with one notable change. The Decadents chose Frederick Wright to lead the parade. This was the beginning of the Grand Marshal tradition.

In *Southern Decadence in New Orleans*, Maureen Block observes, "Frederick simply had to be the first Grand Marshal. There was no question about it."[1] Though he did not live in the city, "he would always make time for a stopover in New Orleans for his job travels . . . Everyone fought to pick him up at the airport. He was the guiding spirit of the group, a natural force. No one knew what he'd do next, the life of the party, but with a huge heart. Just a lovely man."[2]

By 1980, the focus of Southern Decadence had shifted from the house party to the parade. In 1981, the Grand Marshal's Parade began at the Golden Lantern, a tradition that continues today.

Another important tradition began in 1987 when SDGM XV Olive introduced the first official theme. There were no themes in 1988 and 1989, but there has been an official theme every year since 1990. It was also in that year that SDGM XVIII Ruby introduced the first official color. SDGM XV Miss Love secured the first parade permit in 1997. The first official song was introduced in 2000 by SDGMs XXVIII Tony Langlinais and Smurf. There has been an official song every year since 2000. SDGMs XXXVIII Toby Lefort and Julien Artressia introduced the first charity. There has been an official charity every year since. In 2016, SDGMs XLII Jeffrey Palmquist, Felicia Phillips, Tony Leggio, and Derek Penton-Robichaux introduced the first official shot.

After the advent of the internet in the 1990s, Southern Decadence has grown exponentially in both participants and visitors, as well as in terms of economic impact. Over 300,000 revelers are expected to attend Southern Decadence 2018.

According to Southern Decadence founder and SDGM IV Robert Laurent, "Cheers to Southern Decadence! What began in 1972 as an end-of-summer party among a small group of friends has transformed itself into a Quarter-wide weekend celebration. The first costume party was a farewell to Michael Evers, who was leaving New Orleans. Now, forty-one years later, his spirit, wit and sense of frivolity continue, transformed into a celebration of *Laissez les bon temps rouler!*"[3]

Some of the founders of Southern Decadence, and other old-timers, lament the commercialization of Southern Decadence—a topic that forms the basis of the next article.

Ambush, July 3, 2018

NOTES

1. Howard P. Smith and Frank Perez, *Southern Decadence in New Orleans* (Baton Rouge: Louisiana State University Press, 2018).

2. Smith and Perez, *Southern Decadence in New Orleans*.

3. Smith and Perez, *Southern Decadence in New Orleans*.

THE TWO SIDES OF DECADENCE

These are the dog days of summer. The heat is insufferable, and the humidity is oppressive. Ennui hangs in the sticky air. Every step out of doors is a study in sluggishness. Indolence and lethargy rule the day. Summer in New Orleans.

These were the conditions that gave rise to a small house party in 1972. The invitation read, "Ya'll Come to the dress up as your favorite Southern Decadent—Party at Belle Reve, 2110 Barracks, late afternoon, Sunday, September 3."

The host? A group of close friends who dubbed themselves "The Decadents." The place? A run-down home in the Treme neighborhood owned by David Randolph and his lover Michael Evers. The place had become a headquarters of sorts for the Decadents. Robert Laurent remembers noting the decay of the home: "Why, it's like the faded and withered spirit of Blanche DuBois's Belle Reve from *A Streetcar Named Desire*." The name stuck. The guests: about fifty friends and acquaintances.

Randolph was not there. He had left town because of a family emergency, an emergency that would keep him in Michigan and require Evers to leave New Orleans to join him. So, two weeks later, on Saturday, September 16, another party was held, this one a going away party for Michael Evers. The invitation, again designed by Laurent, read, "Come back to Belle Reve."

Thus, the birth of Southern Decadence. From these humble origins, Southern Decadence gradually grew but, for the most part, at least until the mid- to late 1990s, it was, primarily, a local affair—and that only for locals in the know.

By 1980, the focus had shifted from the house party to the parade, and even in the 1980s, the parade was nothing like it is now. Then it was more of an informal bar crawl. The first parade permit was not issued until 1997.

All this is lost, of course, on the 250,000+ out-of-town revelers who come each year to New Orleans for Labor Day weekend. Decadence has, in a sense, outgrown the parade at its nucleus. Many out-of-town revelers probably don't even know there is parade. Nor are they familiar with the tradition of Grand Marshals. They're here to party, and that's great.

Local business owners, especially gay bar owners, love Southern Decadence because of the financial bonanza it brings. Yet sadly, some business owners have no respect for the tradition of the Grand Marshal's Walking Parade. One owner recently told me he wished there would be no parade and no Grand Marshals. Yet another remarked, "No one knows or gives a damn who the Grand Marshal is."

While there is some truth in the remark, the sentiment it captures misses an important point. And the cynicism in such an attitude is disturbing. Southern Decadence, at its fundamental core, is a celebration of friendship. It was never intended to be an opportunity for businesses to make money.

Friendships and profits. The two need not be mutually exclusive, but financial greed cannot be allowed to usurp the very nature of Southern Decadence, which is friends celebrating friendship, hedonism, pleasure for pleasure's sake.

Enter the Grand Marshals and their walking parade. These are the guardians of tradition. Without the SDGMs and their parade, Southern Decadence would be just another circuit party that could be held anywhere in any city. The tradition of the Grand Marshal's Walking Parade is what makes Southern Decadence a uniquely New Orleans tradition. And Southern Decadence is one of the things that makes New Orleans's LGBT+ history distinctive.

So, what is Southern Decadence? To bartenders and servers, it's a mortgage payment or car note. For Billy Bear from Atlanta, it's a chance to get away from the office and cut loose. For the closeted and uninitiated, it's a baptism by fire. For religious zealots, it's an opportunity to condemn and hate. For local allied businesses, it's a bump in slow summer sales. And for Quarterites and other locals, it's a sacred tradition that cannot be duplicated anywhere else.

The next essay takes a closer look at the Grand Marshal institution and how it has evolved over the years.

Ambush, August 14, 2018

GRAND MARSHAL OBSERVATIONS

THIS YEAR SOUTHERN DECADENCE IS EXPECTED TO DRAW OVER 150,000 gay revelers to New Orleans, the vast majority of whom probably have no idea of the annual event's fascinating history or the many rituals associated with it. Of all the traditions associated with Southern Decadence, perhaps the most intriguing is the selection of the Grand Marshal(s). For the first several years (1974–1980), the Grand Marshal was selected by group consensus. And who constituted this group? At its core were those who hosted the original party that grew into Southern Decadence.

The party was a success and they decided to do it again the following year. For the second party, the group met at Mattassa's in the French Quarter and marched back to Belle Reve, thus inaugurating a parade, quasi as it was. The following year, the group decided to name a Grand Marshal for the parade, and the honor went to the late Frederick Wright. The next seven Grand Marshals selected by this method were Jerome Williams 1975, Preston Hemmings 1976, Robert Laurent 1977, Robert King 1978, Kathleen Kavanaugh 1978, Bruce Harris 1979, and Tom Tippin 1980. During these years, the parade started at Mattassa's.

In earlier years, the parade did not have an official route; rather, it meandered around the Quarter at the whim of the Grand Marshal (although there were two Grand Marshals in 1978, the custom of having more than one Grand Marshal is fairly recent). This spontaneity was a source of much of the parade's energy and created some unforgettable moments over the years. In 1986, Grand Marshal XIV Kathleen Conlon led the parade to the Riverwalk, where several drunken revelers jumped in the park fountains, much to the amusement and astonishment of throngs of tourists.

The selection process for naming the Grand Marshal(s) was changed in 1981. From that year on, the reigning Grand Marshal would now have sole authority to select his or her successor(s). Neither qualifications nor criteria for being Grand Marshal have ever been established. All that was and is required is that the would-be Grand Marshal be in the good graces of the reigning Grand Marshal. That being said, unofficial criteria have developed over the decades, and there is no shortage of opinions on what that criteria should be. Some believe the Grand Marshal(s) should be a certain age, certainly not someone too young. Others think the title should go to someone who has lived in New Orleans a certain number of years. Still others believe the Grand Marshal(s) should be someone who has "paid his or her dues." And there are those who view the title of Grand Marshal as a reward or honor for someone who has contributed positively to the LGBT+ community. For a while, the criteria seemed to be the Grand Marshal had to be someone who truly led a drunken, drug-fueled decadent lifestyle. Lately it has been the custom to name at least one drag queen as Grand Marshal, but that is a recent trend. The Grand Marshal doesn't even necessarily have to be gay.

The practice of the reigning Grand Marshal(s) selecting whomever he/she/they desire builds excitement and anticipation, which culminates at the official announcement party. In the days leading up to the announcement party, gay barflies are abuzz with speculation as to who will be named. Some years it's easy to guess; other years it's not. Some designees are a complete surprise; others are fairly predictable. For the most part, whoever is selected ends up doing a fine job of organizing and raising funds for a local charity. Then again, sometimes a Grand Marshal goes horribly wrong. Remember the Steve Miller Band's song, "Take the Money and Run"?

And then there is the question of how many Grand Marshals are appropriate. Of the forty times Grand Marshals have been named, thirty have been single individuals. Two co–Grand Marshals have reigned seven times, and three concurrent Grand Marshals have reigned three times, including this year. Since 1987, the Grand Marshal(s) have selected an official theme, color, and song.

Building on the general observations in this essay, the next piece zooms in on one particular Grand Marshal and offers specific details about the aforementioned observations.

Ambush, August 26, 2014

TIFFANY ALEXANDER AND SOUTHERN DECADENCE 2011

ON APRIL 1, 1996, TIFFANY ALEXANDER (MITCH KINCHENS) MOVED TO New Orleans to retire from doing drag. She had taken a job in the cosmetic industry and, after tremendous success in Baton Rouge as an entertainer, she was ready to move on from performing. But fate had other plans.

Before arriving in New Orleans, Tiffany had amassed a rather impressive drag resume: Miss Gay Louisiana America (twice), Miss Gay Louisiana U.S. of A., Miss Apollo (Baton Rouge and Lafayette), Miss Baton Rouge, Miss Capitol City, and Miss Louisiana Entertainer of the Year.

After a few years of settling into her new life in New Orleans, Tiffany's friend Scarlett O'Hara Butler, who worked at the Bourbon Pub, secured her a job at the pub in 1998. In addition to reviving her drag career and performing regularly, Tiffany eventually became the pub's show director. So much for retiring.

One night after a show in 2011, pub manager Julien Artressia called Tiffany into the office. Tiffany had no idea what the meeting was about and was delightfully surprised when Julien asked her to succeed him as Southern Decadence Grand Marshal. Artressia's fellow Grand Marshal, Toby Lefort, selected Misael Rubio, popular owner of the Quartermaster Deli, to be his successor.

Thus, Southern Decadence 2011 featured Tiffany Alexander and Misael Rubio as Grand Marshals. It was a productive pairing. Each had been very involved in helping their predecessors the year before in producing the parade and each knew what had to be done. And even though they did not know each other very well, they got along with each other, which is not always the case with two or more concurrent Grand Marshals.

Alexander and Rubio selected as their theme "Viva New Orleans: What Happens in New Orleans Stays in New Orleans." Their colors were pink, silver, and black and for their official song they chose "Firework" by Katy Perry. And continuing a tradition established by Toby Lefort and Julien

Artressia the year before, they named an official charity—something every Grand Marshal since has done. Alexander and Rubio selected the NO/AIDS Task Force. Alexander recalled Toby saying, "We raised $5,000. I challenge you to raise more." They met the challenge by raising $8,000.

Another challenge was the weather. As parade day approached, so did Tropical Storm Lee. It stormed all day on Friday and Saturday. On Friday night, during a float parade Toby Lefort organized, Tami Tarmac stood next to Alexander holding an umbrella over her so she would not get drenched as the parade rolled in the pouring rain. On Saturday evening, the police informed them they might not being able to walk on Sunday, but they got the green light on Sunday morning. Sunday morning was very windy and overcast but as the parade started, the rain held. Determined not to get rained on, Alexander set a rapid pace for the parade. She laughingly remembers the police asking her why she was walking so fast. After the parade dispersed, the Grand Marshals proceeded to the *Ambush* headquarters for the traditional Bead Toss, at which point the heavens opened. A torrential downpour ensued for over two hours.

When asked what advice she would give to future Grand Marshals, Alexander replied, "Enjoy every moment because it goes so fast." She also suggested future Grand Marshals pause during the parade and look back on the procession behind them in order to take it all in. The parade, she says, was the best memory of her reign.

And the most challenging aspect of being Southern Decadence Grand Marshal? Alexander didn't hesitate to respond, "Making all the former Grand Marshals happy."

The next essay discusses the COVID pandemic's effect on Southern Decadence.

Ambush, October 9, 2018

SOUTHERN DECADENCE 2020 UPDATE: THE SOUTHERN DECADENCE THAT WASN'T

IN A NORMAL YEAR, THIS COLUMN WOULD INTRODUCE YOU TO THE YEAR'S Southern Decadence Grand Marshals. But as we all know, 2020 is anything but normal. With the bars closed and city hall not issuing parade permits, Southern Decadence 2020 has effectively been canceled. Or has it?

That question has generated a lot of discussion on several Southern Decadence Facebook pages—and not without controversy. Decadence devotees from around the country, and some who have never attended but want to, have asked if it's worth coming to New Orleans this year. The vast majority of responses, posted mostly by locals, is an overwhelming "No. Stay home." Still others, from out of town, have expressed regret about not attending this year but vow to return next year.

Southern Decadence means different things to different people. To purists, it's the traditional Sunday parade. To out-of-towners, it's a chance to get out of their hometowns and cut loose. To bar owners and their staffs, it's a time to work really hard and make a lot of money.

The financial loss of not having Southern Decadence is profound. The Labor Day extravaganza usually attracts upward of 250,000 visitors. In recent years, the economic impact of Southern Decadence has exceeded $300 million. Hardest hit are the gay bars, many of which depend on the weekend to generate significant portions of their annual revenue, and their staffs—managers, bartenders, barbacks, DJs, dancers, security—whose income over the weekend can easily exceed what they would normally make in a month.

But not this year. With bars closed because of the pandemic and large gatherings, even private ones, limited, some bars and entertainers have planned virtual, online events, and as successful as those may be, it will be different.

And it will be historic. Although Southern Decadence has been "canceled" before (in 2005 and 2008 because of hurricanes), this is the first time it has been canceled because of a pandemic. And unlike before, this year, all the bars are closed. If the bars were open, even for to-go drinks only, an informal bar crawl would have been possible. That would have been a return to Southern Decadence's roots in the early years, before parade permits and tens of thousands of revelers packing the bars for days.

So, what will Southern Decadence look like this year? It will look like it did the very first year it was celebrated. This year is a return not to its roots, but its very conception as a house party.

Ambush, August 28, 2020

JOURNALISM AND MEDIA

As QUEER VISIBILITY IN NEW ORLEANS BEGAN TO SURFACE IN THE 1970s, the media played a key role in helping nudge the closet door open. In previous years, media coverage of the LGBT+ community was relegated to newspaper accounts of police raids of gay and lesbian bars. In 1971, the *Times-Picayune* ran a story on the Gay Liberation Front's march on city hall demanding an end to police harassment. A few years later, in the aftermath of the Up Stairs Lounge arson, the *Times-Picayune* ran a weeklong series of six articles on the city's LGBT+ community. Soon thereafter, a queer media presence emerged, both in print and on television. The Gertrude Stein Society produced the first LGBT+ themed talk show called *Gertrude Stein Presents*. *Impact* debuted in 1977 followed by *Ambush* in 1982. In addition, other publications appeared throughout the years. In the late 1980s and early 1990s, *Just for the Record*, a queer-themed magazine format show aired on open access cable television. And in 1995, popular radio personality Michael-Chase launched *Out! with Michael-Chase*. The essays in this section dive into the lives and work of several gay journalists who created and sustained a queer media presence. "Remembering Rip" and "Rip and Marsha: The Early Years" focus on the founders and publishers of *Ambush Magazine*. "Rich Magill and His *Times*" profiles activist Rich Magill and the intersection of journalism and activism. "Valda Lewis and *Just for the Record*" and "Michael-Chase: Out on the Radio" each tell the story of unlikely journalists and their impacts on the community.

REMEMBERING RIP

I KNEW WHO RIP NAQUIN WAS LONG BEFORE I KNEW HIM AS A FRIEND. I had seen him at the bars for years and had even been introduced to him a time or two at various social events. Marsha was always, without fail, at his side. Together, they struck me as an enigmatic couple—mysterious and intriguing, yet aloof and unapproachable. There was something about them that made me want to know them. Rip, gregarious, boisterous, and magnetic, the gravity of his charisma drawing people to him. And Marsha, calm and quiet, surrounding Rip like a forcefield keeping callers at a safe distance. Together, they were a bright star in the gay French Quarter galaxy.

My personal and professional relationship with Rip began one Monday afternoon in 2012 at Lafitte's when Rip asked me if I would be interested in writing a history column for *Ambush*. *In Exile: The History and Lore Surrounding New Orleans Gay Culture and Its Oldest Gay Bar*, a book I cowrote with Jeffrey Palmquist, had just been published and apparently had caught Rip's attention. When he offered me a column, I jumped at the chance.

As an editor, Rip was a joy to write for. He gave me the freedom to write about whatever I was interested in, and he never censored a word I wrote. And even when I wrote about people or places he was not fond of, he was fair and objective. He was a firm supporter of the First Amendment and genuinely believed in the freedom of the press.

Sometime in late 2012, Rip informed me that the fortieth anniversary of the Up Stairs Lounge arson was approaching, and he asked me if I would organize a commemorative event. He told me money was not an issue; he and Marsha would subsidize the ceremony. He then told me why this was so important to him. When Rip came out of the closet to his family, his father derisively told him, "You're going to burn just like those fags in New Orleans." His father eventually came around but Rip never forgot the comment.

Behind all his bravado and shrewd business tactics and sharp tongue, Rip had an incredibly compassionate and generous heart. The hundreds of thousands of dollars he raised for local charities is eclipsed perhaps only by the countless acts of kindness he performed every day for neighbors and those less fortunate—gestures only a few people saw.

I was with Rip helping him lay out the paper at the *Ambush* offices in 2015 when the Supreme Court effectively legalized same-sex marriage. As we learned of the decision, we looked at each other in amazement for a moment and then he called to Marsha, who was preparing lunch. They embraced tearfully and joy filled the *Ambush* headquarters. Rip then instructed me to stop the task at hand and immediately write an article about the landmark decision.

My best memories of Rip, however, are the times we shared on Monday afternoons at Lafitte's. The draw was bartender Jeff Palmquist, one of Rip's best friends. As a handful of Jeff's regulars would gather at the bar, we would all anticipate the arrival of Rip and Marsha. Once situated in their regular barstools, Rip would begin to hold court. Inevitably, hilarious antics would ensue. The more he drank, the louder he became, and the harder Marsha would slap his leg and shush him. Eventually, his acerbic wit turned to me and thus would begin verbal sparring matches that produced side-splitting laughter.

If I was unable to make to Lafitte's on a Monday, Rip would text me the following morning to check on me. We often exchanged early morning texts. I'm not a "morning person" but a text from Rip always put me in a good mood.

When my Twelfth Night Party took on a life of its own and we began the tradition of naming a "Grand Reveler," there was never any doubt I would give Rip the title. What a joy it was roasting Rip at last year's party. I dubbed him "The Award-Winning Reveler" because he was so proud of his award-winning potato salad.

I miss my friend every day. He was a good man and I feel like a better person for knowing him.

The next essay focuses on the little-known early years of Rip and Marsha and provides a context for their later work in and contributions to the queer community in New Orleans.

Ambush, March 1, 2018

RIP AND MARSHA: THE EARLY YEARS

August 8, 2018, marks the one-year anniversary since Rip Naquin passed away. His beloved Marsha joined him four months later on December 14.

Because they were such public figures, the last year without them has been strange. The role they played in the New Orleans community was huge and their absence has left a gaping void, an emptiness felt by multitudes. Their ubiquitous presence, their never-ending social events, their consummate fundraising, their leadership for the community, their profound influence—all that is gone.

But their legacy lives on. It lives in the resurrected version of *Ambush* and the institutions they founded and fostered. And of course, it lives on in the hearts and memories of those whose lives they touched.

Many know Rip and Marsha as the founders and publishers of *Ambush Magazine*, as the founders of the Krewe of Queenateenas and hosts of its annual King Cake Queen Coronation Party, as the producers of the Gay Appreciation Awards and the Gay Easter Parade. What is not so well known is the lives they led before moving to New Orleans.

Marsha grew up in Baton Rouge. Her mother, a police officer, was very supportive of Martin as he discovered his sexual orientation and explored her gender identity. Rip, or Bobby as he was known then, the oldest of seven siblings, grew up in Patoutville, Louisiana, until the family moved to Berwick in 1969. Upon graduating high school, Rip attended Nicholls State University.

While at Nicholls, Rip joined the Pi Kappa Alpha fraternity in 1972. On weekends, it was not uncommon for members of the fraternity to drive to New Orleans and party in the French Quarter. During these excursions, Rip would often find a way to break away from the pack and surreptitiously visit the lively gay bar scene. On one of these occasions, Rip created a scandal when he was spotted at a gay bar. Soon thereafter, the fraternity chapter called a special meeting to address this most serious issue. The first words out of the chapter president's mouth were, "I'd rather have a n****r in this fraternity than a f****t!" The chapter voted unanimously to kick Rip out of the fraternity.

The following year, when Rip came out to his father, shortly after the Up Stairs Lounge arson, his dad responded by telling him he would share a similar fate to those who died in the tragic arson. It was a difficult era for anyone to come out. But Rip had inner strength, an indomitable will, and a wellspring of courage. He took lemons and made rainbow lemonade.

On one of his visits to New Orleans in 1973, he met Marsha just outside the Bourbon Pub. It may sound cliché, but it really was love at first sight. They committed to each other and stayed together for the rest of their lives—nearly fifty years. It was a love story for the ages, and one that Rip's family eventually accepted, including his father.

After finding each other, Rip and Marsha settled into a comfortable life in Baton Rouge. Marsha graduated from the Baton Rouge Beauty College and Rip took a job at the JC Penney department store. By 1977, Rip had cut his teeth in journalism and was the executive editor of *The Zipper*, a monthly gay newspaper published by Alan D. Lowe and George H. Perry Jr. in Baton Rouge.

Early copies of *The Zipper*, its business records, and the personal correspondence of Rip all reveal that Rip and Marsha, during their time in Baton Rouge, were incredibly influential in establishing and promoting the Imperial Court system in Baton Rouge and Miss Gay Louisiana Pageants, Inc.

In 1982, Rip and Marsha launched *Ambush Magazine* and three years later moved to New Orleans, where they settled into the fabled "*Ambush* Mansion" on Bourbon Street. The rest, as they say, is history.

While *Ambush* was important, it wasn't the only queer newspaper in New Orleans. The next essay looks at a short-lived yet important publication—*Big Easy Times*.

Ambush, July 31, 2018

RICH MAGILL AND HIS TIMES

On Friday, May 6, I received a package in the mail from Rich Magill, who died the day before by his own hand.

In the package were fourteen back issues of a gay-themed newspaper Magill published in 1988–1989 called the *Big Easy Times*. These were the years when Magill was at the height of gay activism in New Orleans. Magill moved to New Orleans in 1986 and became involved in LAGPAC (Louisiana Lesbian and Gay Political Action Caucus). In 1991, LAGPAC published Magill's study, *Exposing Hatred: A Report on the Victimization of Lesbian and Gay People in New Orleans, Louisiana*, which was instrumental in the city council's passage of the historic nondiscrimination ordinance.

As I looked at the stack of papers before me, I began to reminisce about my friendship with Rich. I remembered the first time I formally interviewed Magill about his activism, about having cocktails with him at Café Lafitte in Exile, about the parties he threw at his Chartres Street home, about him stopping by my office on St. Ann Street as he walked the Quarter. I thought about him and his friend Stewart Butler smoking marijuana and protesting the pope's visit in 1987. I thought about his dry sense of humor and his keen intelligence and his kindness of heart. I thought about how I would miss him.

Years earlier, Magill assisted his partner John H. Foster in his suicide when complications from AIDS became unbearable. Magill suffered from chronic back and neck pain resulting from an automobile accident decades ago.

And then, as I began perusing the papers he had sent me, I began to think about the gay community in New Orleans in the late 1980s. Newspapers have been described as the first drafts of history. And it's true—newspapers provide historians not just accounts of what happened but also of what was. Advertisements, for example, offer historians invaluable information that may not be found elsewhere—the date of a drag show or political rally or the address of a bar long gone and forgotten. The *Big Easy Times* was published biweekly from August 1988 to February 1989.

It was not the only gay publication in New Orleans at the time; there was also *Impact, Ambush,* and *The Rooster.*

Magill was a regular contributor to the *Big Easy Times,* as was Jerry Zachary, who founded the New Orleans Gay Men's Chorus in 1982; Shelley A. Hamilton, who served as pastor of what was then called the Vieux Carré Metropolitan Community Church; and Henry L. Phillips.

The paper lasted a mere six months, but its fourteen issues provide an insightful glimpse into gay New Orleans in the fall of 1988 and winter of 1988–89. Among those insights:

- An obituary for Paul D. Bond who died of complications from AIDS on August 4, 1988. Bond was an actor best known for his role as Henry Higgins in *My Fair Lady* performed at Le Petit Theatre. He was also a member of the acting ensemble "Nobody Likes a Smartass," which ran for sixteen years on Bourbon Street.
- The cover charge for the Becky Allen Show at the Mint was $1.00. Well cocktails and domestic beers were 90 cents during happy hour.
- Cox Cable Channel 42 was an open access channel that featured a gay-themed show called *Just for the Record.* The show was coproduced by Valda Lewis and Loretta Mims.
- New Orleans briefly had a chapter of ACT UP (AIDS Coalition to Unleash Power).
- Oz almost never was. The property at 800 Bourbon Street had been vacant for two years in 1988 following the closing of Le Bistro (prior to that it had been Pete Fountain's club). Nick Krysalka, who had recently purchased the Great American Refuge, had purchased the property with the hopes of opening a bar called Dixie's. Property owners and area bar owners vigorously opposed Krysalka's application for a liquor license.
- Good Friend's bar, previously the Louisiana Purchase, had just opened and was initially open for just two hours on Friday evenings.
- A cheeseburger with bacon at Quarter Scene (now Eat) cost $4.25.[1]
- Jewel's Tavern was cited for violations of the city fire code.
- Gay Carnival pioneer Bill Woolley celebrated his birthday in 1988 at Le Roundup, which coincided with the bar's twelfth anniversary.
- The Double Play was still Gregory's and not yet The Wild Side.[2]

- Ourelia Manchester and Paulette Coustaut opened Pinstripes and Lace, a bar for Black lesbians.
- An obituary for the legendary Jo Jo Landry.
- There were five lesbian bars in New Orleans in December of 1988: Blue Odyssey II, Charlene's, Diane's, Pinstripes and Lace, and the Other Side.
- The Monster (formerly Menefee's) had its grand opening just before Mardi Gras 1989.

The essays thus far in this section have focused on print media; next, the focus shifts to television media. Continuing with the theme of this essay, the following essay examines the intersection of activism and media.

Ambush, May 24, 2016

NOTES

1. The restaurant at the corner of Dumaine and Dauphine is now called Wakin' Bacon.
2. The bar at the corner of St. Louis and Dauphine is now Crossing.

VALDA LEWIS AND
JUST FOR THE RECORD

IN 1983, VALDA LEWIS MOVED TO NEW ORLEANS AND BEGAN WORKING at a Randall's Record Shop on Toulouse Street importing and selling British punk rock music. Here in New Orleans, she found the freedom to be her true self, a lesbian, that proved so elusive in her hometown of Rayleigh in Essex County back in England.

After Randall's, she took a job bartending and met her first partner, Loretta Mims. The lesbian bar scene was vibrant in those years, and one of its luminaries was Charlene Schneider, owner of the legendary Charlene's. Charlene and Valda became friends and in 1986, Charlene "dragged" Valda to a meeting of the New Orleans City Council. The council was considering a nondiscrimination ordinance to protect lesbian and gay city employees.

The ordinance did not pass that day, and it would be a long fight before finally being adopted in 1991. Before the ordinance was voted down, the council heard testimony from the public. Many spoke in support of the measure but even more testified against it. One woman, a Christian, testified that God had revealed to her that militant, radical homosexuals had met secretly in San Francisco and, for reasons she did not explain, the wicked conclave chose New Orleans as the first city to implement their diabolical plan to usher in the downfall of Western civilization.

Valda was astounded at the misinformation and downright ignorance on display at the council meeting as the ordinance was being debated. Resolved to do something to clear up the prevalent misunderstanding of homosexuality, she and Loretta began producing a television show called *Just for the Record*.[1] She recalls: "We needed a better image."

Just for the Record was a weekly cable access television show produced on cable channel 49 from 1987 to 1993 and was New Orleans's first LGBT+ television show. It covered both local and national topics of interest to the gay and lesbian community. The shows ranged from thirty to sixty minutes. In addition, Lewis and Mims also published a monthly newsletter of the same title from 1989 to 1993. After the show's run, they produced another show called *Queer Street Live*, which ran for thirteen weeks.

Valda fell in love with the camera while producing these shows and began recording other events relating to the LGBT+ community. A sampling of what she recorded includes four annual conferences of the National Gay and Lesbian Task Force Policy Institute, the second HIV/AIDS Regional Summit, the thirteenth National Lesbian and Gay Health Conference, the National Commission on AIDS "Sex, Society, and HIV" Hearings, several Bourbon Street Awards contests, Armeinius and Amon-Ra Carnival balls, and just about anything else queer related that was happening in New Orleans.

After her relationship with Loretta ended, Valda began dating Shelley Hamilton, who served as pastor of the New Orleans Metropolitan Community Church (MCC). The couple left New Orleans in 1993 when Hamilton took a position as pastor of the MCC in Dallas. In Texas, Valda encountered the same type of homophobia she found in New Orleans. When the MCC there tried to purchase a building for their 1,600+ strong congregation, one church official told them he would rather "burn the building" than sell to gays and lesbians.

In 1995, they moved to Wichita to take over the MCC there. While in Kansas, Valda earned a master's degree in women's studies and communication. During her course of study, she fell in love with Dr. Dorothy Miller, a member of the women's studies faculty (the two never had a class together). She would later obtain another master's degree in media studies from the New School for Social Research. Since 2002, Valda and Dorothy have lived in Cleveland, Ohio.

Lewis and Mims's pioneering television show, *Just for the Record*, will be honored later this year at the LGBT+ Archives Project of Louisiana's annual Oracle Gala. Last year, the Archives Project awarded a grant to the Amistad Research Center to digitize *Just for the Record*. Each year at the Oracle Gala, the LGBT+ Archives Project recognizes an individual or organization that has made a substantial donation of material that chronicles LGBT+ history to an area library, museum, or archival repository. In addition to remarks by Valda Lewis herself, clips of the show will be featured at the gala.

The next essay turns its attention to radio by highlighting the story of New Orleans's first queer radio show.

Ambush, June 4, 2019

NOTE

1. With a grant from the LGBT+ Archives Project of Louisiana, the Amistad Research Center has digitized every episode of *Just for the Record* and made those videos available to the public on its Vimeo channel.

MICHAEL-CHASE:
OUT ON THE RADIO

JUNE 1987, A HONDA HATCHBACK ROLLS INTO NEW ORLEANS. A GAY couple was moving to New Orleans. Michael-Chase Creasy and his boyfriend Rusty arrived in town with $232.

Rusty secured a sales job at a popular radio station, Q93. Michael-Chase was leaving a radio career behind, or so he thought. Creasy's father, who once traveled the country as a jazz musician, settled down to start a family and secured a job as a program director and DJ at a radio station in Baltimore. His morning show, *Coffee with Creasy*, was well known on the Eastern Seaboard.

Michael-Chase followed in his father's footsteps and eventually hosted an enormously popular morning show in Richmond, Virginia. His classic "radio voice" and easygoing demeanor endeared him to listeners, and Creasy quickly earned a national reputation in radio circles. His career was taking off, but there was a problem—he was tired of remaining in the closet. In New Orleans, he could be out and free. But radio wasn't finished with Creasy.

As Rusty was setting up his office at Q93, the program director met Michael-Chase and asked him if he was the radio celebrity from Virginia. Stevens offered Creasy a job running the board during Houston Astros games. This led to another opportunity. Creasy remembers, "I eventually filled in for the number one morning team Welch and Woody, and that's where a sales rep for WWL heard me and made sure she taped my morning drive fill in for Welch and Woody and played it for the general manager Dom DeLahoussaye over there at WWL am and JOY 102.9 fm. That's how they found out about me and gave me the job as morning anchor at Joy 102 FM as they change the format to magic 102 and wanted a new host."

Later, Creasy became the program director at WSMV, where he also hosted a sports talk show with Peter Brown. The show was wildly successful, and Creasy's career was skyrocketing just as it had back east. While pleased with the success, he was still in the closet on the air.

Creasy was doing the morning traffic at WYLD when the station manager offered him his own show on their AM counterpart station, WQDT. *From the Pages* aired from 9:00 a.m. to 12:00 p.m. and based its discussion on the Metro section of the *Times-Picayune*. The show caught the attention of Marc Leunisson, the general manager of B97, who called Creasy and said, "I understand you're gay. Would you do a late-night gay show?"

Thus, *Out! with Michael-Chase* was born. The show premiered on July 17, 1995, and aired from midnight to 2:00 a.m. It was one of the first LGBT-themed shows on mainstream, commercial radio.

Creasy remembers struggling with how to handle the first show. His friend Jim Albert advised him, "Pretend you've been on the air six months." It was good advice. The first show was a huge hit. Its topic was a recent *Newsweek* article on bisexuality in high school. After referencing the article, Creasy asked listeners, "Is this true?" And then the calls came flooding in. The response was so overwhelming that after the show, producer Nick Perniciaro, who was straight, looked at Creasy and said, "Your life will never be the same. This is some real shit! Who are you?"

Other memorable topics include "Do Threeways Work?," "On the Job Crushes and Work Relationships," and "One Night, One Star." The show quickly became number one with the eighteen-to-thirty-four-year-old demographic and began generating advertising revenue, which was unusual for late-night spots. One advertiser was Bobby Revere, owner of the Bourbon Pub. Creasy hosted the show from the bar's balcony on Thursday nights. Rubyfruit Jungle was another bar that occasionally hosted the show.

Out! with Michael-Chase lasted only a year. When B97 (along with seventeen other radio stations) was sold in 1996, the new format did not include gay talk shows. Although the show did not last long, it had a profound impact on thousands of listeners, especially people still in the closet. One lady, a nurse, listened to the show during her drive home on the Northshore from work. The show transformed the woman's attitude. She had previously kicked her son out of their home upon learning he was gay. She is now an active member of PFLAG.

Creasy went on to become a media broker and returned to the airwaves as a cohost on B97's show *Wankus in the Morning*. Creasy recalls, "It was fun because I could be out."

LGBT+ visibility in the media is something many now take for granted, especially young people. But before there was *Ellen* and *Will and Grace* and *Queer as Folk*, before satellite radio, and before the internet was widely accessible, there was *Out! with Michael-Chase.*

Ambush, September 19, 2020

PRESERVATION

AT THE TURN OF THE TWENTIETH CENTURY, THERE WAS SERIOUS DISCUS-
sion of tearing down the French Quarter to make way for modern development. The New Orleans City Council actually passed a resolution
in 1895 authorizing the demolition of the Cabildo and, in 1909, an entire
city block was razed to make room for the State Supreme Court building.
Historic preservation was not on a lot of minds then; rather, many viewed
the French Quarter as a run-down slum. The architecture was old and
many buildings were dilapidated; sex workers and drunken sailors were
pervasive, and perhaps most offensively, at least to many, the majority
of French Quarter residents were Sicilian immigrants. Thankfully, it was
gay men who raised their voices and championed the preservation of
the neighborhood. The essays in this section illustrate that without gay
men one hundred years ago, we might not have a French Quarter today.
"Queer Eye for Preservation" looks at several early preservationists, including architect Allison Own. "William Ratcliffe Irby: A Gay Man of
Consequence" outlines the enormous contributions W. R. Irby made to
the city. "The Gay Twenties and the French Quarter Renaissance" recol-
lects the artistic, literary, and intellectual salons that coalesced around
Lyle Saxon during Prohibition. "Remembering Clay Shaw" recalls the
accomplished life of the Quarter preservationist before the infamy of
Jim Garrison's persecution of him. And "LGBT+ National Landmarks in
New Orleans" remembers the National Park Service's initiative to identify and memorialize important sites in local queer history, an initiative
abandoned under the Trump administration.

QUEER EYE FOR PRESERVATION

ELIZABETH WERLEIN, THE DRIVING FORCE BEHIND THE CREATION OF THE
Vieux Carré Commission, is generally credited with saving the French
Quarter from the wrecking ball, but a generation before Werlein's important work, gay men were already sounding the preservation alarm. In
fact, without gay men, the French Quarter might not exist.

Gay men had made their mark on the Quarter as early as 1848, when
Gaston Pontalba, son of the fabled Baroness Pontalba, is thought to have
designed the ornate ironwork "AP" monogram that adorns the cartouche
in the ironwork of the buildings that flank Jackson Square—an early
example of a gay man setting the trend, architecturally at least.

One of the earliest gay preservationists was Allison Owen. After a successful career in the military, he founded the architectural firm of Diboll &
Owen and began sounding the preservation bell. When the city authorized
the destruction of the Cabildo (the Spanish colonial statehouse where the
Louisiana Purchase transfer took place), Owen led the effort to prevent
the venerable old building from being torn down. He also purchased
the Greek Revival home on Chartres Street that would later come to be
known as the Beauregard-Keyes House. He also built the Pythian Temple
and Notre Dame Seminary outside the French Quarter.

As alarming as a proposal to tear down the Cabildo sounds today, historic preservation was not really on many people's minds until the entire
400 block between Chartres and Royal Streets was destroyed in 1909
to make way for what is now the supreme court building. The modern
tourism industry, which depends so much on the "old-world charm" of
the French Quarter, was not yet born. The Vieux Carré Commission was
still years away. It was into this milieu that gay men began restoring and
saving historic properties.

Chief among these men was William Ratcliffe Irby. His lifetime of
philanthropy qualifies him as one of the most significant gay men in
New Orleans history. Irby personally saved several important landmark
French Quarter buildings, the most culturally significant of which was the

old French Opera House at the corner of Bourbon and Toulouse Streets (which unfortunately was destroyed by fire in 1919).

In 1918, Irby purchased and restored the Seignouret-Brulatour Court at 520 Royal Street. Also in 1918, Irby, who was Jewish, donated $125,000 to the Roman Catholic Archdiocese of New Orleans for the purpose of repairing and renovating St. Louis Cathedral, which was already showing its age before being ravished by the great hurricane of 1915.

In 1920, Irby purchased the old Bank of Louisiana building at 417 Royal Street (better known today as Brennan's Restaurant) and donated it to Tulane University. The following year, Irby purchased the lower Pontalba Building on the northeast side of Jackson Square for $68,000 from the grandson of the Baroness Micaela Pontalba. He then donated it to the Louisiana State Museum, which retains it today.

In the 1920s, Irby became a part of what John Shelton Reed calls the "Dixie Bohemia"—a circle of writers and artists and like-minded friends in the French Quarter who would play a vital role in transforming the Quarter from a run-down slum on the verge of being razed into a viable neighborhood that not only fostered creativity but was also worth preserving.[1]

Other gay (and bisexual) men who played a role in this transformation included Lyle Saxon (writer), Richard Koch (architect), Weeks Hall (artist), Sam Gilmore (poet and playwright), William Spratling (Tulane Professor and silversmith), Pops Whitesell (photographer), and Cicero Odiorne (photographer). Among the Dixie Bohemians, Richard Koch and Lyle Saxon, along with Irby, were strong voices for preservation of the French Quarter.

Saxon championed the Quarter as an artistic haven and restored properties on both Royal and Madison Streets. Koch worked closely with Elizabeth Werlein to establish the Vieux Carré Commission and, in the 1930s, also worked with the Historic American Buildings Survey to identify and document endangered buildings throughout Louisiana.

Owen, Irby, Koch, and Saxon were the first in a long line of gay men who have served as guardians of New Orleans architecture. Subsequent generations would see the likes of Boyd Cruise, Arnold Genthe, Clay Shaw, Curt Greska, Lloyd Sensat, Gene Cizek, Randy Plaisance, Larry Hesdorffer, and Bryan Block.

For ages, gay men have served as keepers of culture. That is certainly true in New Orleans. As the Quarter enters its fourth century, the city's founder, Bienville, who lived into his eighties and never married, would be amazed not only at what he wrought, but also at the role gay men have played in preserving it.

Of all the preservationists mentioned in this essay, the most prolific and influential was W. R. Irby. The next essay takes a closer look at his life and legacy.

NOTES

1. For a more detailed discussion of gay men's contributions to the preservation of the French Quarter, and the French Quarter Renaissance in general, see John Shelton Reed's *Dixie Bohemia: A French Quarter Circle in the 1920s* (Baton Rouge: Louisiana State University Press, 2012). Also see John W. Scott's "William Spratling and the New Orleans Renaissance," which appeared in the Summer 2004 volume of *Louisiana History: The Journal of the Louisiana Historical Association* 45, no. 3.

WILLIAM RATCLIFFE IRBY: A GAY MAN OF CONSEQUENCE

WILLIAM RATCLIFFE IRBY IS NOW KNOWN MOSTLY ONLY TO NEW Orleans historians and a handful of tour guides, but he should be a household name in the New Orleans LGBT+ community. His lifetime of philanthropy qualifies him as one of the most significant gay men in New Orleans history. Irby was born in Virginia around 1860 and by the time he was twenty he was living in New Orleans. When he died in 1926, he had been a banker, owned a tobacco company, and served on the board of administrators at Tulane University. As impressive as these personal accomplishments are, his true legacy is as a French Quarter preservationist.

In the 1920s, Irby was part of a circle of people in the French Quarter who would play a vital role in transforming the Quarter from a run-down slum on the verge of being demolished into a viable neighborhood. A group of gay men partnered with society matrons, whose husbands ran the city, and preservation-minded folks to prevent corporate interests and greedy developers from completely destroying the historic buildings of the French Quarter. This group was responsible for the creation of the Vieux Carré Commission.

One of the most culturally significant buildings Irby saved was the old French Opera House. From 1859 to 1919, the French Opera House at the corner of Bourbon and Toulouse Streets served as the epicenter of Creole society during a time when the city was becoming more and more Americanized. At the turn of the twentieth century, New Orleans was the theater capital of the South, and the French Opera House was its crown jewel. Throughout the nineteenth century, New Orleans had a love affair with opera and was considered the "opera capital of North America." But by 1913, the opera house had fallen on hard financial times and went into receivership. Irby bought the building and then generously donated it to Tulane University, along with enough money to keep the place afloat.

When the stately old building burned to the ground in 1919, Lyle Saxon tearfully watched the destruction and lamented in his newspaper column the next day, "The heart of the old French Quarter has stopped beating."

In 1918, Irby purchased and restored the Seignouret-Brulatour Court at 520 Royal Street. The home was built in 1816 for Francois Seignouret, a French wine importer and furniture maker. In 1870, another French wine importer named Brulatour bought the home. By the time Irby acquired it, the property was in disrepair. In 1922, after extensive renovations, Irby donated the slave quarters and the use of the courtyard to the influential Arts and Crafts Club, which used the facility for exhibition space and classrooms. The courtyard, considered one of the most beautiful in all the French Quarter, became the subject of countless paintings. The Arts and Crafts Club, which had been founded a few years earlier in Alberta Kinsey's Toulouse Street studio, was chiefly responsible for introducing modern art to New Orleans.

Also in 1918, Irby donated $125,000 to the Roman Catholic church for the purpose of repairing and renovating St. Louis Cathedral, which was already showing its age before being ravished by the great hurricane of 1915. For a while, the cathedral was closed to parishioners for fear it would collapse on them. Irby made the donation anonymously and was not identified as the benefactor until after his death.

In 1920, Irby purchased the old Bank of Louisiana building at 417 Royal Street (better known today as Brennan's Restaurant) and donated it to Tulane University. The building had been built in 1795 by Don Vincente Rillieux, great-grandfather of French Impressionist painter Edgar Degas. Julian Poydras turned the home into a bank before it reverted to the home of world chess champion Paul Morphy.

In 1921, Irby purchased the lower Pontalba Building on Jackson Square for $68,000 from the grandson of the famed Baroness Micaela Pontalba. He then donated it to the Louisiana State Museum, which retains it today and administers the 1850 House, a replica of a typical 1850s New Orleans row-house residence.

The aforementioned acts of philanthropy are but a few examples of the numerous gifts William Ratcliffe Irby bestowed upon New Orleans. Irby did not live as an openly gay man, nor did he hide his sexuality from other "Friends of Dorothy." Lyle Saxon, for example, occasionally in his writing makes subtle references to Irby's sexuality, using code words and phrases that only gay men would "get."

Historian Buddy Stall notes that Irby's life ended as colorfully as it had been lived. One afternoon in 1926, Irby went to the local bathhouse (yes, there were gay bathhouses then) before spending several hours socializing with friends. Then he went to his favorite restaurant to dine alone before going to a local mortuary to make his funeral arrangements. Then he crawled into the casket he had just purchased and put a bullet through his brain.

The next essay explores a group of artists, writers, and preservationists in the French Quarter one hundred years ago of which Irby was a part.

Ambush, June 25, 2013

THE GAY TWENTIES AND THE
FRENCH QUARTER RENAISSANCE

ONE OF THE MANY CHALLENGES THE GAY HISTORIAN FACES IS RECOGNIZING and recovering the societal contributions gay folk have made throughout history. This is especially true of the pre-Stonewall period when closets were firmly shut and the concept of sexual orientation did not exist. These societal contributions by gay folk may have been philanthropic, political, economic, cultural, literary, or artistic. Because of cultural taboos and criminal laws, many influential gay people never publicly identified as gay. Their contributions may have been significant, and even profound, perhaps even well known (think Leonardo da Vinci), but historically, they have not been credited as "gay."

This is certainly true in New Orleans, especially in the 1920s, when the French Quarter was the site of a literary and artistic renaissance, at the center of which were a number of gay men.

In 1919, Lyle Saxon convinced the Drawing Room Players to move their little theater, which had been located in the lower Garden District since 1916, to the lower Pontalba Building. Within a few years the Drawing Room Players grew into Le Petit Theatre du Vieux Carré and, in 1922, purchased a lot on the corner of St. Peter and Chartres Streets. Architect Richard Koch designed the theater and Sam Gilmore staged three plays there.

Gilmore was also a poet whose work won accolades from the *New York Times*. Gilmore also served as patron, associate editor, and contributor to the *Double Dealer*, a prominent journal of literary Modernism that published writers such as Ernest Hemingway, William Faulkner, Hart Crane, Allen Tate, Robert Penn Warren, and Djuna Barnes, among others.

Also contributing to the *Double Dealer* was William Spratling. Spratling was an artist who had come to New Orleans in 1922 to teach architecture at Tulane University. He lived in the French Quarter and, for a while, shared an apartment with William Faulkner in Pirate's Alley. Spratling would go on to become a famous silversmith and eventually moved to Taxco, Mexico, where he fathered that city's silver-working industry.

While he was in New Orleans, he and his friend Lyle Saxon served as hosts and organizers of many literary and artistic salons, dinner parties, and cocktail soirees. Writing for the *New Orleans States* in 1922, Natalie Scott observed of Spratling's apartment in the French Quarter, "Where he lives with a friend, and performs marvels with tea-pots and tongues, in the role of host." She further described his apartment as one of the "chosen nuclei of the Quarter."

Spratling was also involved in the very influential Arts and Crafts Club, which was founded in 1919, probably at the urging of Lyle Saxon. The Arts and Crafts Club originally met in Alberta Kinsey's Toulouse Street apartment until William Ratcliffe Irby donated the use of the slave quarters at his historic home on Royal Street, the Seignouret-Brulatour mansion. The club operated the New Orleans Art Club and, in so doing, brought modern art to New Orleans. Spratling taught sculpting, clay modeling, and sketching at the school. In addition to providing art classes, the club also offered lectures and hosted exhibitions.

On the board of directors of the Arts and Crafts Club was Weeks Hall, one of the strangest and most interesting gay men involved in the French Quarter Renaissance. Hall was a painter trained at the Pennsylvania Academy of the Fine Arts in Philadelphia, and also in Paris and London. Weeks also owned the Shadows on the Teche, an 1834 plantation in New Iberia, Louisiana. Hall had acquired the plantation in 1919 and hired his friend Richard Koch to restore it. Hall would often invite the writers and artists in the French Quarter to come to the Shadows on the Teche for weekend excursions. Hall had no patience for nosy tourists and, according to John Shelton Reed, would sometimes deal with them "by impersonating a (nonexistent) idiot twin brother. Other times, he just rushed at them in his underwear, shaking his cane and shouting, 'Get out of here, you goddamn silly women!'"

In addition to artists and writers, the French Quarter Renaissance also included photographers, at least two of whom were gay. Pops Whitesell lived in and had a studio at the slaves' quarters behind what would eventually become Preservation Hall. Cicero Odiorne had a photography studio in the Upper Pontalba Building before moving to Paris in 1924. Odiorne's apartment there became a must stop for New Orleanians in Paris.

The French Quarter Renaissance of the 1920s was not an exclusively gay phenomenon. It also included notable straight folk such as William Faulkner, Sherwood Anderson, Grace King, Elizabeth Werlein, Natalie Scott, Hamilton Basso, Louise Nixon, Jack McClure, Flo Field, Caroline Durieux, Louise Nixon, Alberta Kinsey, Roark Bradford, and many others. But the presence of gay men such as Lyle Saxon, Richard Koch, Sam Gilmore, William Spratling, W. R. Irby, Weeks Hall, Pops Whitesell, and Cicero Odiorne demonstrates the French Quarter Renaissance was also not an exclusively straight phenomenon. All these people knew each other, some better than others, and they were all part of a special moment in New Orleans history. Each contributed to the bohemian milieu that gave rise to the French Quarter Renaissance, vestiges of which can still be sensed today.

Fifty years after leaving New Orleans, William Spratling, in an interview, recalled the French Quarter of the 1920s: "The Quarter at that time was not known as a chic place to live . . . many writers, painters, musician, European and American, who came and went, formed a stimulating background. It was a world full of new ideas."

A generation after the gay men of the French Quarter Renaissance, another gay man would make his mark on the neighborhood; sadly, his preservation efforts have been overshadowed by his alleged involvement in the John F. Kennedy assassination. Clay Shaw is the subject of the next essay.

Ambush, December 16, 2014

REMEMBERING CLAY SHAW

ONE OF THE UNFORTUNATE CONSEQUENCES OF THE HISTORICAL CLOSET is that the contributions gay people have made to society in the past have gone unrecognized. These contributions include cultural, scientific, artistic, and economic advancements that have shaped the world we live in today. This is certainly the case in New Orleans. One of the most prominent gay men in New Orleans of the twentieth century was Clay Shaw. Sadly, Shaw's memory has been blemished by his association with the John F. Kennedy assassination. Although he was found not guilty of conspiring to assassinate the president, having been the only person ever charged in the assassination has largely overshadowed Shaw's positive legacy as a war hero, successful businessman, French Quarter preservationist, and playwright.

Born in 1913 in Kentwood, Louisiana, to a prominent political family, Shaw grew up in New Orleans. When the United States entered World War II, Shaw enlisted in the army and eventually rose to the rank of major. Shaw organized and helped distribute supplies to the troops invading Normandy during the D-Day mission, a successful battle that was pivotal in turning back Hitler and the Nazis. For his military service, Shaw was awarded the Bronze Star and Legion of Merit. For helping liberate France, the French government awarded him the *Croix de Guerre* and Belgium named him *Chevalier de l'Ordre du Merite*. Long before the repeal of "don't ask, don't tell," Clay Shaw demonstrated what we've known all along—that being gay has absolutely no bearing on military service.

In 1936, Shaw moved to New York, where he worked before the war, after which he returned permanently to New Orleans. At the peak of his business career, he served as director of the International Trade Mart, which once occupied the tall cross-shaped skyscraper at the foot of Canal Street. The Trade Mart helped modernize international commerce in New Orleans, especially the importation and exportation of goods between New Orleans and Latin America. Shaw's business ventures brought him financial success and afforded him the means to devote himself to one of his passions—historic preservation.

Shaw restored several buildings and homes in the French Quarter (conflicting records indicate between nine and thirteen), the most notable of which is at 716 Governor Nicholls Street. The complex of buildings at that address dates back to 1809, 1814, and 1835 and at various times had been used as a fire station, a private residence, a blacksmith shop, and horse stables. In 1965, Shaw renovated them into upscale apartments. In the last two years of his life, after the public humiliation of the assassination trial and as he was battling cancer, Shaw oversaw the renovation of the historic French Market. A memorial plaque honoring Shaw has been placed at the Governor Nicholls Street address and describes him as a "patron of the humanities." Shaw's restoration efforts in the French Quarter place him in a long line of gay preservationists that began with writer Lyle Saxon decades earlier.

Like Saxon, Shaw also had a lifelong interest in literature and coauthored (with Herman S. Cottman) four plays: *Submerged* (1929), *A Message from Khufu* (1931), *The Cuckoo's Nest* (1936), and *Stokers* (1938). In an excellent literary analysis of Shaw's dramatic works, scholar Michael Snyder notes that all four plays contain strong undercurrents of homoeroticism and often feature "sweaty, muscular men closed together in tight spaces." Shaw's plays have been performed at little theaters across the nation, especially *Submerged*, which was for decades a favorite among high school drama clubs not only because of its quality but also perhaps because Shaw and Cottman wrote it while classmates at Warren Easton High School.

After he retired, Clay Shaw hoped to return to writing, but fate had other plans. In 1967, New Orleans District Attorney Jim Garrison arrested Shaw and charged him with conspiring to assassinate President John F. Kennedy. Shaw was ultimately exonerated, but during Garrison's investigation and the subsequent trial, Shaw was outed as a gay man. Garrison, widely considered by many to have also been a closeted gay man, attempted to explain the assassination as a "homosexual thrill killing" much like the celebrated Leopold and Loeb murder case of 1924.[1] Several writers have speculated that Garrison believed Shaw would commit suicide rather than being publicly outed during a high-profile trial. At the time, it was not uncommon for prominent gay men to choose death over a public outing.

But Garrison miscalculated. Not only did Shaw not kill himself; he bravely faced his accuser with grace and dignity. And because of his tremendous civic contributions, the New Orleans public was generally supportive of Shaw and found Garrison's persecution of him distasteful. Because Garrison's homosexuality was an open secret in the gay community, many gays interpreted his persecution of Clay Shaw as a warning: stay in the closet, don't make waves, and certainly don't try to out me or look what I can do to you. Whether or not that was Garrison's motivation will never be known; nonetheless, the perception was real and, consequently, the gay community in New Orleans remained content to organize socially rather than politically, as gays in other cities were beginning to do.

Clay Shaw died in 1974. The sensational charge of conspiring to assassinate President Kennedy has eclipsed his lifelong service to New Orleans and the nation. And yet even during that ugly episode in which he was vilified and outed, he did not retreat to the closet. And the city who knew him so well respected him for it and stood by him. Thus, Shaw's life was significant not only for his civic contributions but also as an example of grace under pressure.

Shaw and other gay preservationists worked hard to protect many buildings, thus demonstrating the gay community's contributions to the architectural heritage of New Orleans. The next essay demonstrates how the government, one hundred years later, is finally recognizing those contributions.

Ambush, January 8, 2013

NOTE

1. In 2021, Alecia P. Long published *Cruising for Conspirators: How a New Orleans DA Prosecuted the Kennedy Assassination as a Sex Crime*, which examines Shaw's trial as an example of the criminal justice system's preoccupation with homosexuality.

LGBT+ NATIONAL LANDMARKS IN NEW ORLEANS

ONE DOES NOT USUALLY ASSOCIATE THE NATIONAL PARK SERVICE WITH gay history, but that's about to change. On May 30, 2014, secretary of the US Department of the Interior Sally Jewell announced a new theme study to identify places and events associated with the story of LGBT+ Americans for inclusion in the parks and programs of the National Park Service. Secretary Jewell made the announcement outside the historic Stonewall Inn in New York City. Sites may be designated a National Historic Landmark and/or placed on the National Register of Historic Places.

Currently, the only site of LGBT+ interest designated as a National Historic Landmark is the Stonewall Inn, which received the designation in 2000. At present, there are four sites of LGBT+ interest listed in the National Register of Historic Places—the Dr. Franklin E. Kameny Residence, Washington, DC (listed 2011); the Cherry Grove Community House and Theater, Fire Island, New York (listed 2013); the James Merrill House, Stonington, Connecticut (listed 2013); and the Carrington House, Fire Island, New York (listed 2014).

A panel of eighteen scholars has been formed to study and identify landmarks around the country that should be included on the National Register of Historic Places or deemed national historic landmarks or national monuments. Two properties from New Orleans are in the process of being nominated for the project—the site of the former Up Stairs Lounge and Café Lafitte in Exile. The nomination and review process is a lengthy one and not all sites that are nominated are ultimately selected. Nonetheless, the two New Orleans sites are strong candidates.

The Up Stairs Lounge, which was located at the corner of Iberville and Chartres Streets from 1970 to 1973, was the site of the deadliest crime against LGBT+ folk in the nation's history.

Café Lafitte in Exile is the oldest gay bar in New Orleans and arguably the oldest continually operating gay bar in the United States.

The National Park Service theme study has identified the following goals: engaging scholars, preservationists, and community members to identify, research, and tell the stories of LGBT+ associated properties; encouraging national parks, national heritage areas, and other affiliated areas to interpret LGBT+ stories associated with them; identifying, documenting, and nominating LGBT+ associated sites as national historic landmarks; increasing the number of listings of LGBT+ associated properties in the National Register of Historic Places.

According to a press release from the National Park Service, the theme study is part of a broader initiative under the Obama administration to ensure that the National Park Service reflects and tells a more complete story of the people and events responsible for building this nation. The National Park Service has ongoing heritage initiatives to commemorate minorities and women who have made significant contributions to our nation's history and culture, including studies related to Latinos, women's history, and Asian American and Pacific Islanders.

The Up Stairs Lounge and Café Lafitte in Exile sites have yet to receive historical landmark status from the federal government.

Ambush, July 31, 2014

ENTERTAINMENT

FOR MUCH OF ITS HISTORY, NEW ORLEANS HAS BEEN AN ENTERTAINMENT destination. In the eighteenth century, French colonial governor the Marquis de Vaudreuil introduced elaborate masked balls to the city, and a few decades later the first opera ever performed in North America premiered in what we now call the French Quarter. Throughout the nineteenth century, opera houses and performing arts theaters flourished. Nocturnal entertainments such as prostitution also thrived and at the turn of the twentieth century found a vibrant home in Storyville, which also served as an incubator for jazz during its infancy. Music and sex go very well together, especially when lubricated by drinking, a pastime for which New Orleans is well known. The essays in this chapter focus on a number of queer entertainers. "Entertainingly Out: Tony Jackson and Patsy Valdelar" profiles early jazz legend and piano professor Tony Jackson and Patsy Valdelar, the iconic star who hosted shows at the celebrated Dew Drop Inn. "My O My! The Most Interesting Women Aren't Women at All" looks back on the world-famous Club My-O-My, where female impersonators entertained throngs of tourists from around the world. "James Booker: The Black Liberace" examines the troubled life of musical genius James Booker. "Boys on the Bar: The Corner Pocket" tells the story of how a flamboyant drag queen opened a go-go boy bar that endures today. And "John Q. Hustler" highlights the fascinating life of a longtime French Quarter sex worker.

ENTERTAININGLY OUT: TONY JACKSON AND PATSY VALDELAR

New Orleans has a long history as an entertainment destination. In addition to being the birthplace of jazz and home to several legendary nightclubs, the city has always produced colorful entertainers, many of whom were gay. In this edition's column, we remember two of them—Tony Jackson and Patsy Valdelar.

Tony Jackson was a seminal figure in the city's music scene at the turn of the twentieth century. Born in 1876 in Uptown New Orleans, Jackson grew up in a poor African American neighborhood and demonstrated musical ability at an early age. By the time he was thirteen, he was playing the piano in neighborhood bars during the day and quickly earned a reputation as one of the best piano players in town. When Jackson turned twenty-one, Storyville was created, and the brothels/clubs of the infamous red-light district launched his career.

In the twenty years Storyville existed (1897 to 1917), prostitution flourished in "cribs" (dirt-cheap spaces consisting of little more than small bedrooms) as well as elegant mansions that offered full-service bars and elaborate shows featuring exotic acts and music. One brothel, the French House, even offered what was billed as an "Erotic Circus." Many of the madams and prostitutes were lesbians, and at least one house, according to the Blue Book (a Storyville catalogue/guide for visitors), offered live lesbian sex act shows. While lesbianism in Storyville was not uncommon, male homosexuality was strictly forbidden, although there was a not-so-clandestine gay brothel not far away in the Central Business District.

Despite the heterosexual atmosphere of Storyville, Tony Jackson, who lived openly as a gay man, was one of the district's most popular musicians. Jackson's piano playing style was dynamic and mesmerizing. One of his signature moves was to do a high stepping "cake-walk" while pounding the keys. He also dressed to the nines, usually wearing an ascot tie and a diamond pin. Jackson's impeccable sartorial style set the standard for other performers. In addition to being an amazing pianist, he also composed and sang. His repertoire included ragtime, early jazz, pop, opera, blues, and some classics.

His musical genius, incredible versatility, electric style, and theatrical performances earned him the praise of his fellow musicians. Jelly Roll Morton called Jackson "the outstanding favorite" musician of New Orleans and jazz great Clarence Williams said, "We all copied Tony." Similar testimonials also came from Johnny St. Cyr, Bunk Johnson, and Baby Dodds, all significant figures in the early development of New Orleans jazz.

Although Jackson never recorded and never achieved mainstream success, he did tour vaudeville twice (in 1904 and 1910) with the Whitman Sisters Troubadours. Songs attributed to Jackson include "Some Sweet Day," "The Naked Dance" (covered by Jelly Roll Morton), "Pretty Baby" (dedicated to Jackson's male lover), "I've Got Elgin Movements in My Hips with Twenty Years' Guarantee," "Michigan Water Blues," and "I'm Cert'n'y Gonna See About That."

Jackson moved to Chicago in 1912, where he helped established that city's jazz heritage until he died in 1921. In 2011, Tony Jackson was inducted into the Chicago Gay and Lesbian Hall of Fame.

Decades after the decline of Storyville and its famous jazz clubs, New Orleans's rich musical heritage lived on at the Dew Drop Inn on LaSalle Street. From 1939 to 1970, the Dew Drop Inn was considered the swankiest nightclub on the "Chitlin Circuit" (venues in the Deep South for Black musicians who could not legally play in white clubs) and featured local talent such as Tommy Ridgley, Larry Darnell, Earl King, Huey Smith, Irma Thomas, and Allen Toussaint as well as nationally known performers including Ray Charles, James Brown, and Little Richard among many others. Little Richard, who before he became famous performed in drag as "Princess Lavonne" in a traveling vaudeville show, was especially inspired by Patsy's flamboyant style.

For nearly twenty years, the shows were hosted by New Orleans's most famous female impersonator, Patsy Valdelar. Musical acts at the Dew Drop Inn were often preceded by a drag show, one of the more notable of which was Bobby Marchan's "The Powder Box Review." Many of the female impersonators came from out of town, but Patsy was always the star. Around the city, Patsy was referred to as "the Toast of New Orleans," a title that earned her the nickname Toast.

Patsy, originally from Vacherie, Louisiana, had been inspired to become a female impersonator by a well-known New Orleans cross-dresser, the legendary Caldonia.[1] Before working at the Dew Drop Inn in the 1950s and 1960s, Patsy worked briefly at the Gypsy Tea Room and also with the Valdalia Sisters, a group of singing female impersonators. While working at the Dew Drop Inn, she helped organize the annual Halloween Gay Ball, which was also affiliated with the club.

Both Tony Jackson and Patsy Valdelar were remarkable not only for their incredible talent and amazing performances but also because they lived openly gay lives in times that were extremely hostile to gays and lesbians. This fact becomes even more extraordinary when one considers they both worked and thrived in traditionally hyper-heterosexual environments, namely Storyville and an African American nightclub, respectively.

While the Dew Drop Inn was in its heyday, other clubs across the city featured what today would be called drag shows. Many Black drag queens performed at the Caldonia and at the Lakefront; the Club My-O-My was a favorite among locals as well as tourists. The next essay takes us to the Club My-O-My.

Ambush, December 4, 2012

NOTE

1. For more information on the history of Black drag in New Orleans, see Frank Perez's "A Brief History of Black Drag in New Orleans: The Dew Drop Inn, the Caledonia, and Stormé DeLarverie," *Ambush*, November 17, 2023.

MY O MY! THE MOST INTERESTING WOMEN AREN'T WOMEN AT ALL

ONE DOES NOT NORMALLY ASSOCIATE WEST END / BUCKTOWN WITH THE queer community, but for decades the Orleans / Jefferson Parish line at Lake Pontchartrain was home to one of the world's most famous female impersonation venues: Club My-O-My. For nearly twenty-five years the My-O-My hosted three shows a night (four on Saturdays) and attracted not only celebrities such as Judy Garland, Alec Guinness, Bob Cummings, Carmen Miranda, and mobster Frank Costello but also busloads of tourists from Middle America eager for a glimpse into the transgender world. Since it burned down in 1972, the My-O-My has been the subject of academic dissertations, documentaries, and articles, and it has even inspired a musical production. Ephemera from the club (postcards, matchbooks, etc.) sell regularly on eBay and pictures from the club's heyday in the 1950s abound on the internet.

The origins of the club date back to 1935 when Emile Morlet opened the Wonder Bar at 125 Decatur Street. The bar featured female impersonators and was often the subject of police raids. Frustrated with police harassment, Morlet tried to get an injunction to stop the raids, but city officials denied his request because his club was a "menace" to morality. Fed up, Morlet moved the bar to the lakefront and renamed it the Wonder Club, which subsequently became the Club My-O-My under the stewardship of Pat Waters in 1949. Because the club itself sat on pilings over the lake and straddled the parish line, police raids were no longer a problem. A fire destroyed the club in 1948, but it was quickly rebuilt. After the 1972 fire, the club reopened in the French Quarter on Burgundy Street but didn't last long.

A typical show consisted of a four-piece band (which once included Al Hirt) and five or six performers. Performances usually included exotic dancing, singing, comedy, and perhaps a novelty act. Performers employed a variety of props, including ropes, umbrellas, and even a huge python.

It was also not uncommon for the club to feature guest performers from out of town, typically regular stars at other female impersonation clubs like Finocchio's in San Francisco, Club Jewel Box in Miami, and Club 82 in New York. Sometimes international stars made appearances at the My-O-My, such as Cuba's Gene La Marr and London's Louis Hayden, billed as "England's Red-Hot Mama."

Presiding over the shows was the legendary Jimmy Callaway. Callaway moved to New Orleans from Birmingham, Alabama, in 1948 to perform at the Wonder Club. Shortly thereafter, he worked briefly at a club in Florida before returning to Club My-O-My in 1950, where he remained as master of ceremonies until the club's demise in 1972. In addition to working the My-O-My, he also had a contract with Planet Records.

In a 1996 interview with Don Lee Keith in *Tribe*, Callaway recalled what it was like working at the Club My-O-My: "In between shows, performers table hopped and mingled with guests." For Callaway, the schedule was rigorous because he wore a different outfit to introduce each act. After an act, the audience would toss money on the stage. Part of Callaway's duties included collecting the money for the performers, who, in turn, tipped him. The regular pay was around one hundred dollars a week but that income could be supplemented by B-drinking (performers enticing patrons to buy cocktails for them and then being served nonalcoholic drinks in exchange for a cut of the profits). Tricking with audience members was also an option.

While some closeted men went to the club in order to solicit sex from the performers, the audiences at Club My-O-My were, for the most part, straight. For the young among us, it may be difficult to truly appreciate how shocking drag was in the pre-Stonewall era. The notion that gender is not fixed was (and to some extent still is) a radical idea that challenged straight society's core beliefs about sexuality. In her 2004 dissertation entitled *Vintage Drag: Female Impersonators Performing Resistance in Cold War New Orleans*, Thomasine Bartlett argues that clubs like the My-O-My demonstrated that gender is socially constructed and provided a means for exploring new social orders. This may explain the straight fascination with drag.

The fact that times have changed so much may also explain some of the differences between female impersonation then and drag shows now. In an interview with *Times-Picayune* theater critic Dave Cuthbert, Bartlett notes, "The difference between the drag acts of today and the impersonators of the My O My was that these earlier performers didn't go over the top. There was no pretense that they were women . . . To them, the highest achievement was to pass themselves off as beautiful women, the 'girl next door,' a 'lady.' So their make-up was much more subdued than what you see today. They were never more pleased than when they heard someone at a table say, 'That's got to be a girl.'"[1]

In addition to the performers being less flamboyant in dress and make-up, there are, of course, other differences between the drag shows of today and the female impersonation performances of yesteryear. At Club My-O-My, all performances were live; recorded music and lip-syncing were unthinkable. Also, distinctions within the transgender community that we take for granted now were largely unrecognized then. And the title "drag queen" was considered a pejorative term among female impersonators in the 1950s and 1960s.

The term "female impersonator" is passé now and it seems almost every gay bar has a drag show. The fact that the novelty of drag has worn off is ultimately a good thing—a tangible sign that public attitudes have shifted in the right direction. And yet one wonders how the drag shows of today might be different if the stars of Club My-O-My were still performing.

The following essay examines the remarkable career of James Booker.

Ambush, March 5, 2013

NOTE

1. Thomasine Marion Bartlett, *Vintage Drag Female Impersonators Performing Resistance in Cold War New Orleans*, PhD dissertation, Tulane University, 2004.

JAMES BOOKER:
THE BLACK LIBERACE

THE NEW ORLEANS MUSIC SCENE HAS ALWAYS BEEN, FOR THE MOST PART, a place where gay musicians were "given a pass" on their sexual orientation. At the turn of the last century, Tony Jackson was the most popular piano player in Storyville and commanded the respect of all his fellow musicians, even the great Jelly Roll Morton, whom Jackson mentored. In the 1950s and 1960s, Patsy Valdelar was a showstopper at the Dew Drop Inn. Gospel genius Raymond Myles was never fully accepted by his church, but Jazz Festival crowds loved him unconditionally. In more recent years, Davell Crawford, the grandson of James "Sugar Boy" Crawford, has found great success not only here in New Orleans but also internationally. And then there is James Booker, easily the most troubled and perhaps the most fascinating of all the gay musicians New Orleans has produced.

A number of legendary musicians have acknowledged Booker's talent. Rock and Roll Hall of Famer and legendary New Orleans musician Dr. John has described Booker as "the best black, gay, one-eyed junkie piano genius New Orleans has ever created." It was not a destiny his parents envisioned for him. Born in New Orleans in 1939, Booker grew up on the Mississippi Gulf Coast, where his father was a Baptist minister and his mother sang in the church choir. He demonstrated musical talent at an early age, learning to play the piano by the age of six. He immersed himself in a wide variety of styles and listened to everyone from Bach and Chopin to Professor Longhair and Tuts Washington. He especially liked Liberace and would eventually earn the title "The Black Liberace."

After moving back to New Orleans in 1953, Booker attended Xavier Preparatory School, where he met classmates Art Neville and Allen Toussaint. After graduating, his band, Booker Boy and the Rhythmaires, secured a regular spot on a radio show, which eventually led to his first recording, "Doin' the Hambone" and "Thinking 'Bout My Baby" with Imperial

Records in 1954. Booker's contract with Imperial led to some session work with Fats Domino, the label's biggest star at the time.

In 1960, Booker enrolled in the music program at Southern University in Baton Rouge. Also in that year, Booker had a hit with his single "Gonzo," which reached number three on the R&B charts. The song is widely considered to be the inspiration for the nickname that came to describe the avant-garde journalistic style of Hunter S. Thompson.

It was also around this time that Booker began using drugs, most notably heroin, though contemporaries report that he would do whatever he could get his hands on. His substance abuse also began to manifest in what would become chronic alcoholism. Coupled with a lifelong struggle with mental disorders, his addictions took their toll on him as well as the musicians with whom he worked. He was let go from several bands and soon earned something of a reputation among record executives as a con artist. He sometimes overcharged labels for work he had already been paid for, and more than once he was paid in advance for jobs for which he never showed up. Booker's money hustling may explain the loss of his eye. In his autobiography, Dr. John claims Booker lost his eye when a record producer paid someone to rough up Booker for scamming him. Booker himself delighted in telling conflicting stories of how he lost his left eye. The truth may never be known, but in any event, Booker began wearing an eye patch.

In 1970, he was arrested for heroin possession and did six months at Angola, the state prison. After being paroled, Booker resumed his music career by traveling the country and recording with various musicians. In 1975, he gave a memorable performance at the New Orleans Jazz and Heritage Festival, which led to a recording contract with Island Records. He also began touring Europe, where he was enthusiastically received. Upon returning to New Orleans, he began tutoring a very young Harry Connick Jr.

His association with Connick proved advantageous. At the time, young Connick's father was the district attorney in New Orleans—a fact that helped Booker with his numerous scrapes with the law. By this time, Booker was often arrested for public intoxication and disturbing the peace. His mental health, never good, began to deteriorate. Nevertheless, he maintained a regular job as the house pianist at the famed Maple Leaf Bar, though his performances were erratic at best and sloppy at worst.

By 1983, years of substance abuse had taken their toll. On November 8, he died at Charity Hospital sitting in a wheelchair waiting to be treated after suffering an overdose. In many ways, Booker's life was tragic. He was incredibly gifted and talented and yet profoundly troubled and tormented. He didn't fit in anywhere. The piano was his only reality, and he constantly teased it without ever quite apprehending it. He created a unique musical style, combining jazz, gospel, blues, classical, and rhythm and blues into a seamless fusion that today still defies classification. That legacy lives on in those he influenced.

James Booker's life and work is the subject of a documentary currently in production by independent filmmaker Lily Keber. *bayou maharajah* will be released in the spring of 2013.

The next essay expands "entertainment" to include go-go boys by focusing on the Corner Pocket—a legendary gay bar in the French Quarter.

Ambush, February 19, 2013

BOYS ON THE BAR:
THE CORNER POCKET

At one point in *Diary of a Mad Playwright* (1989), James Kirkwood writes about auditioning actors for the part of a male stripper: "I didn't know whether to laugh, cry, blush, shit, or go blind."[1] If we're honest, who among us has not had at least one of those reactions upon, uh, ahem, "auditioning" a male stripper? Let's talk about go-go boys. And in New Orleans, that means the Corner Pocket.

Lee Featherston, better known as Miss Fly, opened the Corner Pocket in 1982 with partner Mike Mayo. Prior to that, the bar at the corner of Burgundy and St. Louis Streets in the French Quarter was called the Post Office and before that the Cruz Inn, both of which were gay bars.

Featherston was born and raised in Panama and came to New Orleans in the late 1970s. The son of a ship captain and a teacher/nurse, Featherston was a true entertainer, both confident and flamboyant. In addition to opening the Corner Pocket, Featherston, along with Miss Do, also opened The Wild Side (formerly Gregory's) at the corner of Dauphine and St. Louis Streets, which eventually became the Double Play.

Miss Fly and Miss Do were quite the duo. Rich Magill, who used to live in the 900 block of St. Louis Street between the Double Play and the Corner Pocket, recalls seeing the pair on an almost daily basis laughing and stumbling down the street, usually around 9:00 in the morning, with three or four hustlers in tow.

Featherston became a beloved figure in the LGBT+ community in New Orleans. Miss Fly served as Southern Decadence Grand Marshal in 1993 and led the first official Southern Decadence Grand Marshal's Bead Toss during the SD parade from the balcony of *Ambush* headquarters. Miss Fly also served as Queen Petronius at the krewe's thirty-ninth Carnival Ball. For a while, Miss Fly also presented the Fly Fashion Awards as part of the Gay Appreciation Awards gala. Featherston's unique brand of humor culminated each year with his "Fashion Victim Award." Over the years, Featherston and his Double Play manager, Miss Do, were most generous with the LGBT+ community, having donated thousands and thousands of dollars to those organizations, charities, and events they cared most about. Featherston's noted yearly "Yellow Party" raised funds for Pride Fest and the Krewe of Petronius. But it did not stop there. Many times, he and Miss Do helped countless individuals who were down and out, without anyone knowing.

Sadly, Lee Featherston was murdered in November 2000 by a young man she had befriended after a verbal argument turned physical. Current Corner Pocket owner Michael Elias summed up the feelings of many when he remembered Lee Featherston as "a good businessperson, funny, witty, and charismatic."

In 2001, Elias partnered with longtime founding bartender Jay Sewell to buy the Corner Pocket. Of all the changes Elias and Sewell made at the bar, the most significant was having dancers on the bar seven nights a week. And from 2002 to 2008, they brought in for Mardi Gras and Southern Decadence the Boys from Montreal, including international porn star Ralph Woods.

In the early years, the Corner Pocket was an authentic neighborhood bar and featured a handful of dancers, usually five to six, only on the weekends. Originally, the boys danced to music played from a jukebox. Also in those early years, Featherston instituted the weekly New Meat Night, which he hosted as Miss Fly. The Friday night show is now hosted by longtime show director Lisa Beaumann and features both amateur and veteran dancers vying for a $100 cash prize. New Meat Night at the Corner Pocket is one of the longest-running shows in gay New Orleans history.

In addition to the long-running New Meat show, the Corner Pocket has, over the years, hosted other productions, including three drag show runs. From 2002 to 2004 there was the Tits and Ass Dragon Variety Show featuring Lisa Beaumann, Klorocks Bleachman, and the dancing boys, which was followed by Potluck Burlesque, hosted by Beaumann and Barry Bareass. After Katrina, there was the Chicken and Dumpster Review, which featured Electra City, Tittie Toulouse, Tami Tarmac, and Starr Daniels. There were also special shows, such as a 2005 all-Disney-themed show called "Lion King," which was directed by Don Russell and starred Lisa Beaumann, Barry Bareass, and the dancing boys. The shows often benefit local charities. For example, in 2002, the bar hosted a show/fundraiser for COPS 8, a nonprofit organization dedicated to the 8th District Police Officers in New Orleans.

Elias points out that even though most people do not initially think of the Corner Pocket as a show bar, that is essentially what it is. Another misconception concerning the bar is that all the dancing boys are slender twinks. While there is certainly a fair share of lean chicken at the Pocket, the bar also features muscled beef and many types of boys in various shapes, sizes, and colors.

The Corner Pocket has been around for thirty-two years because it meets a need; specifically, it's a place where older men can enjoy the company of younger men. In many gay bars, older men are reluctant to approach younger men because of the fear of rejection. This, of course, speaks to the issue of aging and ageism among gay men, but that's a topic for another column.

Over the decades, hundreds, if not thousands, of boys have danced on the bar at the Corner Pocket. The next essay focuses on one of them.

Ambush, February 11, 2014

NOTE

1. James Kirkwood, *Diary of a Mad Playwright: Perilous Adventures on the Road with Mary Martin and Carol Channing* (Milwaukee: Applause Theater and Cinema Books, 2002).

JOHN Q. HUSTLER

THE YEAR IS 1999. A YOUNG MAN, TWENTY YEARS OLD, FROM SMALL-town Ohio, arrives in the French Quarter. A brief stint in the navy didn't work out and he knew he didn't want to work in a factory or on a farm, which, he recalls, is all there was back home.

He soon finds himself dancing on the bar at the Corner Pocket. "I made $125 during one song. And I was wearing Taco Bell boxers," he remembers. "I was hooked." A fellow dancer began "showing him the ropes." At first he declined offers to "go home" with patrons to do "private dances," but he would go bar-hopping with some bar patrons. He accompanied his friend on a private dance and didn't do anything sexual but was paid $200 for his company. His resistance eventually broke down. After being paid $1,200 for oral sex, he became a sex worker—a job he maintains to this day.

"Prostitution allowed me to explore my sexuality." It also helped pay for his drug addiction. "I started using at eighteen years old. That was when I had my first beer, my first cigarette, my first joint, and my first sexual experience." When asked today what his drug of choice is, he responds, "What do you have?"

He is unique in that of all the hustlers that have passed through the French Quarter, he has lasted. Most end up dead, in jail, or transitioning into what some might call "a normal life." And through his seventeen years of hustling the streets, he has attained a certain wisdom that has garnered the respect of other, younger hustlers. He has become an "elder statesman," if you will, of the streets. His assessment of the young working men of today? "They don't know how to converse, and they're dumb. They start shooting up too early. They don't listen. And they don't sleep enough."

Sex work has always thrived in New Orleans, and hustling, whether for money or food or shelter or whatever, has always been an integral part of the city. Some of the city's very first residents were thieves and prostitutes and roguish men who did what they had to do to survive with little regard for the law and conventional morality. The old joke is that here in New Orleans, we don't have laws but rather suggestions. The French

Crown's imperial neglect of the colony made such a carefree attitude inevitable. France never adequately funded or supplied the colony and early colonists did what they had to do. This attitude of the ends justifies the means when it comes to survival has deep roots in New Orleans and makes it the perfect place today for hustlers to thrive.

Many people are familiar with Storyville, the city's fabled red-light district from 1897 to 1917, but there were other, similar districts before Storyville. In the mid-1800s, Gallatin Street at the French Market was called the most wicked street in America. Girls who could not secure work in brothels walked the street with rolled up mats and plied their trade on the sidewalk. And "the Swamp," in what we now call the CBD / Warehouse District, was almost as notorious.

The history of male sex work in New Orleans is less clear. Homosexuality in any form was not something people wanted to document; to do so could land a person in jail or a mental asylum. Consequently, much of local gay history remains in the closet. The earliest reference to any gay-themed business is found in a book on the history of jazz and references a male brothel near what was then Storyville.

As gay bars, or "queershops" as they were called, began popping up throughout the Quarter, hustling found a natural fomenting ground. And while some bars catered to hustlers and johns, street hustling still persisted. The lower Quarter, especially around Cabrini Park, was a particularly active area, as was Exchange Place Alley near Iberville Street. Closeted men would often drive around in circles in the Quarter, slowing down to cruise young men loitering on corners. Often a furtive glance and a head nod was enough; sometimes the liaison was initiated by the ancient symbol of rubbing thumb and forefinger together.

Today, the hustling marketplace still exists on the streets and in the bars but has also moved to cyberspace. Social media and hook-up apps like Grindr and Scruff have expanded the hustling game and made it easier for both hustlers and johns to connect.

John Q. Hustler ends our interview by mentioning he has to get ready to visit a client, one of three long-term regulars. I ask him a final question: What lessons does the French Quarter have for young men who are trying to find their way? His response conveys a wisdom only a life on the streets can confer: "How to make and lose money. How to drink. And patience."

Ambush, March 28, 2017

PRIDE

———⊂⊃———

MODERN PRIDE PARADES TODAY ARE A FAR CRY FROM WHAT THEY WERE when they began in the early 1970s. In those early years they weren't even called parades, but rather marches. And unlike today, they were anything but moveable corporate trade shows; rather, they were angry and defiant demands for equality. Today Pride parades are essentially corporations saying, "Look at our rainbow flag, buy from us." Back then the marchers were screaming, "Fuck you, we have a right to exist." The men and women who founded the first Christopher Street Liberation Day in 1970 would have thought the gains the LGBT+ community has made since Stonewall, such as marriage equality and the repeal of "don't ask, don't tell," are fairly modest and very conservative. Critics of Pride, in New Orleans and elsewhere, claim Pride has become too cisgender, too white, too male, too corporate, and too clueless. The essays in this section focus on the origins and growth of Pride in New Orleans. "The Archbishop, Sissies in Struggle, and Gay Pride" details the origins of Pride in New Orleans and the religious opposition it sparked. "A Pride Parade to Remember" recalls an emotional Pride parade just after the Pulse nightclub massacre in Orlando. "The Politics of Pride" contrasts politicians' embrace of the LGBT+ community and their rejection of the same community after the Up Stairs Lounge fire. "Reflecting on Pride Month" ponders whether or not Pride is still necessary. And "A Brief History of Pride in New Orleans" surveys the tumultuous evolution of Pride organizations in New Orleans.

THE ARCHBISHOP, SISSIES IN STRUGGLE, AND GAY PRIDE

In 1978, the Pink Triangle Alliance hosted the first Gay Pride rally ever held in New Orleans.

The Pink Triangle Alliance was the public face/political name of the Louisiana Sissies in Struggle, a group that came out of the Mulberry House Collective in Fayetteville, Arkansas, when Dennis Williams, Dimid Hayer, Stacey Brotherlover, and Aurora relocated to New Orleans. The Sissies had grown out of the back-to-the-land movement advocated by Milo Pyne and served as sort of a forerunner to the Radical Faeries.[1]

The Louisiana Sissies in Struggle was short-lived, but while it lasted, it was intersectional in nature and advocated for queer issues, but also protested non-gay-specific issues such as racism, police brutality, and socioeconomic inequality. The group also helped edit *RFD*, a quarterly magazine for rural folk that aimed to raise queer consciousness that had been founded in 1974.

After the Pride rally the Pink Triangle Alliance sponsored in 1978, a small group of people met to discuss a Pride event the following year. The Pink Triangle Alliance members in attendance argued that more was needed than just a parade. Activists Dick O'Connor, Charlene Schneider, Mark Gonzalez, and other community leaders agreed, and the group decided on a festival.

Dick O'Connor met with City Councilman Mike Early, who enjoyed the support of the gay community and endorsed the idea, going so far as to even help the group secure a prime location for the first GayFest, none other than Jackson Square. When the Roman Catholic archdiocese learned of the event, however, Archbishop Philip Hannan went to work behind the scenes with his contacts at city hall and had the venue nixed.

Years later, in 1986, Archbishop Hannan pressured Councilman Early, a former priest, to withdraw his support for a nondiscrimination ordinance that would have protected lesbian and gay employees. Early had sponsored the ordinance two years earlier, and his "no" vote in 1986 was viewed by many in the community as a betrayal. The ordinance failed in 1986 but was eventually passed in 1991 over Archbishop Hannan's strong objections.

The archdiocese's opposition to gay visibility in front of its landmark Cathedral was ironic considering that one of its own facilities, a church and building complex that had once been a cloistered convent for nuns on the corner of North Rampart and Barracks, was being used as a de facto gay community center.

Prior to the founding of the Lesbian and Gay Community Center of New Orleans, the St. Louis Community Center in the French Quarter served as a gay-friendly meeting place for various LGBT+ organizations, such as PFLAG, a gay Alcoholics Anonymous group, Dignity, Crescent City Coalition, LAGPAC, and a few other LGBT+ groups. This was made possible because of the tolerance of a gay priest on the downlow who ran the facility. Rich Sacher observes, "For a few years, before the Catholic Church in Rome swung to far-right conservatism, this location was practically a gay community center. When Pope John Paul II was elected, we were all told to leave."

GayFest organizers were not happy at having the venue pulled but found a suitable, alternate location at Washington Square Park not far away in the Marigny neighborhood. When GayFest was organized, part of the idea was to raise money for a community center, which they did. Subsequently, however, the money raised for the community center mysteriously vanished. A lack of financial resources would plague the community center throughout its history.

Like the community center, Pride was not without its financial setbacks. By 1994, Pride was on the verge of bankruptcy when cochairs Robert Brunet and Joan Ladnier asked Stewart Butler and his partner Alfred Doolittle for help. Stewart wrote a check without hesitation.

New Orleans Pride would survive and has been reincarnated under various umbrella organizations. The parade has enjoyed phenomenal growth and popularity in the last several years, and although it has been canceled this year because of the COVID-19 outbreak, organizers have announced that this year's Grand Marshals—Halloween New Orleans, the LGBT+ Archives Project of New Orleans, Princess Stephaney, and yours truly—will resume their duties leading the parade next year.

For good or ill, Pride parades today have strayed pretty far from their roots as angry marches of defiance. The gay liberationists in the early

1970s may not be happy with what their marches have evolved into, but one fact is undeniable—Pride parades are here to stay, even if they are little more than moveable corporate trade shows. As long as homophobia persists, the need for Pride will continue.

The 2020 New Orleans Pride Parade was canceled due to the COVID-19 pandemic. The next essay is a personal reflection of the 2016 New Orleans Pride Parade, in which I marched with Mark Gonzalez, one of the founders of GayFest.

Ambush, May 21, 2020

NOTE

1. Jason Ezell, "Returning Forest Darlings: Gay Liberationist Sanctuary in the Southeastern Network, 1973–80," *Radical History Review* 2019 (135): 71–94.

A PRIDE PARADE TO REMEMBER

THE RECENT NEW ORLEANS PRIDE PARADE CAPPED OFF A VERY EMO-
tional week.

I had traveled the previous weekend to represent the LGBT+ Archives
Project of Louisiana and *Ambush* in the Baton Rouge Pride festivities.
While there, I remembered my life in the closet when I was in high school
in Baton Rouge. I remembered meeting my first lover at LSU and how
we would come to New Orleans on the weekends to drink at Lafitte's.
I remembered how careful we were to guard our deeply held secret. I
remembered the fear of discovery. I remembered the self-loathing. I
remembered the shame.

And so, to participate so publicly in the Baton Rouge Pride celebration,
to think about how far I had come in my personal journey, well, it made
me feel proud. Waking up Sunday to the horrible news of the massacre
in Orlando injected a dose of sad reality into my pride: there were still
people who wanted to kill me just because of who I am. On the ride back
to New Orleans it occurred to me that our past is never too far behind
us—and I wept.

Upon arriving back home, I pulled myself together and went to activist Stewart Butler's home for a StoryCorps/NPR interview that had been
planned for weeks. Then I was contacted by Steven Mora and Chad Boutte,
who asked me if I would say a few words that evening at a candlelight vigil
on the river they were organizing. I said yes and hoped I could make it
through my remarks without breaking down in tears, which I did.

The rest of the week was tough. Monday night was yet another vigil
at St. Anna's Episcopal Church. Throughout the rest of the week, I conducted several gay history walking tours, which were especially poignant
in light of Orlando. And then there were numerous interviews and
requests for interviews.

Then came Saturday and the New Orleans Pride Parade. I marched
with the LGBT+ Archives Project of Louisiana, a nonprofit organization
of which I am privileged to be a part. As we were lining up, we were

joined by some younger folks (Sean Ortolano and John Green) who had attended but never before marched in a Pride parade. As we began walking, I thought of the first Pride parade I marched in years earlier. At that time, the route seemed really long, and I told myself ahead of time that I would peel off before the end and head to the bar. But as I marched, the love and energy of the crowds were absorbing and sustaining, and before I knew it, I had marched the entire route.

This year I almost didn't march at all. I underwent spinal cord surgery earlier this year and while my recovery has been nothing short of miraculous, I'm still not 100 percent. And although I'm walking fairly well, I cannot do it for too terribly long, especially not in the oppressive summer heat. The truth is, I feel fortunate to be walking at all.

Shortly after the parade began, I passed my cousin Trish, who reached out and embraced me. I thought of the night she spent with me at the hospital when I was at my worst, and I wasn't even sure I would ever walk again. I knew then my decision to walk the parade was the right one. In fact, at that moment walking the parade became a mission of personal resolve and triumph—a mission that was reinforced with every face along the way of someone I saw who visited me in the hospital.

But this parade was about so much more than just my personal struggle. It was about more than just publicly declaring my personal pride in being gay. It was about Orlando and how the horrible shooting there a week earlier demonstrated more than ever the necessity and importance of Pride parades. Marching in that parade was a declaration that not only are we proud of who we are but also that we are not afraid.

As we marched, I saw parents with their children lining the parade route. Several times I reached out to tell them that I wished when I was a kid that my parents had brought me to a Pride parade. What a difference that would have made! But times were different then. I thought about how times have changed for the better but also about how much more they need to change.

As previously mentioned, we had some first-time marchers in our group. I took great delight in introducing them to Mark Gonzalez, who was also marching with the Archives Project. Gonzalez (along with Charlene Schneider and Richard O'Connor and others) founded GayFest in 1978. GayFest produced the first Gay Pride Parade in New Orleans in 1980.

As the parade approached the intersection of Decatur and Iberville Streets, I began to think of the Up Stairs Lounge (located a block away) and the thirty-two people who died as a result of the arson there on June 24, 1973. What would those men have thought if they could have seen this parade, this public display of pride? Could they have even imagined it?

The 2016 Pride parade was the largest in New Orleans history, due, in no small part, to the massacre in Orlando a week earlier. The crowds were, for the most part, supportive and enthusiastic. There are, however, always exceptions. As we made our way down upper Bourbon, I heard a frat guy type on the sidewalk make a derogatory comment questioning why they don't have straight pride parades. If I could have talked to him, I would have told him to be thankful they didn't need one. If Orlando teaches us anything, it's that Pride parades are still just as necessary now as they ever have been.

The following essay traces city hall's evolving attitude toward Pride.

Ambush, July 5, 2016

THE POLITICS OF PRIDE

ONE OF THE FIRST POSTS I SAW ON FACEBOOK THIS MORNING WAS A picture of Mayor Cantrell standing in front of city hall smiling broadly under a rainbow flag. It must be Pride month.

I don't know how the mayor truly feels about LGBT+ people. I hope the sentiments expressed in the picture are sincere. What I do know is we've come a long way when politicians are eager to pose with rainbow flags to express their support of our community. It wasn't always so.

A Pride flag waving from city hall. Rainbow banners on North Rampart. Police escorts during the Pride and Southern Decadence parades. A nondiscrimination ordinance. All of this would have been unthinkable to the thirty-two people who died in 1973 at the Up Stairs Lounge.

June 24 marks the forty-fifth anniversary of the Up Stairs Lounge fire. Back then, homosexuality was still considered a mental disorder. Police raids of gay bars were de rigueur, and being outed often resulted in being fired from a job or evicted from an apartment. Jail and mental asylums were a strong possibility too. As far as society was concerned, it was not okay to be gay.

After that terrible arson—the deadliest fire in New Orleans history— the politicians were silent. Moon Landrieu was the mayor of New Orleans then.

Eight months before the fire at the Up Stairs Lounge, there was a fire at the Rault Center, a high-rise office complex, that claimed six lives. Moon hastily left a conference of US mayors he was attending in Indiana to return to New Orleans to address the crisis. Leading the grieving city, he declared the victims were "mourned not only by those who knew them, but by New Orleanians in all walks of life."

A month and a half later, a sniper on the rooftop of the Howard-Johnson hotel killed nine people and injured thirteen. Moon was quick on the scene to help with negotiations. Moon would later say the incident was "perhaps the most tragic criminal act in the history of New Orleans." He also declared a state of citywide mourning and called for blood donors.

Moon made public statements after fire at the Rault Center (six dead) and the Howard-Johnson incident (nine dead), but thirty-two dead at a fire at a gay bar? Crickets.

Moon's silence is odd given his progressive track record. When he ran for mayor in 1969, he actually campaigned at Café Lafitte in Exile and one of his chief supporters was Leon Irwin III, an Uptown insurance man whose gayness was an open secret. After the election, he appointed outed business leader Clay Shaw to the French Market Corporation.

And Moon was well ahead of his time with regard to racial issues. He made good on his campaign promise to integrate city hall and was dubbed "Moon McCoon" by the Ku Klux Klan.

The mayor was out of the country when the Up Stairs fire occurred. He had traveled to Copenhagen, Denmark, to visit its famed Tivoli Gardens, which Moon hoped to use as a model for a park honoring Louis Armstrong, who had recently died.

Moon returned two weeks after the fire. At his first press conference upon returning (July 11), Moon offered an inane comment about the need for sprinkler systems in buildings. Local reporter Bill Rushton (himself gay) of the *Vieux Carré Courier* pressed him on the fact the Up Stairs Lounge was a gay bar; the mayor responded, "I'm just as concerned about that life as any other life. I was not aware of any lack of concern in the community."[1] These comments were not reported in the *Times-Picayune* or the *States Item*.

That life. Not life but "that life." Lord Alfred Douglas's famous line, "The love that dare not speak its name," originally published in 1894 still resonated in 1973. Thankfully, it doesn't resonate quite as much in 2018.

Happy Pride.

In view of the growth of Pride parades and the political climate of the country, the next essay raises the question—are Pride parades still necessary?

Ambush, June 19, 2022

NOTE

1. Bill Rushton, "Fire Three: Who the Victims Were," *Vieux Carre Courier*, July 13, 1973.

REFLECTING ON PRIDE MONTH

IN RECENT YEARS, THE ARRIVAL OF JUNE HAS TRIGGERED A DEBATE IN my head—is Pride still necessary?

As a historian, I think of Stonewall and the lightning bolt struck there by the queer gods. I think of the closet and how pervasive it was. I think of the Mattachine Society and how conservative it was. I think of the Gay Liberation Front and how radical it was. I think of the early Pride parades. I think about how important those parades were for our collective and individual well-being.

I also think of how Pride parades have changed over the years. I think of how they have been co-opted by corporate America in a fevered attempt to capture our rainbow dollars. I think Pride parades today are essentially corporate trade shows.

But is it really that simple? And if it is, is that a bad thing? No, and maybe not. Pride grew out of a terrible need that is gradually but surely diminishing. Much like the role of gay bars has changed as society evolves, so has Pride. Besides, at least here in New Orleans we still have Southern Decadence. May the queer gods help us if that parade ever becomes any more corporate than it already is.

On a personal note, last month was an especially poignant Pride month. The month began with the annual membership meeting of the LGBT+ Archives Project, an organization I helped found five years ago and which I have the pleasure of continuing to lead. History has always been a passion of mine and I consider it an honor to have played a small role in getting some of our local LGBT+ history out of the closet.

Then I spent much of the month preparing for Southern Decadence and the annual Press Party. I'm proud to have been selected as a Grand Marshal. It's thrilling for me to be a tiny part of such a huge New Orleans tradition. And it's fun too, despite all the behind-the-scenes work that is involved.

The Southern Decadence Press Party was held on June 21, and what a night it was! But the jubilation of that night was replaced a few days later by the second anniversary of the Pulse massacre and the forty-fifth anniversary of the Up Stairs Lounge arson. The Archives Project collaborated with St. Mark's Methodist Church to host a commemoration service and second line parade for the victims of the Up Stairs. Having the new mayor attend the service and walk the parade was significant given the city's reaction, or lack thereof, forty-five years ago.

There was also a panel discussion about the legacy of the fire at The Historic New Orleans Collection a few days later. Among the memories and attendant emotions the panel evoked was the commemoration event held in the same room five years earlier, which I also organized. In 2012, Rip and Marsha told me they wanted to plan something special for the fortieth anniversary of the fire but that they didn't have the time to organize it. They then asked me if I would do it. They assured me money was no object and they would anonymously underwrite the whole affair if necessary. That memory made me miss Rip and Marsha more than I usually do, which is a lot.

Then there was Ferris LeBlanc's family. Ferris died in the Up Stairs Lounge fire in 1973, a fact his family did not learn of until 2013. I became acquainted with Ferris's sister Marilyn and her family when they visited New Orleans in 2013 in an attempt to claim Ferris's body and bring him back to California. Since then, I have become friends with the family and was happy to spend the weekend with them while they were in town for the memorial service. I'm sad to report that three years later, they are still fighting the city and the cemetery to recover Ferris's body (more on that saga in a future column).[1]

The month ended on a sour note when Supreme Court Justice Anthony Kennedy announced his retirement. Kennedy was the swing vote in a number of key decisions that favored equality, including *Obergefell v. Hodges*, the landmark 2015 decision that legalized same-sex marriage nationwide. Kennedy's departure from the court is particularly ominous since his replacement will be selected by Trump. This will likely set civil rights back a generation or two.

And that brings us back to Pride. If the Trump disaster has taught us anything, it is that society can devolve backward easier than it can evolve forward. All the hard-fought rights won since the 1960s—everything from civil rights for Black Americans to reproductive rights for women to due process for immigrants to equal protection under the law for LGBT+

people—all of that is now in danger of being lost. And that makes Pride more necessary than ever.

The next essay provides a historical survey of the various incarnations of Pride in New Orleans.

Ambush, July 17, 2018

NOTE

1. As of this writing, LeBlanc's body has still not been located.

A BRIEF HISTORY OF
PRIDE IN NEW ORLEANS

MOST READERS OF *AMBUSH* ARE FAMILIAR WITH THE POLICE RAID, AND subsequent riot, of the Stonewall Inn in New York on June 28, 1969. What may not be so familiar to readers is the Eastern Regional Conference of Homophile Organizations (ERCHO) meeting held a few months later in Philadelphia. At that conference, Craig Rodwell, his partner Fred Sargeant, Ellen Broidy, and Linda Rhodes introduced a resolution that read in part, "We propose that a demonstration be held annually on the last Saturday in June in New York City to commemorate the 1969 spontaneous demonstrations on Christopher Street and this demonstration be called CHRISTOPHER STREET LIBERATION DAY. No dress or age regulations shall be made for this demonstration. We also propose that we contact Homophile organizations throughout the country and suggest that they hold parallel demonstrations on that day. We propose a nationwide show of support."[1] The resolution was enthusiastically adopted, and the first Gay Pride parades were held the following year.

The first Gay Pride parade in New Orleans did not occur until 1980. This may seem odd given the size of the gay population in New Orleans and the fact that New Orleans unequivocally loves a parade. But it's important to remember that New Orleans has never been a hotbed of political activism, gay or otherwise. New Orleanians are prone to organize socially rather than politically, a fact evidenced by the phenomenon of Gay Carnival, which dates to 1958, and the incredible popularity of Southern Decadence, which started rather humbly in 1972.

The first event locally to call itself "Gay Pride" occurred in 1978 when the very radical Pink Triangle Alliance hosted a Gay Pride Rally. The following year saw the birth of "GayFest," organized by Mark Gonzalez, Charlene Schneider, Richard O'Connor, and others. GayFest produced the first Gay Pride parade in New Orleans. The first two GayFests were held at Washington Square; the third, which featured Ellen DeGeneres, was held at Armstrong Park. By the mid-1980s, Gay Fest was plagued by financial difficulties, and in 1988, "GayFest" was changed to "Gay Pride."

A look back at the parade participants from those early years provides a glimpse of not only how the parade has changed but also at what our community was like in those years. Consider the participants in the 1989 parade: Bourbon Pub/Parade, Community Gospel Church, Grace Fellowship in Christ Jesus Church, Happy Hunters, Knights d' Orleans, Krewe of Olympus, M&M Productions, Metropolitan Community Church, Midtowne Spa, Monster/Dixies/Refuge, MRB/Wolfendales, NO/AIDS Task Force, Phoenix/Country Club, Twenty-Six-O-One, Wood Enterprises. In recent years gay-friendly churches still have a presence in the parade but gay bars do not, which is odd considering the prominent role they play in the LGBT+ community.

By the 1990s, Pridefest was being sponsored by the New Orleans Alliance of Pride. Notable parade Grand Marshals in the 1990s include Alan Robinson (1993); Mark Gonzalez, Charlene Schneider, and Richard O' Connor (1994); Father Bill Richardson (1995); and Rip and Marsha Naquin-Delain (1996). Robinson was a longtime activist who owned the bookstore on Frenchmen Street and a cofounder of the Gertrude Stein Society. Gonzalez, Schneider, and O'Connor were the original organizers of GayFest in 1979. Richardson was the priest at St. George's Episcopal Church in 1973 when an arsonist set fire to the Up Stairs Lounge. After the fire, which occurred on June 24, Reverend Richardson, over the objections of the community in general and his parishioners in particular, allowed St. George's to be used for a memorial service. The Naquin-Delains were the first same-sex couple to register a domestic partnership with the city of New Orleans and the owners of *Ambush Magazine*.

Rip Naquin-Delain recalls,

Marsha and I first became involved with Pride in 1985 when we moved from Baton Rouge to New Orleans. In subsequent years, Ambush Magazine would become involved as well, helping promote the celebration in conjunction with the Pride organization. Our community struggled for inclusion, and in 1991, New Orleans made it unlawful to discriminate in commercial spaces, employment, housing accommodations, private clubs, and public accommodations on the basis of age, color, creed, gender or sex, marital status, national origin/ancestry, physical condition/disability, race, religion, or sexual orientation.

Gender identification was added in 1997. In 1996, we were chosen as the seventeenth Pride Grand Marshals and the first couple to serve together. That same year saw Chastity Bono reign as celebrity Pride Grand Marshal, and "disco queen" Thelma Houston live on the Pride stage at Washington Square Park. In 1998, Pride moved to Armstrong Park, where the largest New Orleans Pride celebration would ever be held.

One could argue that Pride celebrations (even if they were not called that) in New Orleans date back to 1971. The very first gay-identified public event in Louisiana took place on February 6 at City Park. The event, sponsored by the newly formed local chapter of the Gay Liberation Front, was a picnic called a "Gay In." On February 20, 1971, three days before Mardi Gras, the GLF presented "Gay In II" at Washington Square Park in the Marigny. In June of 1971, the Gay Services Center and the local chapter of the Daughters of Bilitis organized a "Gay Day Picnic" at Popp Fountain at City Park.

In 1971, the GLF staged a march on city hall demanding an end to police harassment of lesbians and gays. This was the first public demonstration on behalf of LGBT+ rights in New Orleans. Six years later it was announced that Anita Bryant, homophobic superstar and darling of the religious right, was coming to New Orleans in June to perform a concert. The announcement came just after Bryant had led a successful campaign in Miami to overturn a gay rights ordinance. Local activist Alan Robinson spearheaded an alliance of several groups and businesses called HERE (Human Equal Rights for Everyone) to protest Bryant's appearance in New Orleans. The organizers hoped a few hundred people would show up in Jackson Square for a rally and march. The turnout was more like a few thousand. It was the first significant demonstration on behalf of LGBT+ rights in New Orleans. Although the event took place in June, it was not technically a "Pride" event.

Throughout the 1980s and into the early 1990s, annual "Celebration" events, usually held in June, were also popular. Celebrations featured dinners, musical concerts, ecumenical religious services, and workshops. Nationally known speakers were also brought in. Celebration 1983, for example, featured two keynote speakers. Barbara Gittings, founder of the Daughters of Bilitis, gave a talk entitled "Gay and Smiling: Tips from Twenty-Five Years in the Trenches." Bruce Voeller, a biologist and early AIDS activist, spoke on "AIDS: Everyone's Issue—Where Are We Now?"

Workshop titles from that year include "The Crime Against Nature Law: A Crime Against Gay People" (Cynthia Lorr), "Coming Out / Self Esteem" (Richard Devlin and Linda Bush), "Lesbian Visibility, Or, I know One When I See One" (Barbara Gittings). Other topics included alcohol and drug addition, gay unity, the Bible's stance on homosexuality, and NAMBLA (the North American Man Boy Love Association).

Historically, there is a sense among many that Pride in New Orleans has never quite lived up to its potential. The reasons why are the subject of another article but surely the heat and humidity don't help (indeed, Pride was briefly moved to October for this reason). Neither does the enormous popularity of Southern Decadence, which many people erroneously assume to be our version of Pride. And at various times throughout its history, New Orleans Pride has also been plagued by financial troubles and personality conflicts. Nevertheless, the LGBT+ community in and around New Orleans has much to be proud of. With that in mind, Happy Pride!

Ambush, June 7, 2016

NOTE

1. Katherine McFarland Bruce, *Pride Parades: How a Parade Changed the World* (New York: New York University Press, 2016).

HISTORICAL SCHOLARSHIP

UNTIL VERY RECENTLY, THERE WAS PRECIOUS LITTLE SCHOLARSHIP DONE on LGBT+ history in New Orleans, which is odd given that New Orleans is a city in love with its history and given the queer history of the city is so fascinating. The first book-length treatment of any queer topic was not published until 2011. Prior to that, only a handful of unpublished theses and dissertations had been written. But in the last ten years there has been an explosion of research: no fewer than seven books have been published and four documentary films have been released. In 2014, the LGBT+ Archives Project of Louisiana, a locally based federally recognized nonprofit organization that works to preserve local queer history, was founded. Since then, the Archives Project has facilitated the donation of several significant LGBT+ collections to museums, libraries, and archival repositories around the state. It also launched an oral history initiative, which remains active today. The essays in this section feature various efforts at getting our history out of the closet. "The State of Scholarship on Gay New Orleans History" lists all the efforts underway in 2014 to document our history. "The 1995 Panel on Lesbian and Gay History in Louisiana" reflects on a highly controversial panel discussion and the political firestorm it sparked. "The New Orleans Dyke Bar History Project" recounts an important effort to capture the memories of lost lesbian bars. "LaRC: A Treasure Trove of LGBT+ History" highlights the extensive LGBT+ collection in the Tulane University archives. And "October Is LGBT History Month" explores the origins of LGBT History Month.

THE STATE OF SCHOLARSHIP ON QUEER NEW ORLEANS HISTORY

THIS IS AN EXCITING TIME TO BE GAY, ESPECIALLY SO FOR THOSE OF US interested in queer history. Older members of our community rightfully observe with wonder the strides we have made in the last several years. Openly gay elected officials, visibility in the mainstream media, legalized gay marriage—these and other social phenomenon would have been inconceivable to our elders in their closeted youths. Conversely, younger people in the LGBT+ community today cannot possibly fathom the days when being gay was cause for criminal arrest and electroshock therapy. Gay history is being made at break-neck speed, which is great, but much of our history remains in the closet, which is regrettable. Fortunately, interest in researching and uncovering our history is at an all-time high. This is particularly true in New Orleans.

The formal study of queer history emerged from the closet in the academy in the early 1970s. Queer studies was an outgrowth of neo-Marxist interdisciplinary social theory. Scholarship in the field eventually led to queer theory (which focused on literary criticism and philosophy) and lesbian and gay studies (sometimes called sexual diversity studies) and gender studies (which often includes feminism and women's studies). At some universities these fields of inquiry are housed in their own academic departments, while in other cases they are subsumed into other departments such as English, political science, sociology, etc. Regardless of where these programs are housed within the academy, they are all informed by postmodern theory and their research methodologies range from ethnographic to historiographical.

Research into New Orleans's queer history has consisted mostly in the form of theses, dissertations, shorter articles in magazines and journals, and a few books. Much, but not all, New Orleans gay historical scholarship has been undertaken by independent researchers.

No fewer than eleven theses and dissertations touching on some aspect of New Orleans gay history have been written since 1989, most of them since 2004. These treatises cover topics such as the Up Stairs Lounge fire, lesbian bar culture, vintage drag culture, media coverage of the AIDS crisis, surveys of the gay rights movement, the gay gentrification of the Faubourg Marigny, voter attitudes toward gays and lesbians, and the attitudes of social workers toward gay youth.

There are a handful of books and chapters of books dealing with gay New Orleans history, the earliest of which was Edmund White's classic *States of Desire: Travels in Gay America* (1980). While White focuses on the time he spent in the city with artist George Dureau, James Sears's landmark work, *Rebels, Rubyfruit, and Rhinestones: Queering Space in the Stonewall South* (2001) focuses on the origins of Southern Decadence, the Up Stairs Lounge fire, and the Anita Bryant protest rally and march in 1977. Topics of other books and book chapters include the Up Stairs Lounge fire, Café Lafitte in Exile, queer cuisine, lesbian sexuality, and architectural preservation by gay men.

Yet another fascinating source of gay history are the back issues of gay-themed periodicals, magazines, newspapers, and newsletters, most of which are long gone. These include *Ambush*, the *Big Easy Times, Distaff, Impact, New Orleans Gay and Lesbian Yellow Pages*, the *Pink Pages of Greater New Orleans, The Rooster, Sunflower*, and *The Whiz*. These primary sources may be located in various archives and libraries around the city.

After Hurricane Katrina, a number of articles were written about the storm's impact on the New Orleans LGBT+ community, including a cover story in *The Advocate*. Each year, Arthur Hardy's Mardi Gras Guide features an article on some aspect of Gay Carnival.

In 2010, a documentary film about the history of Gay Carnival by local filmmaker Tim Wolff was released, entitled *The Sons of Tennessee Williams*. And last year a short documentary film about the Up Stairs Lounge by Royd Anderson was released.

Currently, two more documentary films about the fire are in production (Robert Camina's *Upstairs Inferno* and Sheri Wright's *Tracking Fire*). In addition, two more books about the fire are currently being written, one of which is by Robert Fieseler, who is currently in town conducting research. Scott Ellis, author of *Madame Vieux Carré*, is currently working on a history of the Faubourg Marigny. Janet Allured, a visiting professor at Newcomb College Institute, is working on a book about second-wave feminism, part of which will deal with lesbian involvement in the women's movement in Louisiana. And Howard Smith, a professor in California, is writing a book on the history of Gay Carnival in New Orleans. In addition to these forthcoming books, an oral history project on old New Orleans lesbian bars called the Dyke Bar Project is also in the works.

As encouraging as all this research is, there is still much to be done. At present, there are gaping holes in what we know about the history of gay New Orleans. Many significant topics have yet to be fully researched and written about. For example, books still need to be written about the following histories: Southern Decadence, the AIDS crisis in New Orleans, the transgender community, drag culture, minority subcultures, lesbian culture, bear culture, leather culture, gay musicians, writers and artists. Biographies need to be written about several pioneers in our community's history (Lyle Saxon, Miss Dixie, Jerry Menefee, Marcy Marcell to name a few). And what about long-gone bars? (A book about Jewel's would be a page-turner, wouldn't it?)

Fortunately, there is now a formal organization fostering the preservation of our collective LGBT+ history. The LGBT+ Archives Project of Louisiana was formed earlier this year to promote and encourage the protection and preservation of materials that chronicle the culture and history of lesbian, gay, bisexual, and transgender community in Louisiana. This project is not endeavoring to create an LGBT+ archive but rather to encourage people in our community to donate any materials they have to an existing archive, library, or museum. In addition, the project offers assistance to researchers interested in gay history. To learn more about the LGBT+ Archives Project of Louisiana, please visit its website or Facebook page.

Since this article was first written, a number of additional books, films, and podcasts have been released, all of which are listed on the bibliography page of the LGBT+ Archives Project of Louisiana's website.

The next essay steps back in time thirty years and examines the controversy surrounding the Louisiana State Museum's first attempt to publicly address queer history. In so doing, it provides a case study in how public attitudes toward queerness have evolved, especially in light of the flurry of research occurring today.

Ambush, July 29, 2014

THE 1995 PANEL ON LESBIAN AND GAY HISTORY IN LOUISIANA

THE LOUISIANA STATE MUSEUM MADE HISTORY ON JUNE 21, 1995, BY sponsoring a panel discussion titled "Pride in Our Heritage: Lesbian and Gay History in Louisiana." The forum was the first of its kind.

The idea for the panel was the brainchild of Wayne Phillips, who at the time was assistant curator of exhibits and programs. Phillips, a gay man himself, is currently the curator of the Carnival collection and of costumes and textiles for the Louisiana State Museum. Today, a panel on gay and lesbian history is barely newsworthy, but times were different in 1995. Back then, the notion of the State Museum sponsoring anything gay related was quite controversial—and politically explosive.

Within the state bureaucracy, the Louisiana State Museum falls under the Department of Culture, Recreation, and Tourism, which, in turn, is under the Office of the Lieutenant Governor. In 1995, the lieutenant governor was Melinda Schwegmann, who, at the time, was running for governor.

One of her opponents, former governor Buddy Roemer, seized on the panel topic to attack Schwegmann by exploiting the widespread homophobia that permeated the state. The Roemer campaign issued a venomous press release questioning Schwegmann's priorities. The press release states: "Melinda Schwegmann needs to get her priorities straight. I recommend that she go to a Wal-Mart—or a Schwegmann's if she prefers—and listen to what Louisiana's families' priorities are. She'll learn that they are concerned about jobs, education, welfare reform and corruption in government. 'Gay and Lesbian History' is not on their list of priorities."

For her part, Schwegmann distanced herself from the program claiming she knew nothing about it. This claim was a manifestation of political cowardice and contradicted a previous statement from Schwegmann's office, which read, in part, "The State Museum is committed to preserving and presenting the heritage of our state including perspectives of the many diverse groups that make our cultural legacy unique."

Roemer's political attack and Schwegmann's anemic response generated a number of headlines, and James Sefcik, director of the State Museum, weighed in, pointing out that the cost of the program—less than $200— was being paid not by taxpayers but rather by the Friends of the Cabildo, a volunteer organization that raises money for the State Museum. That still didn't satisfy Roemer, who complained that taxpayers would be footing the bill for electricity and air-conditioning at the Old US Mint, which is owned by the State Museum.

Sefcik responded in a *Times-Picayune* article, telling reporter John Pope, "I look at it as just another manifestation of the diversity of Louisiana, which is one of the things that makes our state so interesting . . . We're not here to keep everybody happy; we're here to tell the history of this state."[1]

In an interview with Patrick Shannon, Phillips added, "I don't look at this as pandering to minority groups. I look at it as giving credence to a heretofore unaddressed area of cultural interest." Sefcik's and Phillips's comments notwithstanding, the political controversy surrounding the panel generated a lot of publicity and over 350 people packed the event.

The panel featured three speakers. Researcher Roberts Batson spoke on "Telling Secrets: from Ephemera to Anekdota." Political activist Rich Magill spoke on "The Making of an Ordinance." State Museum historian Karen Trahan Leathern spoke on "Reflections on Gay and Lesbian Mardi Gras."

Magill's and Leathern's topics were fairly specific, but Batson, who spoke first, spoke in more general terms and, while providing interesting anecdotes, also discussed the challenges the gay historian faces.

According to a condensed version of Batson's talk that was reproduced in an *Impact* article titled "Claiming Our Past," Batson also addressed the political controversy surrounding the event by making a case for the preservation of gay and lesbian history, "To be a part of our culture, we must know, and remember." Further, Batson noted, "With all due appreciation to the museum staff here today who are responsible for this historic panel . . . the public should not look upon this panel as some great, magnanimous act of generosity on the part of our state. Tonight's presentation is exactly the sort of thing they should be doing."[2]

Not everyone in attendance agreed. Most of the comment cards were favorable, but there were a few notable exceptions. Debra Cox, for example, wrote that the State Museum was "totally out of line hosting a lecture on the sexual orientation of persons contributing to Louisiana history. Sexual orientation, no matter how deviant, is totally irrelevant to history. To glorify sexually deviant behavior as being important to history is wrong."

Despite the factual errors and erroneous assumptions in Cox's comments, most of those in attendance responded favorably to the program. Typical of most comments, one anonymous attendee simply wrote, "Thank you for just giving us equal treatment."

The panel discussion was followed by a reception at the newly opened Mint bar.

The following essay focuses on a specific effort to document the history of lesbian bars in New Orleans.

Ambush, December 20, 2016

NOTES

1. John Pope, "Uproar Draws Fans to Mint," *Times-Picayune*, June 22, 1995.
2. Roberts Batson, "Claiming Our Past," *Impact*, June 1995.

THE NEW ORLEANS
DYKE BAR HISTORY PROJECT

CHARLENE'S. PINO'S CLUB 621. THE OTHER SIDE. DIANE'S. THE GROG. Pinstripes and Lace. De Ja Vu. Brady's. The Blue Odyssey. Les Pierre's. The Soiled Dove. Vicky's. Rubyfruit Jungle. Remember these bars? These were just some of the more popular bars in what used to be a vibrant lesbian bar scene in New Orleans. Sadly, today there are no more lesbian bars in New Orleans.

Bars are not the only thing disappearing. History can be lost too. Much of our LGBT+ history has been lost and still more remains in the closet. Fortunately, efforts are now underway to preserve that history. The National Park Service has begun an initiative to include LGBT+ sites in the National Register of Historic Places, the LGBT+ Archives Project of Louisiana was founded earlier this year, and a number of books and films about the Up Stairs Lounge fire have been released or are in production. One of the most exciting efforts to document our history is the New Orleans Dyke Bar History Project.

This project is incredibly important because even within queer historical narratives, which are scarce, gay men have been traditionally privileged over lesbians. Local lesbian history is fascinating and important but not well documented. The New Orleans Dyke Bar Project is helping to change that.

In the spring of 2013, Rachel Lee was visiting with Alda Talley, who lives in Pascagoula, Mississippi. Talley began reminiscing about being a young lesbian in New Orleans. Later, Lee recounted the conversation with her friend Bonnie Gable. They then had an idea to produce a play based on Charlene's. The two began to brainstorm and invited a mutual friend, Sara Pic, to help. They formally interviewed Alda Talley as well as several other women. Thus, the New Orleans Dyke Bar History Project was born.

Tally was a regular at Charlene's and recalled how bars like Charlene's provided lesbians safe social spaces:

We would get all dressed up like it was Saturday night and we would get in my car, I always had the car, and go drive down, and what we were seeing was this bar on the corner with a mirrored entry one way view door, and Charlene was always outside and of course all the women who wanted to be groupies were standing around and there was this scene, this outside scene, and we would just drive by. We might park across Elysian Fields, which was a very wide street with a neutral ground so could park at the other side and watch from a distance. We did that several times before we got out of the car. We went once and just hung out with Charlene outside. We stood just a little away on the sidewalk like, practiced being lesbians at a bar. How do you stand? We were total babies and totally naïve. There weren't movies, there weren't shows, this was our only visual experience of the dyke bar scene, so we kind of eased our way into it.

In addition to Talley, the New Orleans Dyke Bar History Project has also interviewed fourteen other women ranging in age from fifty to eighty years old. The project focuses on lesbian bars of the 1970s and 1980s. According to project organizers, "The play was the seed for talking to other women and in the process learn of other bars."

The project will eventually create a digital archive of the interviews. In addition, the project has also begun hosting a series of monthly fundraising, networking, and social events. It has also produced a number of small-scale performances, the most recent of which was at the National Coalition of Anti-Violence Programs Regional Training Academy. The academy was sponsored locally by BreakOUT!, Women with a Vision, and the LGBT Community Center of New Orleans. The New Orleans Dyke Bar History Project also made a presentation and shared an interview at the inaugural meeting of the LGBT+ Archives Project of Louisiana in June.

The New Orleans Dyke Bar History Project is currently looking for additional women to interview. It is also in need of creative people to get involved, especially people with fundraising and audio editing skills. To volunteer, donate, or learn more about the New Orleans Dyke Bar History Project, please email dykebarneworleans@gmail.com or visit the group's Facebook page.

The next essay explores the Special Collections Division of Tulane University's efforts at preserving local queer history.

Ambush, September 9, 2014

LARC: A TREASURE TROVE OF LGBT+ HISTORY

ONE OF THE LARGEST CHALLENGES FACING THE LGBT+ HISTORIAN IS A lack of primary source material. For much of the twentieth century, being LGBT+ was not something most people wanted to document; to do so was to essentially amass evidence of a crime that could result in prison sentences and/or commitment to insane asylums. Preserving materials that chronicled sexual otherness could also result in employment and housing discrimination, to say nothing of being ostracized from family and social networks.

In New Orleans, we are fortunate to have the Louisiana Research Collection (LaRC) at Tulane University. Under the longtime tenure of director Leon Miller, LaRC has made a concerted effort to collect LGBT+ themed materials. In fact, LaRC houses one of the largest collections of LGBT+ material in the state. The collection consists primarily of organizational records, personal papers, and ephemera.

Some of the organizations whose records are housed at LaRC include the Knights d'Orleans records, 1993–2006; the LGBT Community Center of New Orleans records, 1992–2010; and the Louisiana Lesbian and Gay Political Action Caucus records, 1980–2001. These records encompass everything from official correspondence to membership rosters to financial records to meeting minutes to bylaws.

In addition to organizational records, LaRC preserves the personal papers of individuals who have played a significant role in local LGBT+ history. Two of the most important collections of personal papers include those of Skip Ward and Stewart Butler.

After coming out as a gay man in 1971, Skip Ward became an advocate for gay rights. In the 1980s, Ward became very involved in LAGPAC (the Louisiana Lesbian and Gay Political Action Caucus), a political activist organization. Ward and his partner, Gene Barnes, began publishing a gay-themed newsletter and formed Le Beau Monde in 1981. Le Beau

Monde was an informal social group of gay people who met regularly to "explore the humanistic and spiritual aspects of being gay." Spirituality had always been an integral part of Ward's life. As a child, his grandmother instilled in him a strong mistrust of organized religion, especially Christianity. Ward eventually became a lifelong Unitarian Universalist and went on to cofound the Unitarian/Universalist Church's Gay Caucus. Ward became associated with the Radical Faeries (a national organization for rural-based gender and sexual nonconforming spiritualists) and in 1994, he and Barnes acquired twelve acres of land in North Louisiana and called it Manitou Woods. It became a retreat space for spiritual communion and meditation.

Stewart Butler was also very involved with LAGPAC. In addition, Butler has also been very involved with the local chapter of PFLAG since its founding in 1982. Around 1988, Butler became a PFLAG board member and remains so to this day. In 1993, Butler chaired the National PFLAG Conference in New Orleans. In the 1990s, Butler led the charge to have transgender people included in the PFLAG mission statement. Consequently, in 1998, PFLAG became the first national gay rights organization to include transgender people in its mission statement. Butler also took the local and national Human Rights Campaign (HRC) to task for their reluctance to advocate for transgender persons. Butler has also participated in three Marches on Washington for LGBT rights, the Southeastern Conference for Lesbians and Gay Men (SECLGM), Louisiana Lesbian and Gay State Conferences/Celebration, AIDS Memorial Marches, the New Orleans GLBT Community Center, and numerous voter registration drives. More recently, Butler helped found the LGBT+ Archives Project of Louisiana and currently serves on its board of directors.

LaRC also houses an extensive collection of ephemera. Ephemera is defined as items designed to be useful or important for only a short time, especially pamphlets, notices, tickets, etc. Many ephemeral items may not seem significant during their brief lifespans, but over time become a wealth of historical information. These items include restaurant menus, posters for drag shows, matchbooks, and a host of other materials.

Yet another source of information are long since defunct publications such as newspapers and magazines. Copies of *Impact, The Whiz, Rooster,* and others may be found at LaRC.

LaRC is located in Jones Hall at Tulane University and is open to the general public for research.

The final essay in this section explains the origins of National LGBT History Month.

Ambush, February 14, 2017

OCTOBER IS
LGBT HISTORY MONTH

In 1994, A TWENTY-NINE-YEAR-OLD HIGH SCHOOL SOCIAL STUDIES teacher in St. Louis, Missouri, named Rodney Wilson did something remarkable. After teaching a lesson about the Holocaust, Wilson came out to his class by telling them the Nazis could have killed him too for being gay. He then did something even more remarkable; he proposed that a month be devoted to gay and lesbian history.

Wilson recalled his motivation for making the proposal in a 2013 interview with Colin Murphy: "I believe it's important to know one's history—personal, family, local, state, national, species—including the history of people like oneself. As an undergraduate and as a budding history teacher at Mehlville High School, I was inspired by Carter G. Woodson, who founded Negro History Week in 1926. When I typed up the proposal that October 1994 be declared the first-ever LGBT History Month, I hoped to do for the LGBT community what Woodson had done for African Americans, which was make LGBT history more accessible."

The idea for a Gay and Lesbian History Month (now LGBT History Month) was quickly endorsed by a number of national LGBT+ organizations, including the Human Rights Campaign, the Gay and Lesbian Alliance Against Defamation, the National Gay and Lesbian Task Force, as well as by the National Education Association. President Bill Clinton declared June 2000 "Gay and Lesbian Pride Month." Nine years later President Barack Obama declared June 2009 Lesbian, Gay, Bisexual, and Transgender Pride Month.

In 2006, LGBT History Month came under the charge of the Equality Forum, an international LGBT rights advocacy group. The group's website, http://www.lgbthistorymonth.com/, features thirty-one LGBT icons (one for each day of the month) in a short biographical video. The site also contains graphics, posters, and ideas for celebrating LGBT+ history. Last year, Governor Jerry Brown of California signed historic legislation that mandates the teaching of LGBT+ history in California schools. California is the only state to enact such legislation. Why October? Wilson thought October would be good because October 11 is National Coming Out Day. Also, the 1979 National March on Washington for Lesbian and Gay Rights occurred in October.

And is LGBT History Month being celebrated in New Orleans? Not really. Some groups and perhaps a few individuals will acknowledge the month on their Facebook pages or other social media outlets. But there is no official governmental proclamation—certainly not one from our homophobic governor. I suppose the mayor might issue a proclamation if someone bothered to ask him. For a city so in love with its history, one would think the LGBT+ community would be more in touch with its own. It is, after all, a very rich, colorful history.

One organization that is trying to preserve and share our collective history is the recently formed LGBT+ Archives Project of Louisiana. The mission of the project is to promote and encourage the protection and preservation of materials that chronicle the culture and history of the lesbian, gay, bisexual, and transgender community in Louisiana. The Archives Project purposes include educating the community on the importance of ensuring that LGBT+ historical materials are archived and made available for future generations to access, research, and study; promoting the proper maintenance and preservation of historical LGBT+ materials; providing an informational directory of archival resources where LGBT+ historical materials may be deposited or accessed for research and study; indexing, publishing, and maintaining a current list of locations of archived historical LGBT+ materials; developing financial resources to assist in the preservation and availability of certain LGBT+ collections. To learn more about the LGBT+ Archives Project of Louisiana, please visit http://www.lgbtarchivesla.org/mission-purpose/.

Ambush, October 21, 2014

LAGNIAPPE

THE ESSAYS IN THIS SECTION COVER A VARIETY OF TOPICS, RANGING FROM New Orleans's influence on Walt Whitman to the South's first gay and lesbian themed bookstore. The section opens with "The Historical Closet: Mid-Nineteenth Century Gay New Orleans," which examines literary depictions of the city's queer scene by focusing on famed poet Walt Whitman, who lived in New Orleans for a while in 1848, and lesser-known writer Ludwig von Reizenstein. The article then questions the sexuality of well-known philanthropist John McDonough. The historical closet is important because in it are the unacknowledged contributions of queer folk to the larger community. Consider Bienville, the founder of New Orleans, who lived into his eighties and never married. "All about the Bears" visits the gay zoo and stops at the bear cage. The article identifies the origins of not only the use of animal nomenclature to describe different types of gay men but also the origins of bear culture. It then examines bear culture's relation to other queer subcultures, such as motorcycle and leather clubs. "Here Cums Mr. Bingle" revisits the department stores along Canal Street in a grander age, particularly their restrooms, which served as a fertile cruising ground for gay men when it was not okay to be gay. The article also recalls other cruising areas as well. "FAB: Faubourg Marigny Arts and Books" tells the story of how a former Episcopal priest opened the South's first gay bookstore. And "Miss Fly, Miss Do, and the Double Play" remembers the unforgettable characters and charm of one the French Quarter's quintessential dive bars.

THE HISTORICAL CLOSET: MID-NINETEENTH-CENTURY GAY NEW ORLEANS

Not long ago, a friend and I were discussing the significance of President Obama's support for marriage equality. He was convinced it wasn't all that important and told me, "What will really be significant is when we elect a gay president." I replied by telling him we already have. He, like many people, was surprised to learn that James Buchanan, our nation's fifteenth president, was and is widely considered to have been gay. Buchanan was the only president to never marry, and he lived with his "good friend" William Rufus King (who was a US senator and vice president under President Franklin Pierce) for twenty-three years. Andrew Jackson referred to the couple as "Miss Nancy" and "Aunt Fancy," and Aaron Brown called King "Buchanan's better half." In his biography of Abraham Lincoln, Carl Sandburg described Buchanan and King's relationship as having "a streak of lavender and spots soft as May violets." Buchanan was president from 1857 to 1861.

In addition to not knowing our gay ancestors, one of the most frustrating aspects of the historical closet is not recognizing the contributions gay people have made to society. The word "gay" and our modern concept of gayness are twentieth-century constructions, of course. The word "homosexual" was not coined until 1869 and then only in clinical, psychiatric contexts. This raises the question of how gay people in previous ages viewed themselves. President Buchanan and his partner would not have thought of themselves as "gay" as we understand that term today. And yet they shared a life, and a bed, together, as did countless other same-sex couples.

One of the earliest known gay men to live in New Orleans was the great American poet Walt Whitman. Whitman arrived in the city in 1848 to work as a reporter for the *Crescent*, one of the city's several daily newspapers at the time. Although he lived only three months in New Orleans, the city profoundly influenced him and his poetry. In his leisure time, Whitman was fond of perusing the French Market before cruising the riverfront, where he delighted in meeting stevedores and longshoremen. The gay graybeard absorbed all the sensory imagery the city had to offer and later immortalized those images in much of his masterpiece, *Leaves of Grass*. The poem "I Saw in Louisiana a Live Oak" is a meditation on romantic male companionship and "Once I Pass'd Through a Populous City" is a poetic tribute to a male lover Whitman met in New Orleans. When the poem was published, the word "man" was changed to "woman"—an unfortunate consequence of the historical closet.

Where Whitman met his trick, and how, is uncertain. Gay social networking for the purposes for finding sex partners has been around for centuries. Fifteenth-century Florence, for example, had quite an extensive network, a Renaissance version of Grindr, if you will. It's safe to assume nineteenth-century New Orleans also had such a network. We do know there was a "gay scene" at the time for it is referenced by Baron Ludwig von Reizenstein, a German expatriate living in New Orleans in the 1850s who wrote a serialized novel entitled *The Mysteries of New Orleans* for a German language newspaper called *Louisiana Staatz-Zeitung*. Von Reizenstein includes a chapter devoted to a lesbian love affair.

Whitman's homosexuality is well documented. Such is not the case with other prominent gay men of the time. Some believe John McDonogh, the great nineteenth-century philanthropist who willed his fortune to the city of New Orleans and his native Baltimore for the cause of public education, was gay. Reclusive and eccentric, McDonogh never married. But was he gay? The reality is we just don't know. Not much has been written about McDonogh. A biography of his life was published in 1886 and a monograph about his legacy appeared in 2002; neither work addresses McDonogh's sexuality. The only evidence to suggest he may have been gay is the fact he remained a lifelong bachelor. If we accept that line of reasoning, we have to also wonder about Jean-Baptiste Le Moyne, Sieur de Bienville; the founder of New Orleans and long-term French colonial governor also never married.

A year after Walt Whitman left New Orleans and the year before John McDonogh died, the famed Baroness Micaela de Pontalba returned to New Orleans from Paris with her two sons to construct the fabulous Pontalba Buildings, which flank Jackson Square. While the buildings were being erected, mother and sons lived in a rented house on Burgundy Street. During the day, headstrong Micaela visited the construction site while her tender and devoted son Gaston sketched scenes of the Vieux Carré. Gaston had a sensitive nature and was something of an accomplished artist specializing in cityscapes as well as portraits. If his sketchbooks are any indication, it was probably he who designed the illustrious AP monogram (denoting the family names Almonester and Pontalba) in the cartouche of the famous cast iron that adorns the buildings' verandas. Pontalba biographer Christina Vella observes, "The letters are perfectly clear and perfectly unobtrusive; they give a focal point to the pattern without detracting in the least from the diffused loveliness of the iron tracery."[1] Noting Gaston's sketchbooks, Vella also says that "it is entirely likely that he designed all of the scrollwork" on the gallery ironwork that would set the trend for cast-iron balconies and galleries throughout the French Quarter. Vella's research has led her to conclude what many have suspected—Gaston de Pontalba was probably gay.

We may never know for certain if John McDonogh and Gaston de Pontalba were gay and, in the grand scheme of things, it may not matter much. What does matter are the untold multitudes of gay men and women in New Orleans's past whose sexual orientations have been lost to the historical closet. Hidden in the dark recesses of that closet are significant parts of our heritage as a community. If McDonogh and de Pontalba were indeed gay, the legacy of public education and architectural beauty both men bequeathed to New Orleans is something for which the gay community should be proud.

The next essay jumps forward in time and examines the emergence of "bear" culture in New Orleans.

Ambush, April 30, 2013

NOTE

1. Christina Vella, *Intimate Enemies: The Two Worlds of the Baroness de Pontalba* (Baton Rouge: Louisiana State University Press, 2004).

ALL ABOUT THE BEARS

ONE OF THE EARLIEST REFERENCES TO BEAR CULTURE DATES TO 1966. According to bear historian Les Wright, the minutes of a Los Angeles motorcycle club called the Satyrs refers to a "bear club," probably the Koalas, which published a newsletter called the *Bear Facts*. In the late 1960s and early 1970s, there were a number of loosely organized chubby and chubby-chaser networks, out of which grew the "Bear Movement." The first chapter of Girth and Mirth was formed in 1976 in San Francisco by a chubby-chaser named Charlie Brown; other chapters soon followed: Boston in 1977 and New York in 1978. In 1979, a landmark article entitled "Who's Who in the Zoo" appeared in *The Advocate* in which George Mazzei classified gay men into seven types of animals, bears being one of the categories. In 1987, Richard Bulger and Chris Nelson founded *Bear Magazine*. The magazine was originally conceived of in 1985 by Bart Thomas, who bequeathed the idea to Bulger before he died of complications from AIDS. In 1989, the Lone Star Saloon opened around the corner from the magazine's offices, and the Lone Star became what might be considered the nation's first "bear bar." Bears are everywhere now: there are bear circuits, bear prides, bear books, bear clubs. There is even such a thing as "bear studies" at some universities.

The advent of a distinct bear culture in New Orleans is difficult to pinpoint. To do so requires defining just what a bear is. This is not as easy as some people suppose because the term "bear" may be subdivided into a multitude of categories (from Wikipedia):

Cub—a younger (or younger-looking) version of a bear, typically, but not always, with a smaller frame. The term is sometimes used to imply the passive partner in a relationship.

Daddy—A mature bear who is often looking for a cub (or a younger man) for a relationship.

Ewok—A bear of short stature, but not younger.

Otter—A slimmer or less hairy bear regardless of age.

Chaser—Somebody who is attracted to bears and/or chubs but is not part of the bear culture.

Chub—A heavy-set man who might be described as overweight or obese. These men are also a distinct subculture within the gay community, and may or may not identify with the bear movement per se.

Teddy—A fully hairy bear. Chest, back, beard, everything is hairy.

Musclebear—A bear whose size derives from muscle rather than body fat.

Ursula—A lesbian bear.

Goldilocks—A straight woman friendly with bears.

Black Bear—A bear of African descent.

Panda (or Panda Bear)—A bear of Asian descent.

Koala Bear—A bear of Australian descent.

Polar Bear—An older bear whose facial and body hair is predominantly or entirely white or grey.

Grizzly—A dominant bear of extreme stature in height, weight, and/or hairiness.

Wolf—A slimmer bear, with the behavioral characteristic of sexual assertiveness or aggression.

Manatee—A hairless, chubby male who is called a bear but does not identify as such.

As in other cities, gay New Orleans has always been home to people who fit into the aforementioned categories. The question is when did these people begin to collectively identify as bears? The Phoenix and Rawhide, bars that are often associated with bear culture, were founded in the 1980s and it was in that decade that a national bear culture emerged. It is generally agreed the rise of the bears was a direct reaction against the mainstream gay community's tendency to privilege bodies that were thin, toned, young, and smooth. Bear culture is a celebration of the hirsute and hefty. But more than physical attributes, bear culture embraces a masculine aesthetic that values good-heartedness.

In 2002, the Cavaliers Motorcycle Club was founded in New Orleans by David Lester, Poncho LaPerle, Mike Ducote, Doug Minich, Guy Williams, Mark Dee, and George Hoxworth. Like many groups, the Cavaliers began to fizzle out after the Katrina diaspora, and by 2010 the Cavaliers were defunct. There has always been a correlation between motorcycle clubs and bear culture. The Lone Star in San Francisco was home to the Rainbow Motorcycle Club, and the bear runs of today are vestiges of the gay biker culture of the 1950s and 1960s. Leather, of course, is an integral component of motorcycle culture and hence the overlap between bear and leather cultures. Historically, many members of the various bear clubs have also belonged to leather organizations, such as the Lords of Leather, the Knights d'Orleans, the Crescent City Outlaws, and others.

In 1994, Mark Thomas, aka Guadalupe (Southern Decadence Grand Marshal XXXIV), and others founded the New Orleans Bear and Bear Trapper Social Club. The NOBBTSC is devoted to social gatherings and charity fundraising. Over the last twenty years, the club has raised money for Project Lazarus, NO/AIDS Task Force, St. Anna's Food Kitchen, Buzzy's Boys and Girls, the Gay Easter Parade, and others.

In 2012, a group of men led by Duaine Daniels, Kelley Terry, and Ron Schofield broke away from the New Orleans Bear and Bear Trapper Social Club to form the Renegade Bears of Louisiana. The Renegade Bears is primarily a social club. The group sponsors two monthly events—a beer bust at the Phoenix and Alphabet Soup, which consists of members going out to eat at restaurants whose names begin with whatever letter of the alphabet the group is at. The Renegade Bears also host steak-night fundraisers at various bars to raise money for local charities and Gay Carnival krewes. The club also provides security at Gay Carnival Balls.

In 2012, Charles Jenkins and Jimmy Mondoro founded the Krewe of Ursus. The Krewe of Ursus has donated teddy bears to Children's Hospital and delivered one thousand candy-filled Easter Eggs to Lazarus House. In addition, the Krewe of Ursus has been a sponsor of the Easter parade in 2013 and 2014. Ursus's most recent sponsorship was with the Miss Gay Mississippi America 2015.

Not all people who identify as bears are members of formal bear clubs. Scott and Jeff Turberville left corporate careers in Birmingham, Alabama, to move to New Orleans in 2011. Scott notes, "Just because I'm a bear doesn't limit me to bear culture. I haven't joined a local bear club because I felt it would pigeon-hole me. We're all one community." Scott is a member of the Big Easy Bears, a local softball team in the NOLA Softball League. He and Jeff are also part of a bowling league that bowls in Kenner.

Today, bears are a sizable and integral part of the LGBT+ community in New Orleans. Their charity fundraising is without parallel, and their loyal patronage of several local gay bars is unyielding. Their visibility in the community dispels the stereotype that all gay men are effeminate.

The following essay explores the fertile cruising grounds of department store restrooms along Canal Street.

Ambush, September 23, 2014

HERE CUMS MR. BINGLE

TAKE IT OR LEAVE IT, CHRISTMAS IS HERE AND ALL WE CAN DO IS EITHER enjoy it or suffer through it, depending on your perspective. As Western society acknowledges the advent of two thousand years of sexual repression and scientific ignorance, my thoughts turn to anonymous sex. Allow me to explain.

For generations of New Orleanians, Christmas meant not only Papa Noel but also Mr. Bingle. Who, you ask? Mr. Bingle was a beloved Christmas icon here in New Orleans for decades. Back in the years before it went all fast food and tacky tourist shops, Canal Street was lined with high-end department stores and specialty shops and was considered the city's premiere shopping destination.

During the holiday season, decorators worked tirelessly to transform store windows into fabulous wintry display cases. One department store, Maison Blanche (now the Ritz-Carlton hotel), outdid all the other stores in 1947. Store decorator Emile Alline created a lovable snowman and called him Mr. Bingle. When the fifty-foot papier-mâché Mr. Bingle appeared on the Maison Blanche building, New Orleans knew the Christmas season had arrived. As Santa's helper, Mr. Bingle was a big hit with children and adults. In the 1950s, Alline hired Oscar Isentrout, a master puppeteer in the French Quarter, to produce Mr. Bingle marionette shows in the Maison Blanche storefront window. Mr. Bingle went on to have his own radio and television shows.

What does all this have to do with anonymous sex? Mr. Bingle recalls the bygone era of the great Canal Street department stores—D. H. Holmes, Maison Blanche, Krauss, Gus Mayer, Kreeger's, and Godchaux's. It may be hard for some to fathom now, but in the 1950s and 1960s, long before sex-networking websites and apps like Grindr, these department stores were prime cruising grounds for gay men. The men's bathroom at D. H. Holmes was a particularly active spot for businessmen looking to hook up during their lunch breaks.

There were gay bars, of course, but that was risky. Just being in a "queer-shop," as they were called then, was dangerous because the police often sent undercover vice squad officers into them to make arrests. And arrests were usually accompanied by a beating and a public outing in the next day's paper. There was also the fear of being seen entering or exiting the bars. It's important to remember that not only were homosexual acts illegal then, being gay was also considered a mental disorder at the time. Horny men looking for some action had to weigh the benefit of getting their rocks off with the potential cost of jail time or a stint in a psychiatric hospital (can you say electric shock treatments—ouch!).

Nevertheless, the few gay bars that did exist did host some sexual activity, especially Café Lafitte in Exile, the oldest gay bar in the city. In fact, by 1966, Lafitte's reputation as a cruise bar had caught the attention of the United States Navy. In that year, the local naval commander sent a letter to the bar's owner informing him Lafitte's had been "declared off-limits and out-of-bounds to personnel of the Armed Forces." To this day, the letter is on proud and permanent framed display on the wall near the front door of the bar.

The ban probably did not have the effect the navy desired because there were a number of "Greek sailor bars" on Decatur Street that were primarily the domain of straight female hookers but also tolerated gay hustlers. There were a few bars that welcomed working boys, notably Wanda's on Iberville, and perhaps more common were certain areas in the French Quarter where hustlers slowly strolled along the sidewalk or hung out on corners waiting for closeted men to drive by and pick them up. These included the lower Quarter on the lakeside of Bourbon Street and the old Tango Belt in the upper Quarter. The bathhouse on Toulouse and cruise bars such as Jewel's Tavern, Rawhide, and the Phoenix would come later.

For those men too timid to go to the bars or pick up street hustlers, there was always the New Orleans Athletic Club on North Rampart Street or the parks. Cabrini Park saw so much action, much of its shrubbery had to be removed to prevent men from having sex in the bushes. In the summer of 1976, seventy men were arrested in City Park and Audubon Park during a one-month period on charges of obscenity or crimes against nature.

Cruising today is not nearly as dangerous as it used to be. Many would say that is a good thing, but others might see it differently. Exchanging body stats and d**k pics online is certainly convenient, but missing in the transaction is the element of suspense that comes with live, face-to-face cruising—the furtive glances, the hope of orgasm, the fear of rejection. And gone, now, perhaps forever, is the slight thrill of fear that comes with uncertainty. Is this guy a vice cop? Is he even gay? Is he going to hit me if I make a pass at him?

So, this Christmas season, as you shop for gifts at the mall, remember your gay forefathers. Remember the ones who were so closeted they had to cruise department store bathrooms, but also remember the ones who proudly paved the way for you to be out today. Open cruising is a great gift that would not have been possible without them.

The next essay highlights the South's first queer and feminist–themed bookstore.

Ambush, December 18, 2012

FAB: FAUBOURG MARIGNY
ARTS AND BOOKS

In 1977, Tom M. Horner, a former Episcopal priest, had two things on his mind—finishing his book on homosexuality in the Bible and opening a gay and lesbian themed bookstore. *Jonathan Loved David: Homosexuality in Biblical Times* was published by the Westminster Press, and in 1978, Horner signed a lease on a space for a bookstore at the corner of Frenchmen and Chartres Streets in New Orleans.

Horner opened FM Books (Faubourg Marigny Books) with less than a hundred titles. At the time, the gay publishing industry was in its infancy. Ten years earlier, gay activist Craig Rodwell had opened the Oscar Wilde Memorial Bookshop in Greenwich Village, but it wasn't until after Stonewall that gay-themed presses and bookstores began to proliferate in order to accommodate the growing number of gay titles. Glad Day opened in Toronto in 1970, followed by Giovanni's Room in Philadelphia in 1973 and Lambda Rising in Washington, DC, in 1974. Then came other, legendary gay bookstores, such as People Like Us in Chicago and the Walt Whitman Bookstore in San Francisco. Glad Day became a chain, as did Lambda Rising and A Different Light. By 1994, there were forty-five gay and lesbian themed bookstores across the nation. Of these, only a handful remain.

Horner ran FM Books for ten years before retiring to California. Well-known New Orleans gay activist Alan Robinson then took over the store and ran it for the next sixteen years. Robinson had demonstrated an acute political consciousness as an anthropology student at the University of Illinois and became active in the local gay rights scene after he moved to New Orleans in 1975. For a while he worked at the Gay Service Center (a short-lived community outreach effort) before cofounding the Gertrude Stein Society with Bill Rushton and Ann Gallmeyer.

At the bookstore, Robinson brought in more titles and hired a staff. He also began hosting signings for gay and lesbian authors visiting New

Orleans. Johnny Townsend (author of *Let the Faggots Burn*, a book about the Up Stairs Lounge fire), who worked part-time at the store in the late 1990s, recalls, "I remember Patricia Nell Warren, and Barbara Peabody (who wrote *The Screaming Room*, an AIDS memoir), and Vito Russo of *The Celluloid Closet*, and Aaron Lawrence (who wrote two books about escorting). I read my one solitary porn story, set in the bookstore, and published in *Indulge*, at a reading while wearing my leather. Alan always had plenty of refreshments for all his signings, though I doubt he made very much money from any of them." In addition to promoting queer authors, Robinson also founded, along with Uptown bookseller Mark Zumpe, the New Orleans / Gulf South Booksellers Association.

By the early 2000s, Robinson was not in the best of health and moved to Texas to be with his family. In 2003, M. K. Wegmann, the owner of the building that housed FM Books, approached Otis Fennell and asked him to help her find someone willing to run the store. Fennell took over the lease in July of 2003.

Fennell changed the name of the store to FAB: Faubourg Marigny Art and Books. In addition to bringing in art, he also began stocking books about New Orleans and creating window displays. When he took over the store, Fennell had no experience in bookselling. "I had no experience, but I wanted to save the institution. Six months later I asked myself what the fuck have I done?" Fennell came to the store with a business background, having earned an MBA at LSU and having served as the director of research for the New Orleans Chamber of Commerce in the 1970s.

Fennell has a keen sense of history, and preserving LGBT+ culture is extremely important to him. Part of that impulse to keep our heritage alive is an awareness of the role the bookstore has played in its thirty-five-year history. Culturally, FAB is significant not only because it is the only predominately gay-themed bookstore in New Orleans but also because it is one of just a few independent gay bookstores in the nation that has survived in the internet age. Before the internet transformed the way everyone lives, gay bookstores functioned as spaces that fostered community building and served as an alternative to bars and porn shops.

Suzanna Danuta Walters, writing about coming out in Philadelphia in the 1970s, says of patronizing gay and lesbian bookstores, "Perhaps we were 'buying gay,' but I think the patronage of those bookstores felt more like 'being gay' in a world in which the spaces for that openness were severely limited."[1]

Thankfully, "being gay" is no longer as difficult as it once was. Unfortunately, selling hardcopy books is. Independent bookstores are virtually extinct in the rest of the country, and independently owned gay bookstores have long been on the endangered species list. Nevertheless, FAB, under the leadership of Otis Fennell, stubbornly refuses to die. May she live at least another thirty-five fabulous years.

Update: In 2018, Fennell sold the bookstore to David Zalkind. While the store retains a significant number of queer titles, it is no longer considered a primarily LGBT+ themed bookstore.

The final essay in this section remembers two unforgettable French Quarter characters and one notorious dive bar.

Ambush, August 6, 2013

NOTE

1. Suzanna Danuta Walters, *All the Rage: The Story of Gay Visibility in America* (Chicago: University of Chicago Press, 2001).

MISS FLY, MISS DO, AND THE DOUBLE PLAY

THE WILD SIDE BAR AT THE CORNER OF DAUPHINE AND ST. LOUIS Streets in the French Quarter for years catered to a rough crowd. One evening a patron began to make trouble when the bartender/manager—a former prize-fighting boxer and trans woman—nonchalantly punched the troublemaker in the face. After the man hit the floor, Miss Do calmly ordered, "Get him outta here."

Miss Do and her lover Gigi arrived in New Orleans in 1972. Gigi had secured a job as a dancer at the Silver Frolics Night Club at 427 Bourbon Street. Miss Do, whose legal name was Jerry Moreland, applied to be a dancer as well, only to be told no but that she could be a bouncer. After six months or so, Regina Adams, who started her career as a performer at the legendary Gunga Din in 1967 and who headlined Silver Frolics, convinced the manager to make Miss Do a bartender. Thus began the bartending career of one of the most colorful characters in recent French Quarter history.

Lee Featherston, also known as Miss Fly, opened the Corner Pocket in 1982. Prior to that, the bar at the corner of Burgundy and St. Louis Streets in the French Quarter was called the Post Office and before that the Cruise Inn, both of which were gay show bars. Featherston was born and raised in Panama and came to New Orleans in the late 1970s. The son of a ship captain and a teacher/nurse, Featherston was a true entertainer, both confident and flamboyant. In addition to opening the Corner Pocket, Featherston also opened The Wild Side (formerly Gregory's and the Playhouse), which later became the Double Play, at the corner of Dauphine and St. Louis Streets. Miss Do managed The Wild Side for Miss Fly, and many people assumed Miss Do owned the bar.

Rip Naquin recalls that one morning he and Marsha were walking to St. Jude Church to light candles and say prayers when they passed Footloose, a bar that had once been Alice Brady's and later the Ninth Circle.

Miss Do and Miss Fly saw them walking by and summoned them into the bar to do shots. The candles went unlit that morning.

Featherston became a beloved figure in the LGBT+ community in New Orleans. Miss Fly served as a Southern Decadence Grand Marshal in 1993 and led the first official Southern Decadence Grand Marshal's Bead Toss during the SD Parade from the balcony of *Ambush* headquarters. Miss Fly also served as Queen Petronius at the krewe's thirty-ninth Carnival ball. For a while, Miss Fly also presented the Fly Fashion Awards as part of the Gay Appreciation Awards gala. Featherston's unique brand of humor culminated each year with his "Fashion Victim Award." Over the years, Featherston and Miss Do were most generous with the LGBT+ community, having donated thousands and thousands of dollars to those organizations, charities, and events they cared most about. Featherston's noted yearly "Yellow Party" raised funds for Pride Fest and the Krewe of Petronius. But it did not stop there. Many times, he and Miss Do helped countless individuals who were down and out, without anyone knowing.

Miss Do had been named Easter parade Grand Marshal in 2001, but she died before the parade.

Sadly, Miss Fly was murdered in 2000 at the age of thirty-nine. George Schaefer III, twenty-four, had been Miss Fly's lover and in the heat of an argument shot her twice in the chest and once in the head.

After her death, Miss Fly's mother was going to give Miss Do half of the Double Play and sell the other half to D. B. and Caroline Carnes. When Do died, Carnes didn't want the bar and offered it to Miss Fly's accountant, Robert Byrd. Byrd didn't want the bar either and offered it to Chuck Turner and Bill Miller, who bought the Double Play in 2001. Michael Elias, Miss Fly's attorney, bought the Corner Pocket.

Turner and Miller were no strangers to the bar business. They had opened their first bars, the Four Seasons in Metairie and Billy's in Slidell, in 1990. Angles, in Metairie, opened in 1992 and in 1994 they opened Chances in Hammond. Today, Turner and Miller own Billy's and the Double Play.

When she sold the bar, Miss Fly's mother said she didn't want the character of the Double Play to change, and Turner and Miller have made every effort to honor that request. They kept Doc on hand as manager during the transition and hung a portrait of Miss Do in the bar. Miller recalls, "Drag queens would treat that portrait like a shrine. They would leave flowers and cry."

Today the Double Play is still going strong and attracts a diverse and interesting crowd. It still has a symbiotic relationship with the Corner Pocket, primarily because of their proximity, and bar manager Will Antill has come to be unofficially known as the Mayor of the Financial District.

Ambush, May 10, 2016

INTERVIEWS

OVER THE YEARS I'VE HAD THE PLEASURE OF CONDUCTING MANY interviews with interesting people who have contributed to the growing body of knowledge concerning local LGBT+ history. This section includes five of the more significant interviews, which were published in *Ambush Magazine*. "Race and Gay Spaces: Remembering the Safari Lounge—An Interview with Robert Fieseler" examines the role of race and privilege in historical research generally by specifically looking at a forgotten Black gay bar called the Safari Lounge and its place in the story of the Up Stairs Lounge. In "Cruising Public Bathrooms: An Interview with Retired NOPD Officer Larry Williams Sr." a former New Orleans police officer recalls his time entrapping gay men in public restrooms and other places and arresting them for "crimes against nature." Williams also offers insight into the homophobia that once permeated the police department. "Decadence Past: An Interview with 2010 SDGMs Julien Artressia and Toby Lefort" highlights the 2010 Southern Decadence parade and the two Grand Marshals that produced the parade, and also yields insights into how SDGMs are selected. In "Local Queer History Goes to the Lammys: An Interview with Deacon Maccubbin," Maccubbin recalls the opening of Lambda Rising and the heady days of gay bookstores, how the Lammys were founded, and his love of New Orleans. "Ricky Everett Recalls the Night He Escaped the Up Stairs Lounge Fire" is the extremely personal, highly emotional recollection of a man who survived the fire at the Up Stairs Lounge.

RACE AND GAY SPACES: REMEMBERING THE SAFARI LOUNGE—AN INTERVIEW WITH ROBERT FIESELER

FRANK PEREZ: SINCE THE PUBLICATION OF *TINDERBOX*, YOU AND YOUR husband have moved to New Orleans. What has living here been like for you?

ROBERT FIESELER: It's been vastly different than just visiting here, even for extended bouts of adventure and misadventure during book research. Setting down roots with my husband has meant realigning our lives with the pace, attitudes, and flavors of this foreign land. At first, I would weep every morning on walks with my dog about how intricately beautiful everything could be. Flowers bloomed in November. I would also, occasionally, shudder at disparities others took as a matter of course. I'm not from the South, and this city can be shockingly up front about class and race.

But then I began to see a fabric weaving it all together and, in a sense, protecting this place from skirmishes of the outside world, the America that begins when you stray a step too far from the Quarter. For the first time in a long time, our first thoughts when we woke weren't some reaction to a president who stage-manages himself into thoughts and imaginations and nightmares. We both exhaled. We didn't even realize we were exhausted, beaten down, becoming censored versions of ourselves. And then we really started creating. My husband Ryan began painting these amazingly queer and sexy self-portraits. And I began to write the story that scared me most to tell, which will come out this summer. We felt that freedom to say "Fuck 'em all" and just do and be.

FP: You have recently done some research into the racial climate in 1970s and 1980s New Orleans. How did you get interested in that topic?

RF: Race, in general, is an underexplored avenue in the historical LGBT+ canon, and many forget that New Orleans gay bars were effectively segregated into the mid-1980s. In *Tinderbox*, I wrote a line about a Black gay bar down the street from the Up Stairs Lounge called the Safari Lounge being the first to close in a fire code crackdown that followed the 1973 tragedy— the notoriously unsolved crime that claimed thirty-two lives.[1] Something about the Safari Lounge's closing stuck in my mind long past the book's publication. How could one fire lead to the disappearance of not just one but two gay bars on the same city street? Why did no one from the white gay community step up to defend the Safari Lounge when it became targeted?

These questions bothered me. It bothered me that I didn't know, and it bothered me that I hadn't fully asked in the book, largely because it would have raked up all the complexities of southern racial politics at a time when my editor was encouraging me to cut half of the material from the original manuscript. (My husband nicknamed the original draft of *Tinderbox* "Gay War and Peace" or "Gaylord of the Rings.")

Honestly, I began to see some amount of privilege in my not attempting to find out more about the Safari Lounge. I am a gay white male who can accidentally "pass" because I hid in the closet into my early twenties, which means I tend to be taken as the "model sexual minority" at churches and barbeques—the least-threatening queer person to white men with golf tans. And I realized that an author in my position, where I'm accidentally presumed to be straight all of the time, had a responsibility to draw attention to unheard queer voices and unheard queer stories, if able, and I decided I was able. I had no excuse.

So, I just started asking. And kept asking. It's not like this isn't a city where people won't tell you if you want to know. You just have to want to know. No archival collections existed to provide obvious answers to my questions, per se, but a solid record of news reports did exist, which nipped at the periphery of this subject. I met figures vital to the local Black gay story like Michael "Fish" Hickerson, Ken Williams, and Rusty Downing. Discoveries accumulated until I had the equivalent of a companion chapter to *Tinderbox* that was ready to publish. I also want to be up front that I intend for an article on this topic to spark conversation about Black gay history, but it's no final word, not by any stretch.

There's more than enough material for a history book on this, but I think my going alone any further on a project like this would constitute "appropriation" or some form of cultural theft. I do hope a queer writer of color from New Orleans takes this idea to contract with a publisher and wins the Pulitzer Prize.[2]

FP: Tell me about the slang words "snow" and "dinge."

RF: "Snow" and "dinge" were 1970s street-speak for white gay men and Black gay men. "Snow" reflected antiquated notions of purity, aka Snow White, and "dinge" commented on dirt and dinginess of skin tone. These terms, especially "dinge," are now understood to be pejorative and offensive and justifiably so. You won't hear them used in the bar scene, and most queer youths aren't even aware they once existed.

But these words were common in the 1970s, and especially in New Orleans, in an era and in a city that both stigmatized and eroticized interracial dating and gay men of color, per se. A white man who sought primarily Black male partners was known as a "dinge queen," and a Black man who sought mostly white male partners was known as a "snow queen." You can find these terms scattered throughout early queer literature. For example, it's in Andrew Holleran's classic novel *Dancer from the Dance*. It was national queer lingo that took on a life of its own in the Creole South.

LGBT+ historians have swept these terms under the rug, in large part because most queer historians are gay white males who assume unexamined activist roles. They, the writers, often curate the past to inspire readers and end up presenting a singsong narrative of LGBT+ citizens joining hands and marching together for mutual rights after Stonewall. Most people, in fact, forget the primary role of queer people of color in the Stonewall Rebellion. But I think the queer community is stronger and more effective when it takes a harder look at uneven advancement. The poisonous legacy of "snow" and "dinge" must be acknowledged.

FP: Bars were segregated in the early 1970s by color as well as by sexual orientation. One of the few bars that catered to Black men was the Safari Lounge. Can you tell us a bit about the Safari Lounge?

RF: In 1973, the Safari Lounge was something of a companion bar to the Up Stairs Lounge on Iberville Street in that both were second-story establishments for gay men, both required a walk up a nondescript staircase to reach safe harbor, both boasted celebrated drag shows, both were popular locales—written about in the international gay travel guide *Bob Damron's Address Book*—and both were frequented by members of the closeted working class.

The major difference between the two bars was that the Safari Lounge served Black gay men, and the Up Stairs Lounge served primarily white gay men, although a few Black patrons did become regulars at the Up Stairs Lounge thanks to the open-minded personality of manager Buddy

Rasmussen. At the time of the Up Stairs Lounge fire, the Safari Lounge had Black ownership, a man named Hayes Littleton, and Black management. When you stepped off the staircase into the bar space of the Safari, according to Up Stairs Lounge survivor Regina Adams (Grand Marshal of this year's Gay Easter Parade), you'd see a T-shaped stage where Black drag queens you never saw elsewhere performed magnificently.

It should be noted that Safari Lounge existed at a time when the Black gay community of New Orleans, persecuted twofold by the white community and the Black church community, mostly hid its existence for protection. The white gay community, also largely in hiding, didn't suffer racism alongside the homophobia. They found hideaways like the Safari Lounge to be so negligible, so separate from their daily concerns, that many patrons of, say, the Up Stairs Lounge down the street were not even aware that the Safari Lounge served gay patrons.

After the Up Stairs Lounge burned to ashes on June 24, 1973, in the deadliest fire on record in New Orleans history, the Louisiana State Fire Marshal and the New Orleans Fire Prevention Division began a fire code crackdown on the French Quarter bar scene, citing at one point more than one thousand violations and associated fines. The first bar shuttered in that crusade, closed by June 28 of that week, was the Safari Lounge—the Black gay bar steps away from the Up Stairs Lounge. In a very real sense, the Safari Lounge was the most vulnerable and obvious target for authorities if they wanted to "make an example" of someone or something.

The white straight and white gay communities seemed either apathetic or oblivious; the *Times-Picayune* reported the Safari Lounge's closing in detail but failed to mention that it was a gay establishment. *The Advocate*, the most heralded queer publication in LGBT+ history, also noted the Safari Lounge's closing in a story but misreported to readers that "the Safari is not gay." The Safari was in fact gay, and it was now gone, wiped from the map as if it never existed.

FP: The Up Stairs Lounge was unique in that it allowed Blacks and women. Did that fact affect the way other bar owners/regulars viewed the Up Stairs Lounge?

RF: That's a question I wish more people would raise. The Up Stairs Lounge nurtured a trailblazing community of patrons in its short existence of about three years, from Halloween 1970 to the summer of 1973. Most people only think of its destruction, not the laughter or the love or all of the hurdles overcome.

Not only was the Up Stairs Lounge unique as a gay institution in that, after the fire, it elbowed its way into mainstream conversation at a moment when no mainstream publication wanted to cover homosexuality, but it also had been an interracial hangout that flouted racial codes by encouraging Black and white gays to meet on a more equal playing field of friendship, erotic courtship, and—at the white baby grand piano—song.

The Up Stairs Lounge set an example as a new kind of gay bar, and its vibe was catching on. When an interracial couple like Up Stairs Lounge victim Reggie Adams, who was Black, and Up Stairs Lounge survivor Regina Adams went to Café Lafitte in Exile in May 1973, five or six weeks before the tragedy, Reggie became the first Black man that Regina ever saw drink in one of the city's most famous gay institutions. Regina remembers a sign at Café Lafitte in Exile that read, "No Blacks, No Fems, No Women."

One wonders whether bar owners like Tommy Hopkins, who ran Lafitte's, were made less sympathetic to the destruction of a competitor bar whose racial attitudes had affected his own. Certainly, Hopkins discouraged talk of the fire and the recent deaths after the incident. Hopkins also, according to Troy Perry, resented the national gay activists holding press conferences in the week that followed the tragedy and blamed gay leaders for decreasing his bar crowd sizes. Sometimes in any community, those in power can't see further than their own bank balances.

I think these should stand as open questions: To what extent was the dismissive reaction to the deadliest fire on record in New Orleans history shaped by the Up Stairs Lounge having a Black gay victim and some Black gay patrons? To what extent was the Safari Lounge's subsequent closing a reflection of those same racial attitudes? Who was least interested in the fire when it happened? Who didn't want to know, and why?

Ambush, April 23, 2019

NOTES

1. Robert W. Fieseler, "The Up Stairs Lounge Fire Killed 32 People. Its Legacy Still Haunts Black Gay New Orleans," *Daily Beast*, May 11, 2019.

2. In 2021, the LGBT+ Archives Project of Louisiana partnered with The Historic New Orleans Collection to commission a book on the history of queer communities of color in Louisiana. Scholar Channing Joseph is writing the book, which is forthcoming from The Historic New Orleans Collection.

CRUISING PUBLIC BATHROOMS: AN INTERVIEW WITH RETIRED NOPD OFFICER LARRY WILLIAMS SR.

FRANK PEREZ: WHAT YEARS WERE YOU A POLICE OFFICER?

LARRY WILLIAMS: I joined NOPD as a police cadet in November 1968 after spending two years at Xavier University of Louisiana studying political science and minoring in history. The police cadet was a New Orleans Civil Service classification created in 1963 to bring high school age persons into NOPD. When I joined the program cadets were required to enter Loyola University and major in criminology while working in clerical jobs in NOPD. However, since I had majored in political science I was assigned to NOPD's intelligence unit. The unit was tasked with infiltrating political subversive groups such as the Movement for a Democratic Society (MDS), the Black Panther Party (BPP), the Ku Klux Klan (KKK), the Republic of New Africa, and other groups listed by the United States attorney general. The unit also tracked the movements of traditional organized crime in the New Orleans metropolitan area. The main groups were the Mafia and La Cosa Nostra.

FP: What rank did you attain?

LW: I attained the rank of patrolman, but when I resigned, I was on the sergeant's promotional list.

FP: Where are you from?

LW: I was born September 7, 1948, in Detroit, Michigan, but grew up in New Orleans.

FP: Why, specifically, did you form the Black Organization of Police?

LW: While on NOPD I noticed the Black officers were treated differently in the areas of where assigned, in promotions and discipline. So, several Black officers formed the Black Organization of Police.

FP: What led to the lawsuit you and others filed in 1973?

LW: The lawsuit sought to correct the manner Black officers were treated. Once the suit was filed in federal court, we expanded the suit to include female officers. I personally approached three Black officers who were known to by gay and asked each of them to join the suit as gay men to complain about the questions on the polygraph. Each declined, not wanting to be publicly "outed." A number of Black officers were opposed to including the gay officers in the suit.

FP: What were your duties when working for the vice squad?

LW: I was never specifically assigned to the vice squad. I was detailed or loaned on an "as-needed basis." My duties included arresting prostitutes, bookies, and persons who engaged in what was known as "crimes against nature." Later included the arrests of gay men who propositioned me to engage in oral and anal sex acts in public restrooms, vehicles, and hotels.

FP: What was the attitude in NOPD at the time regarding homosexuality? Has it changed?

LW: During the selection process for police cadet, I was given a polygraph. One of the questions sought to ascertain my sexual orientation by asking if I had ever had sex with a male. My answer was in the negative. During my time with NOPD I would hear gays referred to as "queers," "homos," "freaks," and "degenerates." I would say most of the officers who expressed feelings about gays were negative.

FP: What was/is your attitude toward homosexuality? Has it evolved?

LW: I grew up in the Hollygrove neighborhood of the city. A gay boy lived next door to us. He would come over and visit, watch television, and cook with my grandmother. He was quite effeminate. Although he was very polite, his visits annoyed my grandfather. However, two blocks down the street lived a gay teenager who was masculine. He too was one of my playmates. Although I understood both of these neighbors were different, I did not really understand until my father explained homosexuality when I was about twelve years of age. The subject came up when I asked him why my uncle (his brother) held hands with another man. My father explained that some men liked men as most men liked women. Also, I attended St. Augustine High School, which was an all-Black Catholic school. In my class there were two gay students and a number of gay students in the student body. Because of my exposure to gays in my neighborhood and my own family, I had no negative attitudes toward gays. In fact, I sought to include gays in the lawsuit against NOPD because growing up I came to understand that in NOPD gays were marginalized as were Blacks and women. My views about homosexuality "evolved" when I was a teenager. It was the conversation I had with my father that shaped my attitudes about gay people.

FP: What did you think at the time of arresting men in bathrooms?

LW: I viewed arresting gay men in bathrooms as the enforcement of public decency just as I arrested heterosexual couples who engaged in "natural" sex acts in cars or cemeteries. It was not because of sexual orientation. I viewed the same sex acts as something that was out of place in a public restroom.

FP: What is your best estimate on the number of men you arrested?

LW: I estimate I arrested about thirty or more men for what was termed as "crimes against nature." My change of heart occurred when I was involved in an arrest that resulted in the arrestee falling to the floor and wailing because he thought the arrest would embarrass him publicly and cause the loss of his employment. I was involved in the arrest of executives, civil servants, military personnel, protestant ministers, and priests.

FP: What was the criteria for an arrest? Eye contact? A verbal suggestion?

LW: On days when we would go out to make "crime against nature" arrests, a three-person team would leave the vice squad office located in the basement of the old police department headquarters at 2700 Tulane Avenue. We would drive river bound first stopping at the New Orleans Public Library located at 219 Loyola Avenue. I would enter the first-floor restroom and stand at the urinal exposing myself until a person stood at the adjoining urinal and started a conversation. I would wait until he made a sexual remark or advance usually admiring my penis. I waited until he asked me if I wanted to have sexual contact. We would enter a stall, he would drop to his knees and unzip my pants. I would then ask him if he was sure he wanted to do this. If he said "Yes," I would reach over his head and unlock the door to the stall and the two other vice detectives would enter and place the gay under arrest. Often, I was "arrested" so as not to "blow my cover." This deception would allow me to return to the restroom in the future and maintain my cover. After the library the vice team would go to Maison Blanche, then located at 901 Canal Street, the Center Theater at 912 Canal Street, and then finally we would visit the public restroom located at Madison and Decatur at the French Market. At times we would look below a bathroom stall door and see two pairs of legs or a person—male or female kneeling down and say we were there to clean the interior of the stall. Once the door was opened, we would arrest the couple whether same sex or a hetero couple. Several cases stand out in my time doing vice work. Once while sitting in the audience in the Center Theater a gay man began flirting with and moved down the row next to me. After introductions, we retired to the restroom. After he kneeled down to perform oral sex he started to masturbate. He stood up and slowly moved close to me continuing to pleasure himself. At that moment I unlatched the stall and my partners entered and shouted, "Vice squad, you're under arrest." The suspect, startled, turned around and ejaculated on one of the entering detectives. In spite of the ejaculate hitting the detective, he remained calm and did seem ashamed to appear in court to testify to the facts. The second memorable arrest occurred one Saturday. We were at Jackson Square when the chef from a very famous French Quarter restaurant approached me as I sat on a bench and started a conversation. He asked if I had some free time and I responded in the affirmative, so he asked me to come home with him. As we walked, my partners walked behind us until we entered a residence. Once inside the gentleman started to massage my crotch and began to undress. He asked me to follow him as he led me to a bedroom, which had a gurney with leather belts attached to both sides. He laid on the gurney face down and asked me to strap him down and beat him with a whip that was lying beside the gurney. When he was not looking, I opened the door and my partners entered. However, we could not think of how a violation occurred, so we left.

FP: What was the department's reaction to the Up Stairs arson?

LW: When the Up Stairs Lounge occurred, I was assigned to the Fifth District as a uniform patrol officer, so I was not privy to discussions about the incident. However, as a part of my duties when working vice cases I would visit 604 Iberville to make prostitution arrests, but I don't recall if the establishment was known as the Up Stairs Lounge.

FP: Did you participate in raids of other gay bars? Lesbian bars?

LW: I never participated in the raid of any bars because of gay or lesbian activities.

FP: Did you ever have to testify at trial? Or did most of these men plea out?

LW: I did testify in "crime against nature" cases but it was very rare because most arrestees pleaded guilty hoping to avoid publicity.

FP: Were you ever assigned to the Southern Decadence parade?

LW: I was never assigned to the Southern Decadence parade.

FP: In the 1970s, there were several types of gay bars, some of which catered to hustlers and johns. Do you remember any of those?

LW: I don't recall the names of bars that catered to gays or lesbians.

FP: Do you remember the Anita Bryant protest in Jackson Square in June of 1977?

LW: Yes.

FP: Gay folk, along with other groups, have long complained about police brutality and excessive use of force. Did you ever witness that? And how effective was/is the "blue code of silence"?

LW: I never witnessed brutality by a police officer against a member of the gay or lesbian community.

Ambush, January 17, 2017

DECADENCE PAST: AN INTERVIEW WITH 2010 SDGMS JULIEN ARTRESSIA AND TOBY LEFORT

FRANK PEREZ: HOW WERE YOU SELECTED TO BE GM? WHEN? WHERE? Did it surprise you?

JULIEN ARTRESSIA: The previous GM was Paloma, who was a bartender at the Bourbon Pub, where I was the manager. She approached me with the honor one day at work, and I was completely flabbergasted.

TOBY LEFORT: Tittie Toulouse selected me as Grand Marshal. I was both her and Paloma's parade lieutenant and the following year Tittie asked me to see if I wanted to be Grand Marshal and I said absolutely. It was something that she and I talked about for years. Paloma then asked me to lunch at Port of Call and asked me if I wanted to be Grand Marshal with Julien and I said Tittie already asked me.

FP: Why did you select your theme, colors, song, charity?

JA: "Bringing the French back to the French Quarter" just seemed like a natural theme, particularly when combined with my love of Marie Antoinette. The colors—purple, powder blue, and black—just happened to be the favorite colors of myself and co-GM Toby Lefort. We also created a sub-theme, "Leather and Feathers," based on our two personalities. Our song was "Tu Es Foutu" by In Grid.

TL: We selected the theme leather and feathers because I was Mr. Louisiana that year and Julien wanted to do feathers. I chose black and purple, and she wanted powder blue. We both agreed on the charity, which was NO/AIDS Task Force because of my past involvement with them. The song I let Julien choose.

FP: Did you get along with your co-GM? Did you know each other before being selected?

JA: Although I knew of Toby, we had never actually met before each being selected as GM. Fortunately, we clicked right away, and were able to create an incredibly successful season via collaborative effort.

TL: We got along fantastically. We knew each other just a little but got very close after.

FP: What is your favorite memory of your year? Least favorite?

JA: Riding on the float in the first-ever Friday night parade as it rolled down Bourbon Street, and marching in the Sunday parade, as it turned onto St. Ann Street; each time seeing the thousands of happy people, all the rainbow balloons everywhere, music blaring from every bar, they were both just overwhelming moments. My least favorite would probably be the butterflies I got each time I was about to speak on a microphone.

TL: Favorite memory was our fundraiser at Cutters with a lot of the older Grand Marshals. My least favorite memory was all the political duties.

FP: What was the most challenging thing about being GM?

JA: Wondering if my liver would survive it!

TL: The most challenging thing was to keep everyone happy, but looking back it should just be about you and the traditions.

FP: In your opinion, what was significant about your year?

JA: We raised more money for charity than any previous year had. Working on a theme of inclusivity, we also managed to include bar crawl visits to every gay and lesbian bar throughout the French Quarter, Marigny, Metairie, and Northshore.

TL: The significance of our year is we totally wanted to make a difference and we did.

FP: What do you want people to remember about your year?

JA: That it just screamed fabulousness!

TL: We wanted people to remember who we were, that we had fun and helped a charity while doing it.

FP: If you had to do it over again, would you do anything differently?

JA: I wouldn't let myself get so stressed out over the little things.

TL: If we were to do it over, we would change one thing: not having a fundraiser almost every night, just do a couple of big ones not fifty small ones.

FP: What advice would you give to future GMs?

JA: Be sure to surround yourself with a really exquisite team of lieutenants. Much like a bridal party, they'll help every detail get attended to.

TL: Have fun and do what you want to make it fun.

FP: How has SD changed since your year? Are those changes good or bad?

JA: It has gotten a lot more corporate sponsorship, which can deter from some of what was the original theme but is pretty much a necessity given the costs involved.

TL: It has changed a lot. The biggest change seems to be a structured event where we just had fun and did not let politics get in our way.

FP: Can you please provide some biographical background? Where are you from? What brought you to New Orleans? What are you up to now?

JA: I was born in Aurora, Indiana, sometime before the 1970s. As a young child I enjoyed competitive swimming and gardening and milking cows. Adulthood found me moving to the University of Cincinnati, where I majored in art, which led to a career at the Contemporary Arts Museum (Cincinnati). I eventually relocated to New Orleans, where I embraced the nonconservative atmosphere with open arms. It wasn't long before I started working as a bartender at the Bourbon Pub, later becoming manager of the bar, which I continued until the year after my GM reign. I currently serve as studio manager for Urban Earth Design Studios.

TL: From Larose, Louisiana. Been here since the early nineties, when I was with my first partner. I'm now bartending at the Bourbon Pub.

FP: Is there anything else you would like to add?

JA: I'm grateful for the opportunities I've had to meet and get to know all the previous GMs at various events, particularly as we discuss the incredible changes in society which have evolved from one person's reign to another's.

Ambush, September 25, 2018

LOCAL QUEER HISTORY GOES TO THE LAMMYS: AN INTERVIEW WITH DEACON MACCUBBIN

I RECENTLY HAD THE OPPORTUNITY TO MEET AND INTERVIEW DEACON Maccubbin, the founder of the Lambda Literary Awards. In 1974, Maccubbin also founded Lambda Rising, a pioneering gay-themed bookstore in Washington, DC. Maccubbin was in New Orleans with his husband Jim Bennett visiting their friend, architect David Dietrich. After a leisurely lunch at Sbisa's, Dietrich, Maccubbin, and I strolled back to Dietrich's very well-appointed home on Orleans Street, where I interviewed Maccubbin about the founding of Lambda Rising, the Lammys, and his love of New Orleans.

FRANK PEREZ: How did Lambda Rising come about?

DEACON MACCUBIN: I was in DC, and I had a business I had started in 1971. Basically, I bought a craft store from a girlfriend I had at the time for $100. The only thing that was really selling at the time were these little pipes and so I started selling them and it became known as one of Washington's premiere paraphernalia stores. In '72 I had been in New York and had gone to the Oscar Wilde Bookshop, which at the time had been at 15 Mercer Street. That was the world's first gay and lesbian bookstore. They only had maybe twenty-five titles on the shelf. It was a real comforting and warm place to be, and I was impressed with the literature they had and I thought, someday Washington should have a store like this. I didn't think I would be doing it. I just thought someone should do it.

In '74, a space became available in the Community Building where I was located. Up until that point we had been selling two shelves of gay books and there had been some interest in them. So, when the space became available, I borrowed $3,000 and spent $1,000 of my own money, which is all I had, and with $4,000 we opened a gay and lesbian bookstore, not knowing for sure if it was going to work. We figured if we could do $25 a day, we would be able to stay open. I'm glad to say we did better than that. The store was successful from the beginning, and we grew relatively rapidly.

Three years later we had outgrown the space and we moved around the corner to a storefront location. In the first stair you could walk up the steps and nobody knew where you were going to go. You could go right to the paraphernalia store, you could go left into the gay bookstore or you could go to any of the many political organizations that were in the building. Every tenant in that building was left-wing (Black Panther offices, antiwar groups, the paraphernalia shop, the gay bookstore; we used to joke that the only thing holding the building together were all the FBI wiretaps). So, people who were closeted felt comfortable about going into the store. When we told them we were going around the corner to a storefront location with wide open windows, several people asked if we were going to put up curtains or somehow cover the windows. We did not put up curtains and eventually, everyone who had raised the issue mustered the courage to come into the store.

By 1984 we had outgrown that space and had to rent a larger space about a block and a half away on Connecticut Avenue, a major shopping thoroughfare with heavy pedestrian traffic, and again some people were unsure if they would be able to come to the store. As before, they did. It helped a lot of people come out. When we opened that store, the mayor declared it Lambda Rising Day and we had two hundred people in line to get in when we opened. The very next day we opened a satellite store in Baltimore. I would never do that again—opening two stores in two days. Eventually we opened a few other stores and bought Oscar Wilde in New York.

FP: Would you call the late 1970s, early 1980s the golden age of gay themed bookstores?

DM: The early '80s particularly. There was an explosion of literature. Remember, when we opened the store in '74 we did it because you couldn't find gay literature easily. I remember going to a bookstore, a good quality general bookstore. I looked around and could not find any gay literature. And I went to the counter where the manager was, and I said I'm trying to find some good gay literature. Where would you have that? And he looked at me over the rim of his glasses and said, "We don't carry that kind of literature." Everybody assumed if you asked for gay literature you were looking for porn.

So, I went to the library to try to find some things and they had a lot of gay books in the card catalog and then I'd go to the shelf and couldn't find them. They weren't there. So, I asked the librarian where the gay books were, and she said, "We can't keep them on the shelf. There are two types of people that prevent us from keeping gay books on the shelf. There are people who don't like gay people and they steal the books and throw them away or deface them, and there are people who are gay and are too embarrassed to check them out." So, I knew there was a demand for LGBT literature and nobody was fulfilling that demand. So that's why I opened the bookstore. I said we're going to open a bookstore that specializes in this literature and we're going to teach the authors that there is a demand for it and we'll convince the publishers they can make money publishing it and we're going to convince other bookstores they can make money selling it. And after thirty-five years we've reached that goal. Mission accomplished.

FP: Tell me about the formation of the Lammys.

DM: I believe it was '89 if I remember correctly. We had been watching the Oscars and we had been watching the National Book Awards and we thought there ought to be an award to recognize excellence in gay and lesbian literature. We mulled that over and, in a few weeks, gathered the staff and said can we pull something like this together? Maybe could do it in conjunction with the American Booksellers Association convention and that way everybody from around the country would be in the same place at one time. It so happened that the ABA was in DC the next year and so that made it easy. So, we got Armistead Maupin to come be the emcee and put together a big dinner party and created this event. It happened. It was beautiful. It was hugely successful. People came from all around the country. We had about 350 people at the first one. It was amazing.

FP: How long did you sponsor the awards?

DM: I think it was the first five years. We did it at a different place each year. It grew to the point where it was self-sustaining. Once it got to that point we had a nonprofit foundation, the Lambda Literary Foundation, and turned everything over to them. And they've been running it ever since.

FP: Who set up the foundation?

DM: It was set up by Jim Marks and several other people.

FP: Here in New Orleans, we have the FAB bookstore, which was founded by Tom Horner in 1977. Did you know Tom?

DM: I did. I knew Tom from the beginning of the founding of his store because he was also an author. He wrote *Jonathan Loved David*, which we carried for some time. Every time we came to New Orleans we would visit with him. And we shared information with him. We were always willing to share information with other bookstores because it was not just to run a business but also to spread the message of gay literature so everybody had access to it. We started a mail order service in 1979 because we wanted to be able to reach everybody in the country with the literature we had to offer. We would get incredible letters from people from really small communities where there were no gay bookstores, no gay people as far as they knew, and they would tell us how we were keeping them sane, alive until they could travel to other places and meet other gay people for the first time in their lives.

FP: When did you start coming to New Orleans?

DM: I believe it was in the '70s. The first time was in the late '70s or early '80s. I came with my husband for a week to Mardi Gras and we had a wonderful time, of course. And then I came when I was the cochair of the Gay Rights National Lobby and they invited me to come to a New Orleans Gay Pride event and so I came and spoke.

FP: You closed Lambda Rising five years ago. Reflecting back and surveying the landscape of gay letters today, what do you see?

DM: Well, good literature is still being written and people are still searching for it. It's not quite as easy to find as it used to be because you can't just go to a bookstore that specializes in it but you can find it on the internet. I wish there were still gay bookstores—at one point there were between one hundred and two hundred gay and lesbian bookstores in the US and Canada. Now there are only two or three left. It is so difficult to sustain a bookstore of any type much less a bookstore with a niche market.

FP: Is there anything else you would like to add?

DM: Only that New Orleans is so welcoming and so wonderful and has such a rich heritage of gay history and I just think it's just wonderful that this place exists. Thank you for sharing it.

Ambush, March 24, 2015

RICKY EVERETT RECALLS THE NIGHT HE ESCAPED THE UP STAIRS LOUNGE FIRE

I RECENTLY HAD THE OPPORTUNITY TO MEET AND INTERVIEW RICKY Everett, a survivor of the Up Stairs Lounge fire in 1973. Here are his recollections of that fateful night.

FRANK PEREZ: What was it like visiting the site of the fire for the first time in forty-plus years?

RICKY EVERETT: It was the first time I've walked in that vicinity since then. I usually just don't go anywhere near it. It was a good experience for me. I thought it would be really freaky and depressing and actually, I've kind of come out of that thanks to Sheri Wright. I've been working with her and her documentary. I've talked about it a lot to different people and it's kind of helped me to overcome the emotional part of it that I've been going through for years—not able to talk about, not wanting to talk about it. So, it was a good experience going back. I was able to meet with you and other people and go through where the Up Stairs Lounge used to be and point out how it was laid out and answer different questions that different people had, so for the most part, I think it was really good for me. It completed a healing process for me. I thought it would be a depressing thing to go through, reliving all that, but it was actually very positive, it was a good thing.

FP: Were you living in New Orleans in 1973?

RE: Yeah.

FP: Did you grow up in New Orleans?

RE: Yeah. I lived on the West Bank and went to West Jefferson High School, and as I got out on my own in my early twenties I moved over to the East Bank and lived there until . . . well, I don't even remember what year it was, maybe 1998, 2000. The partner I had at the time—he and I moved up to the North Shore in Covington and lived there. He died in 2003 and then, of course, 2005 rolled along with Katrina and that destroyed everything for me as far as a job and so I moved on to Dallas. I knew I was supposed to because the Lord was leading me to come here for many years and be involved in Grace Fellowship Ministry here in Dallas and I've been here ever since.

FP: When you were living in New Orleans prior to the fire, was the Up Stairs Lounge your primary bar?

RE: Like everybody else, I went to several bars in the French Quarter. The Up Stairs was more like a home base for me and for many others from what I understand. The Up Stairs was the first bar I'd go to. I'd have one or two drinks and talk with Buddy Rasmussen (the bartender) and other people I was acquainted with and hang out for a little while and then kind of drift off to check out the other local bars in the area. And usually, before I'd go home, I would always stop off again at the Up Stairs and just kind of say goodnight to whoever was there and then head on home. It was kind of a family atmosphere unlike all the other bars. Other people have said the same thing. The Up Stairs was a really great place to meet people, not for cruising, well there was cruising of course, but primarily the Up Stairs was a good social meeting place. People would go there to have fun and good times. It was a good clean bar and well established and professionally run by Phil, the owner, and Buddy Rasmussen, the manager. And they did a very good job. They were clean. It was an all-around fun place with a family atmosphere.

FP: Let's talk about the night of the fire.

RE: I was a member of MCC, which met on Magazine Street. And Bill Larson, who was a very, very close and dear friend of mine was acting as the pastor. That day after church services—I'm not sure exactly what time it was but early in the afternoon, it must have been right after church, Bill Larson, myself and a friend of mine, Ronnie Rosenthal, who was from Smyrna, Georgia, was visiting me. At the time he was kind of like a long-distance boyfriend. The four of us—there was a fourth person, but I can't remember who it was—we had lunch at the Fatted Calf in the French Quarter. While we were eating, I had this horrible feeling that I couldn't get over and I looked at Bill and I said, "Bill, I don't know why but I have a really bad feeling you're going to die." And he looked at me and shook his head and said, "Yeah, I know." And so, I wanted to bring that in because that's what started that day in the French Quarter.

After we ate, we went over to the Up Stairs and joined the beer bust and had a good time with everybody. I don't know exactly what happened with Mr. Nunez. There's apparently more than what I had thought. I knew he had been thrown out of the bar and had made angry threats to come back and burn the place down.

We were having a good time and the beer bust came to an end and quite a few of us remained there and we were relaxing and socializing. And then someone opened the door of the bar upstairs and flames came rushing in. It was very mind-boggling. I was sitting in the middle section of the bar where the dance floor was, and they had tables and chairs where people could sit and talk. I was closer to the door, the large square archway and as you would go into that section of the bar I would be on the righthand side. My back was kind of turned toward the door. I turned to look, and the flames were rushing straight across the bar from the door at the stairwell to the Chartres Street side of the building. The cloth that was hanging above the bar for decorative purposes caught fire and oddly enough the carpeting actually raised up off the floor and flames went under it and that caught fire. Everything happened so quickly.

Before the flames had a chance to shoot across the bar, Buddy Rasmussen, who was tending bar, leaped over the bar, and headed to the middle section and grabbed me by my arm and pulled me up out of my chair. I was just dumbfounded. He led me and somebody said about twenty other people out through the back door by the little theater in the third section and onto the rooftop. I've seen a blog on an LGBT website by a man named Mr. Bill—I can't remember the full name—that said that wasn't true, that it was Courtney Craighead who led people out of the bar and not Buddy. It said Buddy was the one who opened the door, and it was Courtney who led people out of the theater. That was not so. Mr. Bill said in his blog that he was a very close friend of Courtney's and of course being a member of MCC, I'd known Courtney for many, many years and I can't imagine why he would say that. At any rate, the blog went on to say that it was Courtney that led us out, but it wasn't. It was Buddy Rasmussen. To my remembrance, and of course time and the confusion of everything that went on, I really remember Courtney actually leaving the bar before the fire. However, [unintelligible] Villere was pointing out to me that Courtney was interviewed by [unintelligible] the fire department at Charity Hospital where he was saying he was the fourth or fifth person that Buddy led out of the door. However, I kept wondering about that. I know Buddy led me out of the bar, but I couldn't tell you if I was the first person out the door or the last person out the door, much less the fourth or fifth person going out the door. It happened so fast, and I don't know how he could remember so well that he was the fourth or fifth person to be led out. It was amazing.

At any rate, we were out on the roof and there was a window to a bedroom in the building next door. I think it was Buddy that opened the window and we went through there and down a flight of stairs to the street. At the time, Mitch Mitchell and I were standing next to each other and started wanting to find [unintelligible]. I lost track of Ronnie, a friend of mine, when we were coming out of the bar. He was supposed to be behind me, and I turned to look behind me and I didn't see him, and I panicked. When Mitch went back into the bar, I went in with him and Mitch just vanished off into the flames. I couldn't even see him and by that time I was totally surrounded by these flames. One of the main points of my story is that I was standing in the middle of that, and the fire department estimated the fire reached 2,000 degrees and it melted a steel padlock that was hanging on their liquor door in their storage area and the little tables we sat at that had steel columns. Those were all melted. And at that very moment it seemed like it all just happened all at one time. At that moment standing in there I felt the presence of God covering me. It was a [unintelligible] spiritual feeling or healing. It was a physical feeling, something covering me, like a blanket from head to toe and I knew it was God. At that moment, I knew Ronnie had gotten out and that Bill had died in the fire and so I turned and walked out of the bar out onto the rooftop and I gotta say I didn't have one burn or singed hair and I was standing in those flames. That was my miracle. I think it's so important that people know that not to make me seem so special because we're all special people in the eyes of God. He loves us all. At the time and even to this day the quote-unquote religious people claim that we're gonna burn in hell and at the time people were saying the reason the bar burned down was because of homosexuality. If that were so, then I would have burned also. I am a homosexual. I know the love of God. He created us.

Ambush, March 11, 2014

INDEX

ABOUT THE AUTHOR

FRANK PEREZ IS THE COFOUNDER AND EXECUTIVE DIRECTOR OF THE LGBT+ Archives Project of Louisiana. He is also a writer, teacher, tour guide, and public speaker. He has authored several books on LGBT+ history in New Orleans. His publications also include a number of scholarly articles in academic journals as well as a number of poems and short stories in various literary journals. More information at https://frenchquarterfrank.com/.